# Phrase Structure Composition and Syntactic Dependencies

# Phrase Structure Composition and Syntactic Dependencies

Robert Frank

MIT Press
Cambridge, Massachusetts
London, England

This book was set in Times New Roman on 3B2 by Asco Typesetters, Hong Kong and was printed and bound in the United States of America.

Library of Congress Cataloging-in-Publication Data

Frank, Robert, 1965–
  Phase structure composition and syntactic dependencies / Robert Frank.
    p.   cm. — (Current studies in linguistics; 38)
  Includes bibliographical references and index.
  ISBN 0-262-06229-1 (alk. paper)
  1. Grammar, Comparative and general—Syntax. 2. Generative grammar.
I. Title.
P291 .F73   2002
415—dc21                                              2001057917

To Raffaella

# Contents

# Preface

This book explores the role of the Tree Adjoining Grammar (TAG) formalism in syntactic theory. The idea that TAG might be useful in this context is of course not new. So, before starting, I think it would be useful to lay out a bit of history, and some reasons for my writing this book.

The TAG formalism was first defined in a 1975 paper by Aravind Joshi, Leon Levy, and Masako Takahashi. TAG provides operations for composing pieces of tree structure to form larger structures, in a manner reminiscent of Chomsky's (1955) generalized transformations, which in part inspired Joshi's proposals. Since the publication of this paper, Joshi has continued to study TAG's formal and computational properties with a number of students and colleagues at the University of Pennsylvania. However, work directly investigating the importance of TAG for linguistic theory began only in the early 1980s when Anthony Kroch, working with Joshi, observed that the transformational analyses of a number of constructions could be elegantly recast into the TAG formalism. Kroch and Joshi showed that the TAG reanalyses not only retained the explanatory power of the originals, but also were able to derive without stipulation the effects of a variety of constraints on transformational derivations. The most comprehensive presentation of Kroch and Joshi's work was a 1985 technical report entitled "The Linguistic Relevance of Tree Adjoining Grammar," which was accepted to appear in *Linguistics and Philosophy*, but never did. Pieces and elaborations of this work, dealing with *wh*-movement and extraposition, ultimately appeared in Kroch 1987, 1989b, and Kroch and Joshi 1987. However, these publications differed from the more comprehensive, but unpublished, technical report in lacking a general statement of the TAG perspective on syntactic theory. Perhaps as a result, Kroch and Joshi's work went largely unnoticed by the wider community of theoretical syntacticians. Nonetheless, work on TAG approaches to syntax continued within a small community of researchers largely centered at the University of Pennsylvania. Though this line of work has resulted in numerous articles and PhD dissertations, including my own, much of the research has been published in settings outside the usual purview of most generative syntacticians.

The appearance of Chomsky's (1993) paper on the Minimalist Program marked the reintroduction of generalized transformations into mainstream syntactic theory. This change meant that the TAG conception of syntactic derivation was now more directly compatible with a more widely adopted approach. With recent developments in minimalist syntax, especially the introduction of derivational *phases*, the possibilities for cross-fertilization between TAG and minimalist syntax have increased still further. Yet, as mentioned above, with only a couple of exceptions, researchers in minimalist and other generative approaches to syntax remain largely unaware of the detailed empirical and conceptual advantages afforded by the TAG system of phrase structure composition. One goal of this book, then, is a bit of bridge building, by providing an accessible and comprehensive presentation of "TAG syntax" for the broader community of theoretical syntacticians.

I must hasten to point out that the perspective I adopt here in incorporating TAG into syntactic theory is my own, growing out of Kroch and Joshi's early proposals and those from my 1992 dissertation and my 1994 and 1995 papers (coauthored with Tony Kroch), and as such it represents only one of a range of possibilities. Depending on one's perspective, it is either a great vice or a great virtue of the TAG formalism that it remains silent on many issues of grammatical analysis. Thus, one can pursue TAG syntax using the basic ontological assumptions of any number of frameworks. Because of the close connections noted above, in this book I have adopted many of the leading ideas of minimalist syntax into a TAG setting, as the possibilities for theoretical integration are clearest to me in that context. Nonetheless, it is my hope that this book will also prove useful to researchers with other tastes in grammatical theories and will mark the beginning of productive interaction with the TAG tradition of syntactic analysis for syntacticians of a variety of stripes.

# Acknowledgments

Before moving on, I would like to take up the pleasant task of expressing my appreciation to those folks who have been crucial to the development of the ideas in this book. First and foremost on this list are Aravind Joshi and Tony Kroch, who initiated the research program that I explore here. Since my days in graduate school at the University of Pennsylvania, I have been lucky enough to work closely with both of them, and I remain grateful to them for the example of their work and for their intellectual generosity, sage advice, and encouragement. I should note my special indebtedness to Tony, with whom a wealth of the ideas discussed here arose during our joint work, which is cited throughout the book though no doubt insufficiently.

A number of other scholars have graciously shared their insights with me during the lengthy period in which I have carried out the work reported here. Though I am no doubt forgetting some, for their helpful comments and suggestions I would like to specifically thank Steve Abney, Bill Badecker, Judy Bernstein, Tonia Bleam, Luigi Burzio, Rich Campbell, Memo Cinque, Robin Clark, Peter Cole, Michel DeGraff, Tom Ernst, Naoki Fukui, Lila Gleitman, Paul Hagstrom, Dan Hardt, Michael Hegarty, Gaby Hermon, Caroline Heycock, Jack Hoeksema, Norbert Hornstein, Hans van de Koot, Seth Kulick, Dave Lebeaux, Young-Suk Lee, Jeff Lidz, Mitch Marcus, Michael Niv, Dick Oehrle, Bill Philip, Paul Portner, Owen Rambow, Beatrice Santorini, Giorgio Satta, Carson Schütze, Mark Steedman, Arhonto Terzi, Juan Uriagereka, Enric Valduví, K. Vijay-Shanker, Amy Weinberg, Colin Wilson, Raffaella Zanuttini, and the anonymous reviewers of Frank and Kroch 1994, 1995. Much useful commentary also came to me from audiences at presentations at the 16th GLOW colloquium at the University of Lund; at the 3rd and 5th TAG+ Workshops, at the University of Pennsylvania and the University of Paris 7, respectively; and at colloquia and seminars in the Departments of

Linguistics at the University of Maryland at College Park and UCLA, the Jersey Syntax Circle at Rutgers University, the Department of Computer and Information Sciences at the University of Pennsylvania, and the Institute for Formal and Applied Linguistics at Charles University, Prague. Thanks to all who attended. I have also had the good fortune to teach a number of seminars and short courses on the material in this book at various stages in its development. For their incisive questions and commentary, as well as good humor in listening to my not always completely worked-out proposals, I am indebted to the participants in seminars at the University of Pennsylvania in the fall of 1991, at the University of Delaware in the spring of 1993, at the University of Campinas in the summer of 1995, at Johns Hopkins University in the fall of 1997 and the fall of 2000, and at the University of Padova in the summer of 2001.

For patience and generosity in sharing their knowledge of some of the world's languages, I am grateful to Hrönn Gunnarsdóttir, Viola Miglio, Mar Orlygsson, Kjartan Ottósson, Halldór Sigurðsson, Sten Vikner, Verner Egerland, Christer Platzack, Max Guimarães, Mary Kato, Eduardo Raposo, Željko Bošković, Carmen Dobrovie-Sorin, Marina Todorova, Luigi Burzio, Raffaella Zanuttini, Rajesh Bhatt, Henry Davis, Paul Hagstrom, Caroline Heycock, and Paul Portner.

This book has moved from my head to the printed page only because of the invaluable help I have received. The support of my colleagues in the Department of Cognitive Science at Johns Hopkins, among whom Luigi Burzio and Paul Smolensky deserve special mention, was crucial in keeping me moving ahead. The patience and encouragement of Amy Brand, Carolyn Anderson, and Tom Stone at MIT Press were similarly vital. Once I turned over the manuscript to the Press, Anne Mark worked copyediting wonders on my prose. The final result owes much to her justifiably renowned skill and attention to detail. I am also grateful for the financial support of the National Science Foundation in the form of grants SBR-9710247 and SBR-9720412.

And beneath it all, there is my family. My heartfelt gratitude goes to my parents, my sister, and the rest of my extended family spread across two continents for their support, encouragement, and love. To Gabriel and Daniel, who arrived on the scene during the writing of this book, I am indebted for a great many example sentences and for a continuously renewed appreciation of the wonders and joys of life. And finally, I owe more than words can say to Raffaella, whose wisdom, generous spirit, and loving heart I count as my most precious treasures.

# Chapter 1

## Setting the Stage

### 1.1  Phrase Structure Composition in Grammatical Derivation

Within the generative paradigm, our ability to exploit the system of connections between form and meaning afforded by human language is taken to derive from the existence of a mental grammar. A grammar, as understood here, is a specification of the possible connections between form and meaning. I assume that these form-meaning connections are encoded as some sort of formal object, called a *linguistic expression*. Since a given language provides an infinity of connections between form and meaning, a grammar must specify an infinity of possible linguistic expressions. Consequently, grammars are typically specified in some sort of recursive fashion.

This abstract conception of grammar permits a wide variety of instantiations. To at least a first approximation, these can be classified into two categories. *Representationally oriented grammars* determine the set of linguistic expressions using a system of well-formedness constraints. Each of these constraints provides an evaluation of some part of the linguistic expression. The ultimate well-formedness of the entire linguistic expression is determined by combining the evaluations of the individual constraints. Much as logical axiomatizations do not specify how to go about determining which statements are theorems, representationally oriented grammars do not specify how one should find the well-formed linguistic expressions, but only what properties such well-formed expressions must have. *Derivationally oriented grammars*, in contrast, focus exclusively on the process by which well-formed linguistic expressions are found, by providing a procedure for constructing them. In other words, a linguistic expression E is well formed under a derivationally oriented grammar D only if D can construct E.[1]

A derivationally oriented grammar generally includes a set of structural atoms, which I call the *basis* of the derivation. This basis is fed into the derivational procedure, which constructs syntactic structures using operations of two types. The first type, which I call *structural composition*, allows either previously constructed syntactic representations or elements of the basis to be combined to form larger representations. In a derivationally oriented grammar with a finite basis, such operations play a fundamental role, in that they provide a way to generate the requisite infinity of possible structures. Operations from the second class, which I call *transformations*, modify an individual syntactic representation in some specified fashion. Such operations have been implicated in the establishment of morphological and syntactic dependencies, as, for example, between a head and its inflectional morphology or a dislocated expression and its locus of interpretation.

The earliest model in generative grammar (Chomsky 1955, 1957) was derivational in character. Here, we can take the basis to consist of a set of lexical items.[2] Through context-free rewriting, which we can view as a form of structure composition (but see McCawley 1968), the derivation produces simple syntactic tree structures, which I call *kernel structures*.[3] In this theory, kernel structures underlie simple monoclausal active declarative sentences. To derive other sentence types, kernel structures can be modified using a number of transformational operations, called *singulary transformations*, such as Subject-Aux Inversion, Question Formation, and Passive.[4] Such derived kernel structures can also be combined using operations called *generalized transformations* to produce, for example, structures involving relative and complement clauses and coordination. The essential details of the resulting derivational system are depicted in figure 1.1. In the figure, square boxes signify representations, while rounded boxes correspond to application of derivational operations. Among the latter, transformational operations are colored white, while structural composition operations are gray.

Consider how an example like (1) would be generated in this model.

(1) The book is believed to have been written by the Etruscans.

The derivation begins with two independent sequences of context-free rewriting to produce the kernel structures in (2) that underlie the simple sentences *The Etruscans have written the book* and *Mary believes it*.

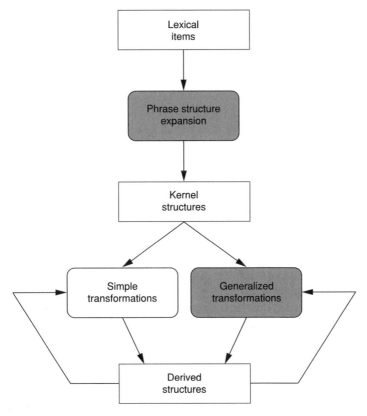

**Figure 1.1**
Derivational system of Chomsky 1955, 1957

(2) a.

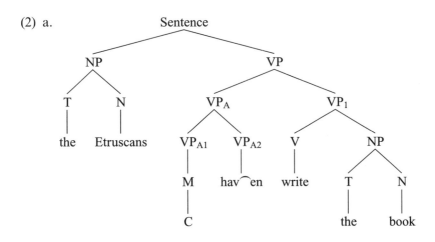

b.

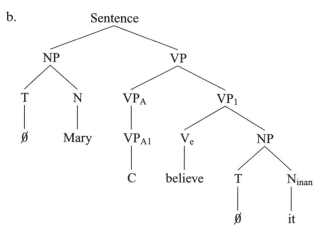

The Passive transformation is then applied to the first of these kernel structures, yielding the phrase marker for the sentence *The book has been written by the Etruscans*. This result is next inserted into the kernel structure in (2b), replacing *it*, using one of a family of generalized transformations that are responsible for embedding clausal arguments. This insertion produces the structure for *Mary believes the book to have been written by the Etruscans*. The Passive transformation applies again, to this structure, producing *The book is believed by Mary to have been written by the Etruscans*. Finally, a transformation of Agent Deletion is applied to yield the sentence in (1).

   Observe that in this system, there are two distinguished processes of structural composition, one responsible for building kernel structures, the other for combining them. Note as well that the process of building kernel structures is completely segregated from the application of singulary transformations. This means that those singulary transformations that are ordered earlier than generalized transformations are guaranteed to apply to phrase markers as large as, but no larger than, kernel structures. Thus, the domain of application of these transformations will naturally be restricted to the structural domain of a kernel structure. Since it is the class of singulary transformations that is responsible for the formation of syntactic dependencies, this means that the kernel structure is the locus in which the dependencies formed by these "early" singulary transformations must obtain (Chomsky 1955, 534). Indeed, Chomsky uses precisely this localization of application for certain transformations to argue in favor of the conception of kernel sentences that he adopts. In Chomsky's transformational analysis of English, Passive and Reflexivization are among these early singulary transformations, and he uses this ordering to ensure that these dependencies are properly locally constructed. In our example derivation of (1), for example, Passive applies crucially to the embedded kernel structure prior to its insertion via generalized transformation into the matrix. If Passive did not apply locally in this way, the further application of Passive in the main clause would be impossible, as the structure would not meet the structural description necessary for application of Passive.[5] Chomsky (1955, 531–532) makes similar arguments concerning the application of the Subject Inversion and Reflexivization transformations.

Subsequent theoretical developments moved away from the use of generalized transformations as devices for structural composition. This was driven by the observation that generalized transformations did not seem to behave in the same fashion or exploit the same kind of expressive power as singulary transformations, in spite of their comparable derivational role. Fillmore (1963) notes, for example, that in spite of the arbitrary interleaving that Chomsky's (1955) model allows between applications of singulary and generalized transformations, no cases appear to necessitate ordering a singulary transformation that applies to a matrix sentence prior to a generalized transformation that embeds a complement within that sentence. Additionally, generalized transformations never need to be extrinsically ordered with respect to one other. These stand in sharp contrast to the extrinsic orderings that at the time were considered necessary among singulary transformations.[6] Additionally, in comparison to the complex use that singulary transformations make of elementary permutation and recombination operations, the generalized transformations that proved grammatically necessary combined structures in the simplest of fashions. The final nail in the coffin of generalized transformations stems from Chomsky's (1965) observation that the function of generalized transformations, that of building arbitrarily large pieces of phrase structure, can be taken over by the base component once recursive phrase structure rules are permitted. Chomsky's (1955) prohibition on recursive phrase structure rules was at least formally odd, and thus a theory that avoids this stipulation gains in simplicity.

In the model proposed in Chomsky 1965, then, the initial stage of the derivation involves creating an unboundedly large syntactic structure by applying a now recursive set of phrase structure rules. The derivation proceeds by applying singulary transformations to this *deep structure* representation. This derivational model is depicted in figure 1.2. Here,

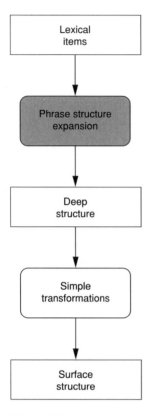

**Figure 1.2**
Derivational system of Chomsky 1965

structural composition and the transformational operations are completely separate. Since all applications of structural composition precede all applications of transformations, there is no longer any way to derive predictions about the domains over which transformationally derived dependencies will be formed. That is to say, since the phrase structure rules can apply recursively, there is no longer any distinguished structural subunit analogous to the kernel structure over which (certain) transformations might apply. Instead, the effect of forcing certain singulary transformations to apply locally is achieved through imposing a number of stipulations on the application of transformations. For one, the sequence of transformations is required to apply cyclically: first to the substructure containing the lowest sentence domain, next to the larger substructure containing the next lowest sentence domain, and so on, up through the matrix clause. Additionally, explicit locality conditions are imposed to prevent a single transformation from forming a dependency over too large a structural domain (see Chomsky 1964, 1973; Ross 1967; and much subsequent work).[7]

The lack of interaction between transformations and structural composition in this model means that the proper formulation of transformations does not depend in any way on the manner in which structural composition takes place. As a result, subsequent developments of Chomsky's model up through Chomsky 1981, 1986, though adopting the basic architecture of the framework of Chomsky 1965 in which structural composition precedes transformations, pay less and less attention to the processes by which structure is built. Indeed, with the elimination of an explicit set of phrase structure rules (Stowell 1981), the initial syntactic structure is no longer even seen as deriving from the application of structural composition operations. Instead, the grammatical architecture that is adopted in Chomsky 1981 is a hybrid of the representational and derivational approaches, with the initial phrase marker, now called D-Structure, specified through a set of well-formedness conditions rather than a derivational algorithm. Even with the introduction of well-formedness constraints, however, the grammar remains derivational in one crucial respect: other levels of representation are constructed from D-Structure through cyclic applications of a single general transformational operation, called *Move α*, which accomplishes the dislocation of syntactic elements.

Simultaneously with these developments, another group of researchers moved in the opposite direction, maintaining or increasing the role of structural composition in grammatical derivations while minimizing or entirely eliminating the role of syntactic transformations. In Lexical-Functional Grammar (LFG) (Bresnan 1982b), the lexical basis of the grammar is enriched to allow lexical representations with richer hierarchical structure. In turn, the structural combination operation of context-free phrase structure expansion is strengthened with the additional mechanism of unification. This operation provides a means for combining feature-value information from a variety of sources and can be used to allow complex passing of information during the construction of a syntactic representation (Shieber 1986). Together, these two changes allow syntactic transformations to be eliminated entirely from the derivational system. The formation of previously transformationally established dependencies is instead taken to derive from the application of structural combination to complex lexical entries that have been transformed by lexical rules. For example, two distinct lexical entries exist for the active and passive forms of an individual verb, and the distinctive combinatory properties of these lexical entries are coupled with unification-driven linkages so as to yield the appropriate thematic dependencies. For long-distance dependencies, unification is used to pass the features of a displaced element back to its θ-role assigner, thereby establishing the proper semantic dependency and ensuring compatibility of, among other things, case and agreement properties. Generalized Phrase Structure Grammar (GPSG) (Gazdar et al. 1985) also eliminates the role of syntactic transformations in grammatical derivations, but takes a different approach to the elimination of transformations. Here, derivation proceeds by context-free phrase structure expansion. In GPSG, dependencies are established not via modification of lexical entries, but via the application of metarules that modify the context-free base rules themselves. Thus, the possibility of, for example, *wh*-question formation derives not from a transformation, but from additional phrase structure rules generated from question-forming metarules. Combinatory Categorial Grammar (CCG) (Steedman 1996) takes yet a third approach, adopting an enriched, universal set of operations for structure composition. The additional combinatory options provided by these operations yield the possibility of generating nonstandard constituent structures, which, in certain cases, avoid the need for transformationally derived dependencies entirely.[8] For example, no filler-gap dependency needs to be explicitly established in the formation of a relative clause, as the structural composition operation of function composition allows the "fronted" relative operator to combine directly with the remainder of its clause.

Despite the continued role of phrase structure composition, these non-transformational systems share with the transformational models deriving from Chomsky 1965 the property of having no privileged intermediate level of syntactic structure, like the kernel structure, over which dependencies are formed.[9] Consequently, some analogue of the cyclicity principle needs to be incorporated to prevent nonlocal dependencies from forming.

Recent work in the transformational paradigm has returned to the idea that phrase structure composition, in the guise of generalized transformations, is a central player in syntactic derivations. There have been a variety of reasons for this shift. One stems from the constraints that have been assumed to govern the well-formedness of D-Structure representations. Under standard assumptions, the only argument positions that can be filled at this level are those to which θ-roles are directly assigned. The synonymy between examples (3a) and (3b) implies, then, that the subject position of (3b) must not be filled at D-Structure, since (3a) tells us apparently that the subject of (3b), *the Matterhorn*, is in fact assigned its θ-role lower in the structure in the object position of *climb*.

(3)  a.  It is tough to climb the Matterhorn.
     b.  The Matterhorn is tough to climb.

However, it is also usually assumed that this subject does not raise transformationally from a base position as the verbal object to the matrix subject. Such movement would violate well-attested locality conditions that block movement past one subject position to a higher one, as seen in examples like these:

(4)  a.  *John appears [(it) is certain [*t* to win]].

     b.  *John is likely [(it) has been persuaded *t* [to come]].

Chomsky (1981) suggests a solution to this puzzling complex of facts in which the object of *climb* in (3b) does not raise to the subject position. Instead, the subject position is filled by a process of lexical insertion that takes place during the application of transformations between D-Structure and other syntactic levels, so that the subject is introduced after D-Structure. Chomsky (1993) notes, however, that under any reasonable understanding of the term *lexical insertion*, this solution is inadequate.[10] Such non-D-Structure subjects can be arbitrarily complex, containing even other instances of such *tough*-movement, as seen in (5).

(5)  That the Matterhorn is tough to climb is easy to see.

To derive such examples under the framework of assumptions just sketched, Chomsky argues that the grammar needs to allow for parallel derivations of the subject clause and the remainder of the sentence, proceeding from distinct D-Structure forms that are integrated prior to S-Structure. In other words, derivations need to make use of a device similar to generalized transformations.

A second reason for the return of generalized transformations to grammatical theory stems from an empirical argument given by Lebeaux

(1988). Lebeaux, along with Freidin (1986), notes that relative clauses that are fronted along with the DP they modify do not exhibit the interpretive effects of having been present in the base position of the *wh*-phrase. That is, whereas in the example in (6a), the subject pronoun may not corefer with *Dave*, a name that it c-commands, such coreference is possible when the relative is fronted as in (6b).

(6) a. *He$_i$ lived in [the house that Dave$_i$ built] for ten years.
    b.  [Which house that Dave$_i$ built] did he$_i$ live in for ten years?

This situation contrasts with that involving clausal complements to nominals. Here, for the purpose of interpretive effects like pronominal coreference the fronted example behaves just like the version in which the phrase is not moved.

(7) a. *He$_i$ has been hearing [the claim that Dave$_i$ forged the building permit] for ten years.
    b. *[Which claim that Dave$_i$ forged the building permit] has he$_i$ been hearing for ten years?

Lebeaux explains the contrast between the examples in (6) and (7) by assuming that adjuncts, since they are not assigned θ-roles, are not licensed at D-Structure. Instead, Lebeaux suggests that they are introduced during the transformational derivation with an operation of structural composition he labels *adjunction*. Since adjunction of the relative clause is free to take place after the fronting of the *wh*-phrase in (6b), there is never a point in the derivation at which the structure includes the illicit configuration of the pronoun c-commanding the coreferential name. On the other hand, since clausal complements are assigned θ-roles, they must be present at D-Structure. Hence, the D-Structure representation in the derivation of (7b) will look much like that of (7a), thereby inducing the effect of noncoreference.

Finally, Chomsky (1993) advances a conceptual argument for bringing generalized transformations back into grammatical theory. Chomsky outlines a research program that attempts to formulate what he calls a minimalist theory, in which the only levels of grammatical representation are those that are conceptually necessary. Since the function of grammar is to provide a link between form and meaning, there are minimally two such levels: one that provides an interface with the cognitive systems of articulation/perception, Phonetic Form (PF), and another that interfaces with conceptual/intentional systems, Logical Form (LF). In the

framework of Chomsky 1981, these two levels of representation constitute the outputs of a derivation that begins with the noninterface level of
D-Structure. In a minimalist theory, then, there can be no D-Structure
starting point of the derivation. Instead, a derivationally oriented minimalist theory that produces PF and LF outputs must include some mechanism of structural composition with which such structures can be built.

In the model proposed in Chomsky 1993 and refined in Chomsky 1995,
structures are built out of a set of lexical items, constituting the basis of
this system. Chomsky suggests that the grammar includes a single structural composition operation, which he calls *Merge*, that functions by
combining two structural elements, either lexical items or previously built
structures, into a more complex structure. The usual syntactic tree is now
understood to be a representation of a (partially ordered) sequence of
applications of Merge, much as in Categorial Grammar derivations. The
resulting structure's syntactic properties, like its categorial label or agreement features, are inherited from one of the two elements given to Merge
as input. The tree in (8), then, reflects three applications of Merge. First,
the lexical item *the* combines with the lexical item *book*, with the properties of *the* being inherited. Next, this result combines with the lexical
item *read*, with the properties of *read* being inherited. Finally, this complex combines with *John*, with *read* projecting its properties once again.

(8)

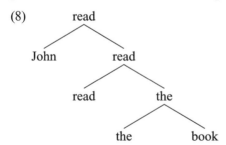

Chomsky distinguishes two subcases of Merge, *substitution* and *adjunction*, corresponding to the traditional distinction between combination of
a syntactic head or phrase with a complement or specifier, and combination of a head or phrase with a modifier or "adjoined" element. The difference between these operations is reflected, essentially, as a diacritic
that is added to the label of a structure resulting from adjunction.

In addition to the Merge operation, this system includes a single transformational operation, *Move*, just as in Chomsky 1981 and subsequent

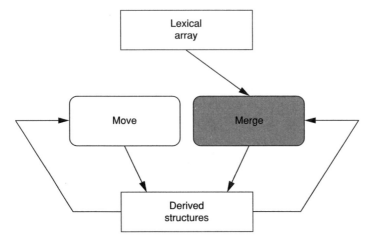

**Figure 1.3**
Derivational system of Chomsky 1993, 1995

work. With the reintroduction of a structural composition operation, however, the possibility is now open for the application of transformations to interleave with structural composition, as in the model of Chomsky 1955, 1957 (see figure 1.1). This possibility is indeed exploited in the conception of derivation adopted in Chomsky 1993, 1995, which is depicted in figure 1.3. It is important to observe that the objections raised earlier against the presence of generalized transformations in such an interleaved grammar do not apply to this more recent proposal. Those objections related to limited types of interactions occurring between generalized and singulary transformations, as compared to the power offered by the possibility of extrinsic ordering. Under the current conception, the generalized and singulary transformations, Merge and Move, are of such a general form as to eliminate the utility of extrinsic ordering.

There is another important difference between this model and that originally proposed by Chomsky (1955, 1957). Recall from our discussion of that earlier system that no cases of structural composition accomplished by the rewriting of the (nonrecursive) phrase structure rules could be interrupted by application of transformations. I suggested that this separation had the beneficial effect of providing a privileged structural domain, the kernel structure, over which grammatical dependencies might be localized. In the current model, however, there is no such privileged domain. Structure composition is accomplished in a uniform fashion, via Merge. As a result, transformational movement may apply to structures produced at any point in the derivation, large or small. This means that once again locality restrictions on syntactic dependencies will arise in this system only in virtue of explicitly stipulated constraints on the application of movement.

Most recently, Uriagereka (1999) and Chomsky (2000, 2001) propose models in which there is an intermediate structural unit having a privileged derivational status, much like the kernel structures of old. These systems share with Chomsky's (1993, 1995) model the property that applications of structural composition, in the guise of Merge, and applications of transformations, in the guise of Move, may freely intermingle. These models differ, however, in that derivations are not permitted to manipulate structures beyond a certain size, which Uriagereka calls a *derivational cascade* (henceforth, DC) and Chomsky calls a *phase*. The common intuition that Chomsky and Uriagereka pursue is this: once a DC/phase has been constructed, it is sent off for interpretation at the PF and LF interfaces. Consequently, from the point of view of the subsequent derivation, the DC/phase is frozen: subsequent derivational operations may not modify its internal structure, but must treat it as an atomic entity. A completed DC/phase may be merged with other elements, or it may be moved in its entirety; but it may not be altered. In its strongest form, this style of derivation imposes a severe locality condition on the formation of dependencies: namely, they must obtain within a single DC/phase.

Of course, the empirical implications of such a derivational model depend on the size of DCs/phases. Uriagereka proposes that the DCs arise from the need to produce the linearly sequenced representation that is required to interface with the articulatory/perceptual systems. He suggests that syntactic structure is unordered and that the simple procedure by which structure is linearized, which reverses the order of Merge operations, functions only with particularly simple structural configurations, in particular, those that are uniformly right branching. When two complex structures are merged, this simple procedure will not suffice to determine linear ordering. To avoid this problem, Uriagereka suggests that the derivation first "spells out" one of the complex structures, so that it is treated subsequently as a sort of complex word. When this complex word is merged with the other complex structure, the simple linearization procedure is now able to determine an ordering between these elements, the complex word preceding the complex structure. As Uriagereka notes, this proposal derives so-called left branch effects, in which dependencies like *wh*-movement may not extend out of a complex substructure on the left. That is, an example like (9a) is not generable since the DP subject *a critic of who*, as a left branch, must be spelled out before it is combined with *see you*, leaving it syntactically frozen. As a result, the subsequent extraction of *who* out of this DP to the specifier of CP is impossible.

(9)  a.  *Who did a critic of see you?

     b.

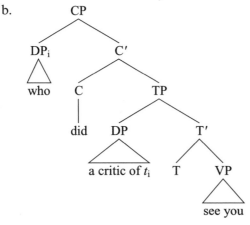

Uriagereka's proposal does not, however, explain a number of other well-known locality restrictions on dependency formation. For example, it captures neither Relativized Minimality effects, like that seen in the *wh*-island in (10a), nor the class of adjunct island effects in which the adjunct is rightwardly attached, as seen with the relative clause in (10b): both of these structures form a single DC with a higher clause, and consequently they should form domains that are transparent to movement.[11]

(10)  a.  *Why did you see [what a critic wrote $t$ $t$]?
      b.  *Who did you see a critic [that wrote about $t$]?

   Chomsky's conception of the limitation on phase size is different. He suggests that phase boundaries are the reflection of breaks between semantically saturated phrase structures. CP, corresponding to a saturated Davidsonian event structure, constitutes one type of phase boundary, and *v*P, as the phrasal instantiation of a saturated lexical predicate, constitutes the other.[12] Under this proposal, then, a single derivational phase may contain at most one such semantically saturated head, that is, either a C or a *v*. Chomsky argues that phases provide the appropriate context for computing derivational economy of the sort I discuss in chapter 4.

Following the intuition that phases are immutable once they have been completed, one would expect on Chomsky's proposal that movement of a *wh*-element out of a CP should be impossible. Yet, as is well known, this movement may apply across an unbounded number of CP boundaries.

(11) What$_i$ do you think [$_{CP}$ that Alice would suggest [$_{CP}$ that Peter ask us [$_{CP}$ PRO to do $t_i$]]]?

To avoid this undesirable result, Chomsky weakens the degree to which phases are frozen. Chomsky (2000) proposes a Phase Impenetrability Condition stating that only elements within the complement domain of a phase's C or *v* head are inaccessible to operations outside the phase. This leaves, roughly, a phase's head and its specifiers as accessible to operations outside the phase. For cases of unbounded *wh*-movement, then, it is sufficient for the *wh*-phrase to move successive cyclically through the specifier of each phase's head, a position that plays the traditional role of an escape hatch for movement out of an otherwise closed domain.[13]

Chomsky's approach to the apparent bleeding of dependencies across phase boundaries bears a striking resemblance to conditions from older theories. Under the Subjacency Condition, for example, transformational movement could only proceed within a certain type of domain, but could escape one domain by moving first to a position at its left edge. While this way of opening up the walls of phases may be empirically desirable, it significantly reduces the explanatory force exerted by the derivational modularity of the distinct phases. Indeed, the ease with which Chomsky is able to introduce an escape hatch to phases emphasizes the fact that in his system, phase immutability does not arise from any general property of the grammatical derivation. Once the grammatical architecture permits the internal constituents of distinct phases to interact with one another, the degree of such interaction becomes simply a matter of stipulation.[14]

The main proposal of this book is that there is in fact a way to maintain the idea that the locality of movement-derived syntactic dependencies stems from the derivational independence of structural units that are bounded in size. The key to doing this, I argue, lies in reconsidering the set of operations that the grammar makes available for structural composition. I propose that we make use of the derivational machinery of Tree Adjoining Grammar (TAG), a formal grammatical system that bears certain interesting relations to Chomsky's oldest and most recent derivational models. By using the structural composition operations that TAG provides—namely, *Adjoining* and *Substitution*—we can overcome the problems posed by examples like (11), without sacrificing the strict separation between independent derivational units. Such cases, rather than involving iterated movement across multiple structural domains, necessitate only local movement over a single derivationally distinguished structure, which is then combined with other independently derived domains using the TAG machinery for structural composition. We will see how this conception of the grammar leads to considerable simplification in the principles of grammar. The remainder of this chapter outlines the fundamentals of the TAG formal system and sketches its potential role in linguistic description.

## 1.2  TAG Basics

Tree Adjoining Grammar (TAG) (Joshi, Levy, and Takahashi 1975; Joshi 1985) was developed some twenty-five years ago as a mathematically restrictive formulation of a mechanism for structural composition, inspired in part by Chomsky's earlier work on generalized transformations. Unlike the well-known grammar formalisms from the Chomsky hierarchy that operate by rewriting strings (i.e., regular, context-free, context-sensitive, and unrestricted grammars), TAG is a system of tree rewriting in which a derivation manipulates a set of predefined pieces of tree structure, called *elementary trees*. During a TAG derivation, the elementary trees are expanded and combined with one another, a conception that is closely related to frameworks in which structures are built up through generalized transformations.

   TAG provides two operations for the expansion of an elementary tree T. The first of these, *Substitution*, rewrites a node N along T's periphery, or *frontier*, as another tree S that is rooted in a node having same label as N (say, X). Alternatively, one can think of Substitution as a tree combination operation in which the root of a structure S is identified with a node N on T's frontier. Such an application of Substitution is depicted schematically in (12).

(12)

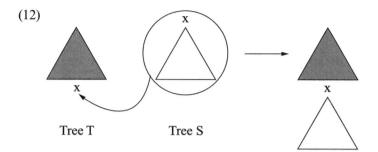

For an application of Substitution like this, we say that *S is substituted into T at N.*

Substitution can be used to derive complex sentences involving clausal complementation. Substituting the tree in (13b) into the CP complement node of the tree in (13a) produces the structure in (13c).[15]

(13) a.

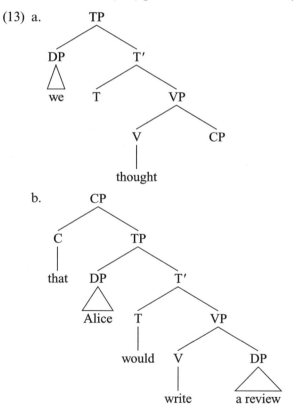

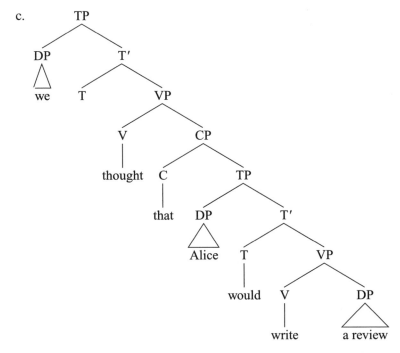

Used in this way, Substitution accomplishes effects similar to those of
(some of) the generalized transformations from Chomsky 1955 and the
Merge operation from Chomsky 1995: it inserts XPs into the argument
positions of syntactic predicates. Substitution differs from Merge, although not from the original generalized transformation proposals, in
that the argument site "inhabited" by the substituted elementary tree in
the derived structure is present prior to Substitution, while such a position is created under Merge.[16]

   While Substitution rewrites or expands only nodes along the frontier,
the second TAG operation, *Adjoining*, is capable of rewriting or expanding any node in an elementary tree. To do this, Adjoining makes use of a
special class of recursive structures called *auxiliary trees*. An auxiliary
tree is a structure whose root is labeled identically to some node along its
frontier, the *foot node*. Given an auxiliary tree A recursive on X, Adjoining operates by rewriting as A some node N within an elementary tree T
that is also labeled X. Any structure that originally appears below N in T
is attached below the foot node of A in the derived phrase marker. This is
depicted schematically in (14).

(14)

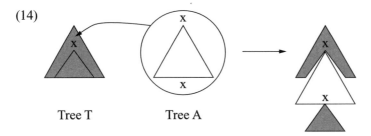

Tree T                       Tree A

When such adjoining takes place, we say that *A adjoins to T at N*. As
with Substitution, Adjoining can also be conceived of as a tree-combining
operation. In such terms, adjoining at a node N labeled X of an elementary tree T first removes the subtree of T dominated by N, then attaches
an auxiliary tree A in place of T, and finally reattaches the subtree of T
to the foot node of A.[17]

Adjoining is crucially involved in the TAG derivation of a variety of
grammatical structures. The first of these is the class of structures underlying modification. By adjoining a VP recursive auxiliary tree like that in
(15a) to the VP node of the clausal structure in (15b), we derive the tem-
porally modified clausal structure in (15c).

(15) a.

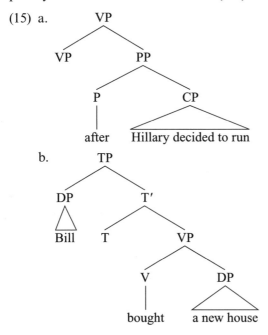

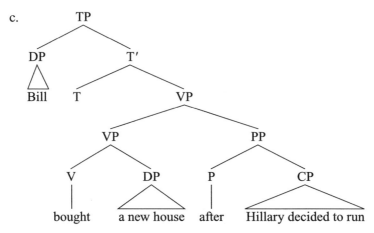

c.

Here, the VP recursion between the root and foot nodes of the auxiliary tree is used to introduce a Chomsky-adjunction structure into the VP in the main clause.

This use of Adjoining in constructing adjunction structures suggests a possible similarity between the TAG Adjoining operation and the adjunction operation familiar from recent work (Lebeaux 1988; Chomsky 1993, 1995). Despite the similarity of name and the overlap in function between the two operations, however, there are a number of significant differences between the two. The first is analogous to the difference observed earlier between the operations of Substitution and Merge. During application of Adjoining, no nodes are added, as the "modification" auxiliary tree in (15a) already includes both segments of the VP to which it attaches. A second difference derives from the greater generality of Adjoining. The derivation in (15) makes use of a restricted form of auxiliary tree in which the foot node is the child of the root. When there is instead greater structural distance between the root and the foot of an auxiliary tree, the output of Adjoining no longer resembles that of adjunction. To see why not, consider again the generation of a structure involving clausal complementation, like that in (13c). Observe that if the matrix clause is represented with a CP-rooted elementary tree, as might be the case in a tree like (16) where an auxiliary verb has been moved to C, this elementary tree has the necessary recursive structure to function as an auxiliary tree: the CP complement is categorially identical to the structure's root.

(16)

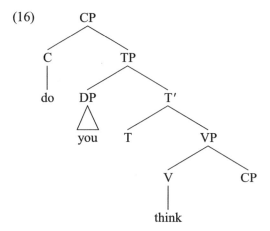

Now, although the CP embedded clause in (13b) may still be substituted into the CP complement position of (16), this combination may also take place by adjoining (16) to the CP root node of (13b). Quite clearly, this structure could not have resulted from an application of the traditional adjunction operation. As a result of these differences, I will use the term *Adjoining* to refer uniquely to the TAG operation, reserving *adjunction* to refer to the more traditional operation.

Conspicuously absent from this review of the TAG machinery has been any mention of transformations. In fact, this is the most central difference between TAG derivations and those in both Chomsky's oldest proposals and his most recent ones. As formally defined (see section 1.3), TAG derivations operate by combining a fixed set of elementary trees with Adjoining and Substitution. I assume that the incorporation of TAG into a grammatical theory entails that this derivational structure should remain unchanged. That is, in a TAG-based theory, no other operations, whether transformations or structural composition, may be interleaved with applications of Adjoining and Substitution. Thus, it is not possible in the TAG context to create dependencies spanning two elementary trees via the application of transformational movement.[18] Since we take operations of structural composition not to be implicated in the creation of syntactic dependencies, this means that any dependencies that are expressed in a syntactic representation R must be expressed within the elementary trees that make up R. This observation leads to the fundamental hypothesis underlying the application of TAG to syntactic theory:

(17)  *The fundamental TAG hypothesis*
Every syntactic dependency is expressed locally within a single
elementary tree.

In evaluating the fundamental TAG hypothesis, it is crucial that we
know what constitutes the syntactic domain of an elementary tree. Yet,
to this point, we have said nothing about this topic. Since elementary
trees are not composed during the TAG derivation but are instead provided to the TAG operations in their final form, the TAG formalism itself has nothing to say about what they will look like. If we are to apply
the TAG machinery to grammatical theory, then, we must provide some
independent specification of the elementary trees that make up the grammar of a language. Since we take Substitution and Adjoining to be a
universal component of the grammatical architecture, any differences that
exist among the grammars of different languages must reside entirely in
what elementary trees they take to be well formed. Since this set of elementary trees must be finite for any particular language, one could in
principle specify the set of elementary trees that are present in the grammars of English, Italian, Japanese, and so on, merely by listing them. Of
course, it would not be surprising if such a listing approach turned out to
be the best way at present for constructing grammars for practical applications, given our limited understanding of abstract grammatical principles.[19] However, explanatory adequacy demands that we do more than
this. We must characterize the commonalities and limited differences
that exist among grammars, with the aim of overcoming the argument
from the poverty of the stimulus. I assume, therefore, that a TAG-based
grammatical theory must include some additional component that determines the well-formedness of elementary trees in a principled fashion.

In developing a theory of elementary tree well-formedness, we will be
guided to a large degree by the fundamental TAG hypothesis in (17): our
conception of elementary trees must allow for the necessary localization
of dependencies. However, the adoption of the TAG operations does
not implicate any particular conception of a theory of elementary tree
well-formedness. One can imagine a variety of ways in which such a
theory might be expressed, ranging from transformational derivations
to unification-based constraint satisfaction to optimality calculations to
categorial inference. In fact, the TAG formalism is perhaps unique in
having attracted a rich variety of perspectives on the proper characterization of structural well-formedness including Lexicon Grammar (Abeillé

1988, 1991; Abeillé and Schabes 1989), Head-Driven Phrase Structure Grammar (Kasper et al. 1995), Categorial Grammar (Joshi and Kulick 1997), and Government-Binding Theory (Kroch 1989b; Kroch and Santorini 1991; Frank 1992; Hegarty 1993a,b).[20] Regardless of which of these is chosen, the basic TAG architecture constrains any mechanism or well-formedness condition to apply strictly within an elementary tree.

I will adopt here the general perspective of principles-and-parameters theory in which universal linguistic principles, as instantiated by the values of parameters set for a given language, determine which elementary trees are licit in a TAG derivation. Beyond this, I assume that the specification of well-formed elementary trees is given at least in part in terms of a derivational process. In chapter 4 especially, I will entertain the hypothesis that elementary trees are constructed using derivations much like those considered in Chomsky 2000, involving Merge and Move. This gives rise to the model depicted in figure 1.4. From this perspective, the set of elementary trees that may take part in TAG derivations (i.e., that are combined by Adjoining and Substitution) in a given language has no more status than the set of well-formed phrase markers in the theory developed in Chomsky 2000. Such a set is an entirely derivative object, and focus on it obscures the primacy of the underlying principles of grammar.[21]

Note that in the model of figure 1.4, the Merge/Move portion of the derivation cannot interact with the TAG portion of the derivation, involving applications of Adjoining and Substitution. That is to say, Merge and Move may manipulate representations only as large as the domain of a single elementary tree. Once the derivation reaches a stage in which it has constructed a representation larger than this, the only operations that may apply are the mechanisms for structure composition provided by the TAG formalism. TAG elementary trees, then, provide the sort of intermediate structural domain long missing from grammatical theory that determines the structural context in which transformational operations may apply.

The degree to which localizing Merge and Move to elementary trees is empirically desirable obviously depends to a great degree on what one takes to be the domain of an elementary tree, a topic to which I turn in chapter 2. For the moment, let me tentatively suggest that elementary trees should be thought of along the lines of the kernel sentences in Chomsky's (1955) model, essentially clausal in extent. This suggestion

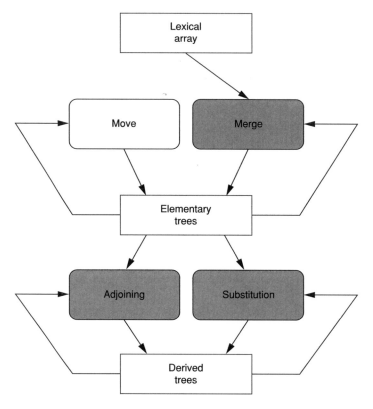

**Figure 1.4**
TAG-based derivational model

goes some way toward supporting the fundamental TAG hypothesis, as it
allows the thematic dependencies of the predicate heading the clause to
be localized within an elementary tree. Moreover, we can see why it is
crucial that elementary trees like the one in (13a) must have a preexisting
position for their complement: it yields a structural basis for the expression of the verb-complement dependency within the elementary tree.
Similarly, the existence of the lower VP segment within the auxiliary tree
in (15a) allows for the structural expression of a predication relation between the PP and the VP within this tree.

Unfortunately, as soon as we set our sights on a wider range of phenomena, the tenability of the fundamental TAG hypothesis seems to
erode, as there are a great many syntactic dependencies that can cross

clausal boundaries. For example, the relationship between the base and surface positions of a phrase that undergoes *wh*-movement, topicalization, or raising can span a number of clauses, as seen in the following examples:

(18) a. (I wonder) [which book] Gabriel had thought his friends should read *t*.

    b. [A meal cooked by Steve], I can't believe that you would turn down *t*.

    c. [That tyrant] is likely *t* to defeat Alice in the election.

It is assumed in this and all other linguistic investigations in the TAG framework that such violations of the fundamental TAG hypothesis are only apparent. In fact, there is a natural TAG derivation of examples like those in (18). To derive (18a), for example, the elementary tree representing the embedded clause will already contain a dependency between the fronted DP and the position of its trace.

(19)

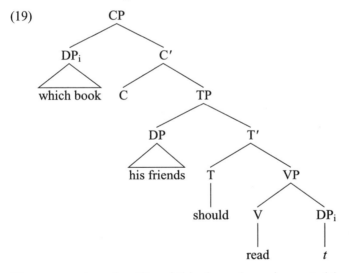

The apparent nonlocality of this dependency is created by adjoining the auxiliary tree in (20a) to the C′ node in (19). The result is the structure in (20b).[22]

(20)  a.

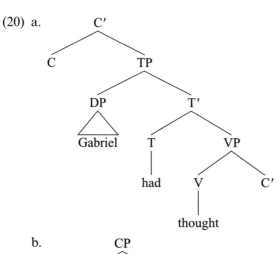

b.

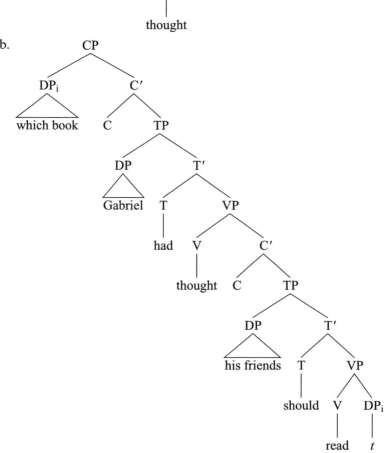

By interposing the auxiliary tree in (20a) between the *wh*-moved DP and its trace, we effectively stretch an originally local relation to one that is no longer clause bounded. As we shall discuss at length in subsequent chapters, similar derivations are possible for the other cases in (18). For (18b), we use Adjoining to interpose an auxiliary tree containing the lexical material *I can't believe* between the topicalized DP *a meal cooked by Steve* and the clause *that you would turn down* that form part of the same elementary tree. Likewise, for (18c), we adjoin an auxiliary tree containing the lexical material *is likely* between the subject DP *that tyrant* and the rest of its clause *to defeat Alice in the election*.

Recall that Adjoining functions by rewriting some node of an elementary tree as a recursive piece of structure, an auxiliary tree. This means that whenever local dependencies are stretched in the manner just sketched, such stretching may result only from the introduction of recursive structure. Thinking about this from the point of view of decomposing nonlocal dependencies, one can state the following corollary of the fundamental TAG hypothesis:

(21) *Nonlocal dependency corollary*
     Nonlocal dependencies always reduce to local ones once recursive structure is factored away.

Much of the remainder of this book will be devoted to showing that this corollary accurately characterizes the types of dependencies present in natural language.[23]

## 1.3  The Structure of TAG Derivations

With the basic ideas of TAG laid out, let us now turn to the task of characterizing the notion of TAG derivation. Note first of all that by *TAG derivation*, I mean only the combination of elementary trees via Adjoining and Substitution and not the process of elementary tree construction using Merge and Move envisioned in figure 1.4. The basic intuition is this: a TAG derivation consists of a sequence of combinations of elementary trees using Adjoining and Substitution. To formalize this idea, we will make use of a representation of the sequence of derivational steps, called a *derivation structure* (Vijay-Shanker 1987). The idea of a derivation structure has a long history within generative grammar, going back to the T-marker in the theory of Chomsky 1955. A TAG derivation structure is a tree in which each node corresponds to an elementary tree.

The daughters of a given node N represent the trees that are adjoined or substituted into the elementary tree represented by N. Since there may be ambiguity about where in an elementary tree another tree is substituted or adjoined (owing to the presence of multiple nodes with the same categorial label within a single elementary tree), the links connecting any pair of nodes are annotated with the location in the mother elementary tree where Adjoining or Substitution has taken place.

Let us briefly consider some examples of derivation structures. For the VP modification derivation in (15), the root node of the derivation structure will represent the main clause elementary tree. Its only daughter will be a node corresponding to the VP modifier auxiliary tree. This yields the derivation structure in (22).

(22)    Bill bought a new house
                VP |
        after Hillary decided to run

The picture becomes more interesting when we consider the somewhat more complex example in (23).

(23)  Bill bought a new house after Hillary decided to run because their fight was over.

This sentence is ambiguous: the *because* adjunct clause may be construed as modifying either the act of buying or the act of deciding. Let us assume for present purposes that the *because* adjunct is introduced into the derivation with a TP-modifying auxiliary tree, similar in structure to the one in (15a). The two readings of the sentence are distinguished by their derivations. The first derivation involves the *because* tree first adjoining into the *after* tree, with the result adjoining into the *bought* tree. This derivation is depicted in (24).

(24)    Bill bought a new house
                VP |
        after Hillary decided to run
                TP |
        because their fight was over

In the second derivation, both adjunct clauses adjoin separately into the main clause elementary tree at the VP and TP nodes. The resulting derivation structure, shown in (25), is quite different in shape.

(25)                                Bill bought a new house

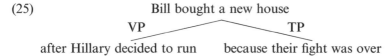

after Hillary decided to run       because their fight was over

The fact that the derivation structure concisely encodes the distinction between the two readings suggests that we might want to follow Chomsky's (1955) line in taking the derivation structure (T-marker) to constitute the interface with the interpretive component.[24] Derivation structures have largely been ignored in recent work in the Minimalist Program, perhaps because in a system that builds structure one level of projection at a time, as with the Merge operation, the derivation structure is to a large extent indistinguishable from the derived structure. It is therefore unclear whether it is the derived phrase marker or the derivation structure that is the object of grammatical interest in these more recent proposals. If I am correct in taking the derivation structure to be the interpretive interface, this raises the question of what role, if any, is played by the derived phrase marker. Though pursuing this matter would take us far afield, it may be that the derived phrase marker's unique function is that of providing an input to the phonological component. I return briefly to such speculations in chapter 6.

   Once the TAG derivational system is provided with a set of elementary trees, any combination of these trees using Substitution and Adjoining will be representable in terms of a derivation structure. This free combinability is, however, subject to one formal restriction that ensures that derivation structures maintain a certain formal simplicity. Recall that since a derivation structure is a tree, the daughters of any node in the derivation structure may have daughters of their own. That is, they may themselves be the locus for the adjoining or substitution of other elementary trees. We have already seen an example of such embedding in the derivation structure in (24). Note, however, that neither this nor any other derivation structure specifies whether the derivation has taken place in a top-down or a bottom-up fashion. For the derivation structure in (24), one can imagine either that the two auxiliary trees have first combined, the result being adjoined into the main clause elementary tree, or that the *after* auxiliary adjoins first into the main clause, the *because* auxiliary then being adjoined into this complex. There is little reason to prefer one of these derivations over the other given the derivation structure, and it therefore seems reasonable to assume that both derivations ought to be possible. To guarantee that this will always be the case, it is sufficient to require that every combination of elementary trees τ and τ′ indicated by a mother-daughter relation in a derivation structure must be possible independently of other combinations indicated by the derivation structure. For the derivation structure in (24), this requirement has the effect of ensuring that the combination of the *after* auxiliary tree with the *bought* elementary tree is possible independently of the prior combination of the *after* and *because* auxiliary trees. This restriction on possible derivations imposes a context-free or Markovian character on these derivation structures, and indeed it can be proven that TAG derivation structures are strongly context free. I return to empirical implications of this restriction in chapter 3.

In a TAG-based grammatical theory, certain grammatical constraints will turn out to have their effects by imposing additional restrictions on derivations. A simple example arises in enforcing selectional properties, as in a verb like *regret*'s requirement that its CP complement be finite. Since the grammar presumably contains both finite and nonfinite CP-rooted elementary trees, we will need to find some way of permitting only finite ones to be inserted—say, via Substitution—into the complement position of an elementary tree containing the verb *regret*. Let us make the standard assumption that nodes in a phrase marker bear certain features. In particular, let us assume that the CP roots of elementary trees like those in (26a) contain a specification of the finiteness of these clauses, and that the CP frontier node of the elementary tree in (26b) bears a finiteness feature as a result of *regret*'s selectional properties.[25]

(26) a.

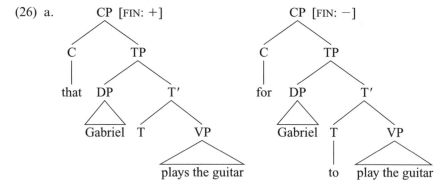

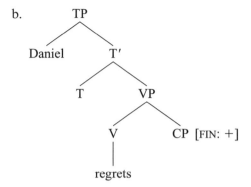

Suppose now that in identifying the root of the substituted structure with the frontier node into which substitution takes place, Substitution also merges the feature sets of the two nodes, where this Merge operation is understood as feature unification. This yields the desired result that certain substitutions that would be possible on the basis of node label compatibility are in fact no longer possible. In the case at hand, the nonfinite CP in (26a) cannot substitute into the CP node of (26b), because of the feature clash. Other derivational constraints might arise from interface conditions, in the sense of Chomsky (1993, 1995). Suppose, for example, that we take the conceptual system that interfaces with syntax to be capable of interpreting only structures that carry complete propositional interpretations. This would mean that the output of a derivation that failed to produce a phrase rooted in CP would not be interpretable. Finally, as I will discuss in detail in chapter 4, a class of restrictions on applications of Adjoining derives from a certain notion of derivational economy.

In the context of this discussion, it is important to note that the TAG formalism tolerates only constraints on derivations that have a local character. That is, the well-formedness of a derivation must be determinable on the basis of consulting only mother-daughter relations between elementary trees in the derivation structure. The formalism does not permit restrictions on derivation structures that make reference to global structural properties (e.g., binary branching or restrictions on certain c-command relations) or global constraints on the derived phrase markers. This limitation of the TAG formalism has a significant impact on the nature of grammatical constraints and processes that may form part of a TAG-based theory of grammar: they may only specify properties of individual elementary trees.[26]

This limitation on allowable grammatical principles is quite restrictive, but appears to capture the kind of constraints that are generally taken to hold in human grammars. Indeed, truly global conditions on syntactic well-formedness have rarely been proposed, and for those that have been, alternative analyses suggest that they should be seen as extrasyntactic constraints. For example, binding theory Condition C, which requires that names, or R-expressions, not be c-commanded by a coreferential element, has been reconceptualized as a morphological condition (Burzio 1989), pragmatic constraint (Reinhart 1986), or interpretive principle (Chomsky 1993). If one of these suggestions is on the right track, then the fact that TAG cannot encode global principles provides empirical support for the link between the formal restrictiveness of the TAG formalism and the properties of human grammar.

## 1.4  Formal Grammar and Human Grammar

In addition to investigations of the sort we are engaged in here concerning the relevance of TAG to linguistic theory, the TAG formal system has been well studied as a mathematical object (Joshi 1985; Vijay-Shanker 1987). Perhaps the central question in such work on formal grammars concerns generative capacity, that is, the range of languages for which a given formalism can provide grammars. Language can be understood here as a set of strings, in which case we talk of weak generative capacity, or a set of structural descriptions, in which case we talk of strong generative capacity. For the formalisms in the Chomsky hierarchy, generative capacity has been well characterized. It is known, for example, that while context-free grammars can be given for the string languages in (27), none can be given for the closely related string languages in (28).

(27)  a.  $L_1 = \{ww^r \mid w \in \{a, b\}^*\}$ (where $w^r$ is the reversal of $w$)
      b.  $L_2 = \{a^n b^n \mid n \in \mathbb{N}\}$

(28)  a.  $L_3 = \{ww \mid w \in \{a, b\}^*\}$
      b.  $L_4 = \{a^n b^n c^n \mid n \in \mathbb{N}\}$

Where does TAG fall with respect to generative capacity, then? It is not difficult to show that every context-free (string) language is also a tree adjoining language (TAL). Moreover, for each of the languages in (28), there is a TAG (i.e., a set of elementary trees) that generates it. These are given in (29) and (30) for the languages $L_3$ and $L_4$, respectively.

(29)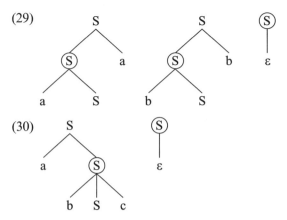

(30)

The grammar in (30) generates strings in $L_4$ by repeatedly adjoining one copy of the auxiliary tree on the left to another at the circled S node. For each such adjoining, the number of $a$s, $b$s, and $c$s increases by one. Finally, to complete the derivation, the derived auxiliary tree adjoins to the S node of the $\varepsilon$-tree. Such a derivation for the string $a^2b^2c^2d^2$ is depicted in (31).

(31)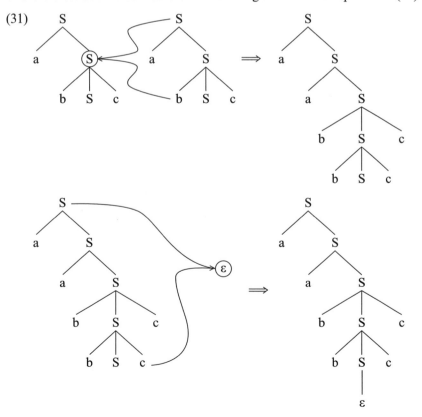

It should be clear how this sort of derivation can be extended to generate any string in $L_4$. To ensure that this grammar does not generate strings outside of $L_4$, we must guarantee that the *a*s, *b*s, and *c*s remain properly partitioned. To do this, we must prevent Adjoining from taking place anywhere other than at the nodes indicated in this derivation. This can be accomplished by adopting the system of derivational constraints proposed by Vijay-Shanker and Joshi (1985), which allows the nodes of an elementary tree to be marked as null adjoining (NA), indicating that nothing may adjoin at that node. Adopting the convention that all non-circled nodes in an elementary tree are marked NA, the grammars given in (29) and (30) indeed generate $L_3$ and $L_4$.

Though the weak (and strong) generative capacity of TAG extends beyond that of context-free grammars, its extension into the realm of the context-sensitive languages is extremely limited. So, the languages in (32), while closely related to those in (28) and well within the realm of the context-sensitive languages, are not generable by any TAG (Vijay-Shanker 1987).

(32) a. $L_5 = \{www \mid w \in \Sigma^*\}$
    b. $L_6 = \{a^n b^n c^n d^n e^n \mid n \in \mathbb{N}\}$

The potential linguistic interest of discussions of generative capacity lies in the degree to which a limitation on generative capacity plays a role in characterizing grammatical competence. As Chomsky has pointed out on numerous occasions (e.g., Chomsky 1965, 60–62; 1981, 11–13), there is no reason a priori to expect that formal properties like generative capacity should be relevant to such a characterization. Indeed, for the classes of grammars in the Chomsky hierarchy, the corresponding generative capacities do not appear to match up with the properties of natural language in any interesting way. Chomsky (1956, 1957) demonstrates that regular grammars are not sufficiently powerful in either their weak or their strong generative capacity to describe natural language, and similar arguments have been made more recently for context-free grammars (Culy 1985; Shieber 1985). The next step in the hierarchy, context-sensitive grammars, is however so expressive that it offers little limitation on what could count as a natural language. It is interesting to note, however, that the "mild" context-sensitivity of TAG is sufficient to allow treatment of grammatical phenomena whose analysis has been shown to lie beyond the power of context-free grammars.[27] One such case, discussed by Culy (1985), concerns a reduplication phenomenon in Bambara. Culy shows that this gives rise to a sublanguage that is in formal respects identical to $L_3$, a language for which a TAG is already provided above. Shieber (1985) brings up the case of Swiss German cross-serial dependencies, in which nominal arguments and their associated verbs appear in crossing rather than nested orders. A TAG of the form in (33) is adequate to generate sentences of this type, assigning them well-motivated structural descriptions (Kroch and Santorini 1991).[28]

(33)

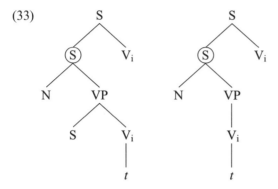

I take the possibility of analyzing these non-context-free phenomena within TAG to suggest that there is a correspondence between the limited formal power of TAG and the expressive demands of natural language.[29]

Let me emphasize that I am not contending that the restricted weak or strong generative capacity (or any other formal property) by itself recommends the use of some grammatical formalism in a theory of human linguistic competence. Similarly, I am not claiming that the existence of a polynomial-time parsing algorithm lends any increased plausibility to the place of some formalism in human grammar (cf. Gazdar et al. 1985). Rather, I am claiming that by considering a significant range of empirical data, we are led to conclude a posteriori that exactly the sort of formal restrictiveness embodied in TAG constitutes a part of grammatical competence (cf. Chomsky's (2000) argument for limited computational complexity, appropriately defined, in the grammar).[30] As discussed above, the adoption of TAG substantially limits the range of possible grammatical principles to those that can be expressed over the domain of elementary trees. As we find ourselves continually able to analyze grammatical phenomena in these terms, our confidence that TAG forms part of the grammar should correspondingly increase. A second type of support for the adoption of TAG comes from the fact that TAG's formal restrictiveness allows us to simplify or entirely eliminate the statement of previously complex grammatical restrictions. For example, as I will discuss in chapter 5, there is no need in a TAG treatment of *wh*-movement for an analogue of a principle governing the locality of movement like Subjacency, as its effects already follow from the mechanisms of the formalism.

The discovery that human language can be simply and naturally characterized in terms of the limited formal power of TAG, if correct, would reveal a rather abstract and very surprising property of human language indeed. Therefore, just as any grammatical theory must explain the existence of other empirically discovered constraints, so we should expect that any theory should also explain why the computational system of human language is limited in its formal power.

# Chapter 2

# The Nature of Elementary Trees

At least since the appearance of Ross 1967, it has been recognized that there are substantial limitations on the structural contexts over which grammatical processes take place. Indeed, much of the subsequent research in generative syntax has focused on characterizing precisely the local domains over which grammatical processes apply. Within a TAG-based syntactic theory, such a characterization is of fundamental importance. The fundamental hypothesis of TAG-based work in syntax states that grammatical dependencies must be expressed within the structural context of an elementary tree. In order to characterize the basic building blocks of the derivational system, then, it is necessary to come to terms with the notion of local domain. In this chapter, I take up this central issue of determining what structural domain can count as an elementary tree.

In doing this, I build on an intuition that has been pervasive in syntactic theory, namely, that basic predications or clauses form the foundation of syntactically local domains. I discuss a number of ways of making this idea precise in the TAG context, ultimately fixing on the notion of extended projection. I then turn to a number of well-formedness conditions on elementary trees and how these affect the course of TAG derivations.

## 2.1 Elementary Trees as Thematic Domains

A great deal of work in syntactic theory has assigned a privileged status to the syntactic analogue of predicate argument structure. Such a domain, which we can call a *thematic domain*, consists of a single lexical predicate along with the structural context in which it takes its arguments. This notion takes a variety of forms and names, but the same essential idea seems to underlie kernel sentences in Harris 1957 and Chomsky 1955, 1957, cyclic domains in Chomsky 1965, strata in Relational Grammar (Perlmutter 1983), f-structure nuclei in LFG (Bresnan

1982b), and governing categories in Government-Binding Theory (Chomsky 1981). Since the earliest linguistic work in the TAG tradition (Kroch and Joshi 1985), it has been assumed, if only implicitly, that elementary trees consist of precisely one such domain, though no characterization of thematic domain has been given.

We can start the process of rendering the idea of thematic domain more precise by taking the idea quite literally, supposing that a thematic domain is exactly the syntactic context in which lexical predicates take their arguments—or, stating it differently, over which they assign θ-roles. Let us focus on verbal heads, with predicates of other categories falling into place afterward. One traditional view of θ-role assignment is that internal arguments are assigned their θ-roles in complement position of the verb, while external arguments' θ-roles are assigned in the surface subject position, which we will assume to be the specifier of a T(ense) projection.

(1)

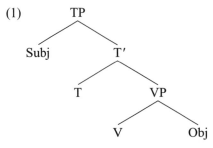

A more recent trend, as seen in the work of Fukui and Speas (1986), Koopman and Sportiche (1991), and Kuroda (1988), has been to follow suggestions by McCawley (1970) and Fillmore (1968) in taking the subject's surface position to be derived, the base thematic position being located within the projection of the lexical predicate.[1]

(2)

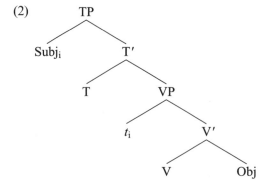

Note that the T head plays no role in θ-role assignment here; instead, it acts as a sort of raising predicate, bearing no thematic relation to its specifier.

If we now equate elementary trees with thematic domains, the two views of the structural context for θ-role assignment lead to two different conclusions: (verbally headed) elementary trees should project up either as high as TP or as high as VP. Unfortunately, both of these conceptions of elementary trees face significant problems when we try to apply them to a system of derivations based on the TAG operations. The first problem relates to the generation of those portions of clausal structure that lie outside the thematic domain. A wide array of recent work has established the need for the syntactic realization of grammatical morphemes that express properties such as tense, negation, mood, aspect, and illocutionary force (see, e.g., Abney 1987; Pollock 1989; Ouhalla 1991; Zanuttini 1997; Cinque 1999). This work argues that each of these functional elements serves as the head of its own syntactic phrase, a functional projection. As functional elements are distinguished from their lexical counterparts by their inability to assign θ-roles, they will never be able to serve as the predicate core of an independent elementary tree under the conception of elementary trees we are exploring. Consequently, the only way that these functional projections can enter into a piece of phrase structure is by "piggybacking" on the thematic domain established by some lexical predicate. We have seen one way this can happen: if we assume that external θ-roles are assigned to the surface subject position, the thematic domain of the tense head includes the projection of the tense head, and therefore this functional projection will be included in the verbally headed elementary tree.[2] Even under this extended view of thematic domain, functional heads that are higher in the clause than the subject, such as complementizers, will not form part of a verbally headed elementary tree and consequently will not be incorporable into a phrase marker.

Two possibilities can be pursued at this point. One involves rejecting the basic assumption that a lexical predicate must form the core of each elementary tree. This would allow elementary trees in which functional heads and their projections could appear independently from lexical heads and therefore could be incorporated into a syntactic representation during the course of a TAG derivation. This is the line of analysis adopted in Hegarty 1993a, where it is suggested that any syntactic phrase may constitute a distinct elementary tree, combined using the TAG combinatory machinery.[3] For reasons that I outline in Frank 1992, I do not believe that this is the right path to pursue (but see Hegarty 1993a for a response). In brief, these arguments center on phenomena, such as the interaction of verb raising and adverb placement, that are not naturally localized within a single phrasal projection and for which Adjoining does not provide a simple solution. The alternative we are left with, then, is that elementary trees must grow: they will need to include not only the thematic domain of a lexical predicate, but also additional functional material.

## 2.2   Extending beyond the Thematic Domain

Elementary trees, like their organic counterparts, can grow in one of two places, either from the root or at the leaves. If we must extend elementary trees beyond their basic thematic domains, we need to determine the direction in which growth should proceed. As our use of TAG leads us to expect that syntactic relations should be localized within an elementary tree, one way to proceed is by determining the sorts of relations that exist between lexical and functional heads and the degree to which upward or downward growth succeeds in localizing them within an elementary tree.

One potentially relevant sort of association between lexical predicates and functional heads concerns the relationship between a lexical predicate and the functional head(s) that appear lower in the structure, as a result of the selectional requirements of the lexical predicates. For example, the verb *think* selects a clausal complement headed by the functional head C, *expect* selects either a C- or T-headed clausal complement, and *take* requires a T-headed clausal complement.

(3) a.   Harold thought/expected/*took [CP that Maude was causing all the problems].
    b.   Harold *thought/expected/took [TP Maude to be causing all the problems].

Indeed, such selection also restricts properties of the complement more specific than syntactic category: *think* requires a CP headed by *that*, *take* requires a TP headed by *to*, and so on. If we take as fundamental this kind of downward association between lexical and functional heads, essentially the traditional notion of government of functional elements

by a lexical head, we are led to a view of elementary trees, advocated by
Abeillé (1991, 1993), in which they include not only the projection of a
single lexical predicate and its thematic domain, as before, but also the
projections of the predicate's selected functional complements. The
elementary tree headed by the verb *think* might then be represented as
in (4).[4]

(4)

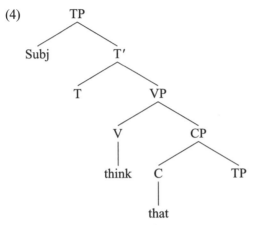

In this "downwardly extended" elementary tree, I have assumed that the
thematic domain of a verb extends as high as TP. Consider what happens, though, when we are faced with a verb like *expect* that selects for a
TP complement headed by *to*. In the generation of an example like (3b),
it is not clear whether the embedded TP projection ought to be included
within the elementary tree headed by the matrix verb *expect* as a result of
being selected, or within the elementary tree headed by *causing* as a result
of being part of its thematic domain. One could of course stipulate a resolution to this conflict to the effect that functional heads are preferably
included within a thematic domain, say, but it is not clear what principled grounds there are for this move. If we instead pursue the alternative
view of thematic domains as including only the projection of the lexical
predicate, we are led to posit downwardly extended elementary trees like
the one in (5).

(5)
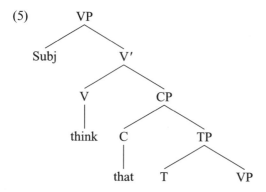

Here, I have included both the CP and TP projections of the embedded clause in the elementary tree headed by the higher verb, as neither forms part of the embedded thematic domain any longer. This conception of elementary trees faces two difficulties, however. First, there is the issue of how unselected clauses—for example, matrix clauses—could acquire CP and TP functional projections. The second, and more serious, problem concerns the placement of the subject. Suppose we want to use the elementary tree in (5) in a derivation, combining it with the elementary tree headed by (what will become) an embedded verb.

(6)
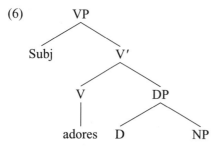

Using the operations of Substitution and Adjoining, there is no way to perform this combination in such a way that the embedded subject finds itself in a position above the lower clause's T head, while still remaining below the verb *think*. Substitution of the embedded clause would leave the subject too low, while adjoining of the matrix clause just below the subject (which would be rendered possible if, say, V′ were assimilated to VP as in Kayne 1994) would leave the embedded subject above the higher verb.[5]

A second type of association between lexical and functional heads that could serve as the basis for elementary trees derives from the upward selectivity of lexical heads for the functional heads with which they co-occur inside a clausal domain. In analyses of a wide range of languages, we see example after example of verb phrases being embedded within projections of tense, mood, negation, complementizers, and the like. Similarly, we see projections of nouns embedded within projections of determiners and prepositions. However, one almost never comes across suggestions that a language exhibits structures in which a noun is embedded within the projection of a tense or complementizer head, or in which a verb is embedded within the projection of a determiner.[6] Grimshaw (1991) characterizes the linkage between lexical and functional projections via a notion she labels *extended projection*. In essence, the extended projection of a lexical head includes the projections of all those functional heads that embed it (up through but not including the next lexical head). The structure in (7), then, includes five separate extended projections, corresponding to its five lexical heads.

(7)

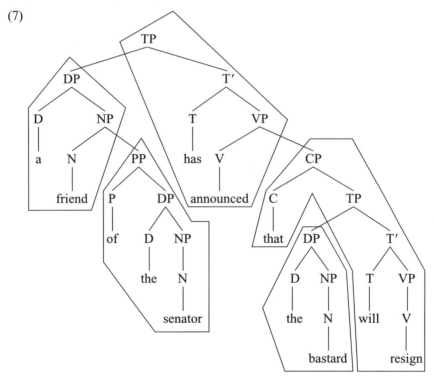

The extended projection of the nouns *friend* and *bastard* includes a D projection, while that of *senator* includes the projection of the preposition

*of* as well.[7] The extended projection of the verb *announced* includes the
projection of the matrix T, while that of the embedded verb *resign* con-
tinues up to the level of the embedded CP. Note that the degree to which
an extended projection extends for any particular head is not fixed; instead, it depends on the syntactic context in which the extended projection occurs. That is, while extended projections of nouns may include the
projections of D and P and extended projections of verbs may include
the projections of T and C, none of these functional heads is obligatory
and indeed an extended projection might include only the projection of
the lexical head itself.[8] What is required, however, is that extended projections preserve the associations and hierarchical orderings between
lexical and functional heads, which Grimshaw formalizes in terms of an
extended notion of categorial features (see also Van Riemsdijk 1996).[9]
Thus, the sequences of projections in (8a) standing in complement relations would constitute well-formed extended projections, while those in
(8b) would not.

(8) a. CP–IP–VP, IP–VP, VP, PP–DP–NP, DP–NP, NP
    b. CP–IP–NP, PP–IP–VP, PP–DP–VP, DP–VP, VP–CP–IP,
       DP–NP–PP

By taking extended projections as the basis of elementary trees, we run
into none of the problems that arise if we assume downwardly extended
elementary trees. To derive a structure involving CP complementation,
like that in (7), we need only substitute the elementary tree given in (9a)
into the CP complement node of the *announced*-headed elementary tree in
(9b).[10]

(9) a.

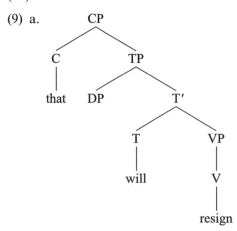

b.

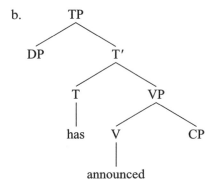

The ease with which extended projections can be combined to produce complex sentences suggests that they constitute a promising candidate as the basis for elementary trees. Since elementary trees localize grammatical dependencies under a TAG-based grammatical theory, it would be reassuring to find evidence that extended projections provide a natural characterization of the locus of a wide variety of syntactic phenomena. Consequently, before turning to the implications of taking extended projections to characterize elementary trees in section 2.4, I explore the unifying nature of extended projections.

## 2.3   The Unity of Extended Projections

I have just suggested that the notion of an extended projection can plausibly be taken to determine the domain of an elementary tree, the primitive structural context within TAG. If the TAG formalism is the appropriate mechanism for separating structural recursion from local grammatical relations, then the architecture of the theory leads us to expect to find many such relations that are entirely localized within the domain of its basic structural units, that is, within the domain of extended projections. Grimshaw (1991) argues that there are in fact many such phenomena. In this section, I will review a number of these cases, involving selectional properties, feature percolation, and head movement, summarizing and extending Grimshaw's original discussion. It is worth noting that Grimshaw's proposal on its own does not explain why any of these processes ought to be localized within extended projections as they are. Instead, extended projections, as derived from preexisting phrase markers, are simply stipulated to localize certain processes. We see then that adoption of the TAG-based derivational system coupled with the view of elementary trees as extended projections deepens the explanation for the existence of certain kinds of locality effects.

### 2.3.1 Selection

The relation of selection is usually assumed to hold between a head and its complement. Under this view, a head can require that its complement have particular values for any of the features it can bear, in the most extreme case down to the choice of a particular lexical item. As already noted, verbs selecting for clausal complements can specify features of the embedded CP projection: the verb *think* takes CPs headed only by the complementizer *that*, the verb *want* demands that its CP complement be headed by *for*, and the verb *wonder* requires either that its complement CP be headed by the [+wh] complementizer *if* or *whether* or that the CP's specifier bear features appropriate to identify the C head as [+wh].

There are in addition many cases where (semantic) selection does not appear to be as local as between a head and its complement. Consider for instance English verbs such as *require* that take a subjunctive complement. This property does not appear to be reflected in the C projection, since both subjunctive and indicative clauses exploit the complementizer *that*. Rather, the distinctive features of the two moods apparently reside in a lower head, say, T. To preserve strict locality of selection, one might posit an ambiguity in the complementizer *that*, so that a subjunctive version of *that* selects a subjunctive T and an indicative *that* selects an indicative one. Even leaving aside the lack of appeal of such a solution, there are other cases of nonlocal selection that do not seem amenable to this sort of treatment. Grimshaw (1991) points to examples of the following sort:

(10) They merged/combined the files/*file.

Verbs like *merge, combine,* and *gather* require semantically plural arguments, arguably a property of N. One line of reply might say that this plurality is in fact a syntactic feature on the determiner. It would simply be a fact about English, then, that such plurality is not expressed phonologically on the definite determiner. However, this plurality need not be syntactically expressed at all. In English, a syntactically singular but semantically plural noun like *army* is sufficient to satisfy the selectional properties of these verbs.

(11) They gathered the army together.

Moreover, in the indefinite determiner system, where number is syntactically expressed, the syntactic number on the D head is singular.[11]

(12)  They gathered an/*some/*∅ army together.

If these nominal complements are projections of a determiner head, as we have been assuming, then the process of selection must somehow be able to "ignore" features in the projection of D and directly inspect properties of the head N. From a perspective in which the features of a nominal extended projection are shared throughout, this is as expected.

An example of a similar phenomenon involves the English verb *serve*. Higgins (1973) demonstrates that *serve* is quite particular about which verbs may appear within its infinitival complement.

(13)  a.  *The ice served to melt.
      b.  The ice served to chill the beer.

Though these examples suggest that *serve* demands a transitive verb, closer inspection reveals that not all transitives can occur as complements.

(14)  *Edison served to invent the light bulb.

Pollard and Sag (1987) show that transitivity is not even a necessary condition, as there are intransitive predicates that can be the verbal head of a complement to *serve*.

(15)  A pair of nines will serve to open in this game.

Higgins suggests instead that *serve* requires the subject of its infinitival complement to be interpretable as an instrument of the action that the embedded clause describes. In other words, the embedded verb must assign an instrumental θ-role to its subject.[12] Assuming that such thematic properties are represented uniquely on the embedded verb, this means that *serve* is able to select for a thematic property of the verb embedded in its infinitival complement, across the intervening CP and TP.

The following contrasts in complements to the verb *decide* provide a final example of this sort of nonlocal selection:

(16)  a.  *Lester decided to know French.
      b.  *Lester decided to be tall.

(17)  a.  Lester decided to speak French.
      b.  Lester decided to be available to his students.

The subordinate clauses in (16) are headed by individual-level predicates (ones that express properties of individuals that persist over time such as *knowing French* and *being tall*; see Carlson 1977). In contrast, the subordinated predicates in (17) are stage-level predicates (ones that express properties of an individual at a certain point in time). I suggest that the contrast between the cases in (16) and (17) is due precisely to the fact that the verb *decide* selects for a clause containing a stage-level predicate. Hence, *decide* must be able to directly select for a stage-level predicate.

Each of these cases points to the conclusion that selection need not be so local as between a head and its complement.[13] If, instead, we say that a head can select for features that are present on any of the heads within its complement extended projection, that is to say, somewhere within the elementary tree the head takes as its complement, then we can account for the *serve*, *decide*, and *gather* cases, as well as the selection for indicative as opposed to subjunctive mood.

This extended view of selection makes clear predictions about which elements a head may not select. In particular, a head may not select any properties that are expressed further down within a complement than the first elementary tree or extended projection. It is easy enough to imagine what such cases might look like. For example, a verb $V_1$ may not select for particular properties of a DP complement to a verb $V_2$ that heads the extended projection of $V_1$'s complement, as in (18).

(18)  $V_1$ [... [$_{VP}$ $V_2$ DP]]

A verb might, for example, require the embedded object to be definite. Similarly, an analysis of *serve*'s subcategorization requirements in which it directly constrains properties of the embedded subject, an analysis I take to be incorrect (see note 12), would similarly violate the extended projection view of selection. What is striking is that such cases do not appear to exist.

### 2.3.2  Agreement and Feature Percolation

The morphosyntactic realization of lexical features is another process that is sensitive to extended projection boundaries. If extended projections are taken to be domains inside of which features percolate freely, we would expect that features borne on one head might also surface on another head within the same extended projection. Grimshaw (1991) discusses a number of cases that are relevant here. I will briefly describe three of them: subject agreement with verbal heads, agreement among nominal heads, and percolation of *wh*-features.

In the verbal domain, Grimshaw observes that the morphological realization of agreement with the syntactic subject can appear on any of the heads within a verbal extended projection. In English, finite clauses containing lexical verbs show subject agreement on the verb occupying the head position of VP, while clauses with auxiliary verbs reveal agreement in a higher inflectional head, which we assume to be T. Grimshaw cites data from West Flemish (Haegeman 1992) as a case in which the complementizer itself shows (number) agreement with the subject DP.

(19) a. ... da   Jan noa Gent   goat
           that Jan to   Ghent goes
        '... that Jan goes to Ghent'
     b. ... dan    Jan en   Pol noa Gent   goan
           that.PL Jan and Pol to    Ghent go
        '... that Jan and Pol go to Ghent'

The analysis of all of these cases is straightforward: once the subject has entered into the structural relation necessary to establish agreement with the relevant head within the extended projection, which we assume to be in the specifier position of TP, these agreement features are then free to percolate to the V or C heads, as they are part of the same extended projection as the T.

Extended agreement is also found within nominal extended projections. In this case, functional heads within the extended projection of a noun agree in features with which the noun is lexically associated. Thus, in a wide variety of languages, determiners share the gender and number features associated with the head noun.[14]

To bring to light another case of extended feature realization, Grimshaw points to the well-known fact that in English wh-questions, prepositional phrases can pied-pipe along with a [+wh] DP to the specifier of CP.

(20) a. Which stone did they find a note under?
     b. Under which stone did they find a note?

(21) a. I was wondering which stone they found a note under.
     b. I was wondering under which stone they found a note.

Let us assume that [+wh] heads, the complementizers in these cases, must satisfy a well-formedness condition along the lines of Rizzi's (1996) Wh-Criterion which requires that they enter into a certain structural relation with a [+wh] element, say, specifier-head agreement. In the (a) examples in (20) and (21), this is straightforwardly satisfied: the projection of the [+wh] D *which* moves into the specifier of the CP. In the (b) cases, however, satisfaction of this condition is not so straightforward since the DP projection bearing morphological *wh*-features is embedded within the projection of a preposition that does not carry such features. If we assume that this *wh*-feature is able to percolate all the way through an elementary tree or extended projection, then under the assumption that P forms part of a single extended projection with the DP, this result is explained.[15]

This proposal predicts that *wh*-features should not be able to percolate beyond an extended projection or elementary tree boundary. This prediction appears to be borne out, as evidenced by the following contrasts:

(22) a.   I wonder which rock star they wrote a book about.
     b.   ?I wonder about which rock star they wrote a book.
     c.   *I wonder a book about which rock star they wrote.

In the (a) and (b) cases, an extended projection of the [+wh] D element is moved to the specifier of CP position as before. However, in the (c) example, a DP that takes this PP as its complement is the element that moves. This DP cannot form an extended projection with the lower PP and therefore cannot constitute a single elementary tree. Consequently, this DP cannot inherit the *wh*-feature from the lower DP and hence cannot enter into specifier-head agreement with the [+wh] complementizer selected by *wonder*.[16] A similar pattern of percolation within extended projections is found in the phenomenon of neg-inversion. As (23) shows, the inversion of an auxiliary verb is triggered when a negative DP is fronted.

(23) a.   Not one single paper has he written all year.
     b.   *Not one single paper he has written all year.

This inversion is also triggered even when the fronted constituent is a PP within which the negative DP is embedded.

(24) a.   About none of her friends has she told a lie willingly.
     b.   *About none of her friends she has told a lie willingly.

Since DP and PP form a single extended projection, we expect the negative features of the DP to be visible at the PP level. In contrast, if the fronted constituent does not form a single extended projection with the negative DP, we expect that inversion should not be possible. The following examples suggest that this is the case:

(25)  a. *Lies about none of her friends has she told willingly.
      b. *Over lies about none of her friends has she gotten upset.

### 2.3.3  Head Movement

The previous two sections have dealt with the representational questions of the realization and visibility of different types of syntactic features. Grimshaw (1991) argues that extended projections localize a more strictly derivational operation as well, specifically that of syntactic head movement. In recent discussions of verb movement, the range of movements involved has almost invariably involved some combination of movement from V to T to C: Italian and French finite verbs move from V to T, English auxiliaries in root interrogatives move only from T to C, and German finite verbs in verb-second clauses move from V to T to C.

(26)  a. Paolo [$_{TP}$ vuole$_i$ subito        [$_{VP}$ $t_i$ un caffè]].
         Paolo      wants right away        a   coffee
      b. [$_{CP}$ Does$_i$ [$_{TP}$ Paul $t_i$ [$_{VP}$ want some coffee]]]?
      c. [$_{CP}$ Jetzt will$_i$   [$_{TP}$ Paul [$_{VP}$ einen Kaffee $t_i$] $t_i$]].
         now wants      Paul     a       coffee

Within the nominal domain, there have been a variety of proposals suggesting that N raises sometimes to D, sometimes to functional projections posited between N and D (Ritter 1991; Bernstein 1991; Cinque 1994; Longobardi 1994; examples in (27) and (28) from Norwegian and French, respectively).[17]

(27)  a. [$_{DP}$ hans [$_{NP}$ bøker om     syntaks]]
         his        books about syntax
      b. [$_{DP}$ bøkene$_i$   hans [$_{NP}$ $t_i$ om     syntaks]]
         books-the his            about syntax

(28)  a. [$_{DP}$ une large [$_{NP}$ vallée]]
         a    large      valley
      b. [$_{DP}$ une vallée$_i$ large [$_{NP}$ $t_i$]]

What is striking about these cases is that they all involve movement in which the base position and ultimate landing site lie within a single extended projection. Movement of heads has widely been assumed to obey the Head Movement Constraint (Travis 1984; Baker 1988), which allows a head to move only as far as the next higher head. Yet, if this constraint is the only thing that restricts head movement, we ought, for example, to expect complementizers or determiners to move to the verbs that embed them. Yet, such movements are largely unattested. Moreover, those cases of head movement that have been argued to violate the Head Movement Constraint, so-called long head movement (Rivero 1991, 1993), nonetheless obey the requirement that head movement remain within the confines of a single extended projection.[18]

There are a number of apparent counterexamples to Grimshaw's claim that head movement is always localized to a single extended projection. The first of these involves incorporation of one lexical head into the other. Since each lexical head must be in its own extended projection, movement of one such head into the position of the other would cross an extended projection boundary. Two cases that have been argued to involve such a derivation are noun incorporation and causativization (West Greenlandic example in (29) from Sadock 1991, and Chichewa examples in (30) from Trithart 1977).

(29) ... kisiannimi usi      nassata-qar-punga
         but        in fact baggage-have-INDIC.1s
     'but I just remembered I have some luggage'

(30) a. Mtsikana ana-chit-its-a      kuti mtsuko   u-gw-e.
        girl        AGR-do-make-ASP that waterpot AGR-fall-ASP
        'The girl made the waterpot fall.'
     b. Mtsikana anan-gw-ets-a      mtsuko.
        girl        AGR-fall-made-ASP waterpot

Baker (1988) analyzes noun incorporation as involving the syntactic movement of the head of an NP complement to the head of its embedding verb (see also Sadock 1991). Similarly, he takes causativization to involve the movement of an embedded verb to a higher verb (see also Marantz 1984). Grimshaw argues that these counterexamples are only apparent and suggests that such cases ought to be treated as resulting from lexical rather than syntactic processes (Rosen 1989; Grimshaw and Mester 1985).

A second problem for the idea that head movement must remain within a single extended projection arises from the behavior of clitic pronouns. To account for their curious distributional properties, these nominal elements are often assumed to occupy some functional head position within the extended projection of the verb of which the clitic is an argument. In some Romance languages, such as Italian, the clitic can attach to the verb of a higher clause, in the process crossing extended projection boundaries.

(31) a. Gianni vuole vederli.
         Gianni wants to see-them
     b. Gianni li vuole vedere.

Grimshaw suggests that clitic climbing should be analyzed not as an instance of head movement, but as phrasal movement, which under her assumptions can move beyond extended projection boundaries (see also Sportiche 1996). I take this option to be unattractive, since on a TAG view all movement must be localized to an elementary tree, and hence an extended projection. I return briefly to the issues posed by clitic climbing in the TAG framework in chapter 6.

## 2.4   Elementary Trees as Extended Projections

We have just seen evidence that extended projections localize a number of grammatical processes. Recall that the function of elementary trees within a TAG-based derivational architecture is to provide the domain over which grammatical well-formedness conditions and syntactic operations apply. Consequently, the evidence we have just reviewed for the localizing nature of extended projections leads us as well to the conclusion that elementary trees should consist of extended projections. In this section, I turn to the task of making this hypothesis more precise. I consider a number of conditions on elementary tree well-formedness and their implications for the structure of elementary trees. I also aim to show that the possibility of combining extended projection domains with the TAG Adjoining operation enables us to uncover an even wider range of extended-projection-local grammatical processes than had previously been observed.

Let us begin by instantiating the idea that elementary trees are extended projections in the most direct manner possible.

(32)  *Condition on Elementary Tree Minimality (CETM) (preliminary version)*
      Every elementary tree consists of the extended projection of a single lexical head.

Strictly speaking, the elementary tree in (9b), repeated here as (33), does not abide by this condition.

(33)

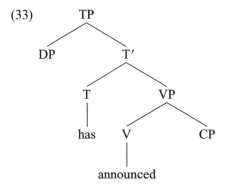

Although the VP and TP projections together form an extended projection, the DP and CP nodes, included to function as slots for the insertion
of the arguments to *announced*, lie outside this extended projection. Yet,
if we are to retain the intuition that elementary trees encompass thematic
domains within which all of the roles of a lexical head are assigned, the
DP and CP nodes must be present in the elementary tree. Furthermore,
even putting aside the issue of the locality of θ-role assignment, the absence of such argument slots from elementary trees would leave θ-roles
unassigned quite generally, as neither Substitution nor Adjoining allows
for the introduction of new sisters to a (nonroot) node in an elementary
tree. We must therefore reformulate the CETM so as to ignore these nonterminal argument slots, but still impose an extended projection bound
on the remainder of the structure.

(34) *Condition on Elementary Tree Minimality (CETM)*
      The syntactic heads in an elementary tree and their projections
      must form an extended projection of a single lexical head.

This statement of the CETM refers only to projections that are associated
with syntactic heads present in the elementary tree. Consequently, in determining whether the elementary tree in (33) satisfies the CETM, we may
disregard the CP node that is complement to the verbal head as well as the
DP node in subject position, as the head of neither projection is present.

   Now that we have allowed for the possibility of argument slots in an
elementary tree, let us next formulate the idea that elementary trees must
include the thematic domain of a lexical predicate. To ensure that all θ-
roles of an elementary tree's lexical head are assigned within the elementary tree, I assume the following TAG analogue of the θ-Criterion:

(35) *θ-Criterion (TAG version) (part 1)*
   If H is the lexical head of elementary tree T, H assigns all of its
   θ-roles within T.

What do we mean here by θ-role assignment within an elementary tree?
After all, in the elementary tree in (33), the structure and the phonological and semantic content of the arguments are not present in the tree, but
are instead only represented by nonterminals that appear along the frontier of the elementary tree. In fact, no more of these arguments' structure
can be present in the elementary tree if it is to satisfy the CETM. An
argument will consist of an independent extended projection, of a noun
in the case of a DP argument and of a verb in the case of a CP argument.
If the content and structure of such an argument were "filled in" within
the elementary tree headed by the lexical predicate, the result would run
afoul of the CETM, as the headed projections that it includes would now
comprise two extended projections, one for the lexical predicate and one
for the argument. Consequently, the CETM forces us to conclude that
local θ-role assignment is to frontier nonterminal slots, argument content
being inserted in the course of the TAG derivation.

   In addition to the condition in (35), I will assume a TAG version of
what is often thought of as the θ-Criterion's "other half," which blocks
the generation of more arguments than there are θ-roles to be assigned.

(36) *θ-Criterion (TAG version) (part 2)*
   If A is a frontier nonterminal node of elementary tree T, A must be
   assigned a θ-role in T.

This condition ensures that only frontier nonterminals that are thematically dependent on the lexical head of an elementary tree may appear
along its frontier. That is, such frontier nonterminals must serve as slots
for the insertion of thematic arguments.

   The CETM, coupled with the θ-Criterion, provides the TAG-based
theory of grammar developed here with an upper bound on the size of a
well-formed elementary tree. This bound derives from two things: first,
the limit on the number of heads and projections that can occur within
a single extended projection, as a result of the CETM; and second, the
limit on the number of θ-roles any lexical predicate can assign, restricting the number of (nonprojected) frontier nonterminal nodes whose presence is mandated by the θ-Criterion. This is crucial, as any TAG-based
grammatical theory must provide such a limit. If grammatical theory
allowed elementary trees to grow arbitrarily large, the set of well-formed

elementary trees, the "grammar" in the formal sense, would become infinite in size. Such a system would no longer be a TAG, in the formal sense
of being a finite set of elementary trees, and consequently it would cease
to have TAG's well-understood restrictions on expressive power. Instead,
the power of such a system would be determined by the complexity of the
constraints or principles that determine the set of well-formed elementary
trees. Such a situation is, of course, not unusual. It is just the one that
obtains in theories that do not compose phrase structure out of smaller
chunks whose well-formedness is independently determined—that is to
say, the vast majority of theories that have been proposed. The combination of the CETM and the θ-Criterion, therefore, plays a central rule in
the enterprise of exploring the consequences of a grammatical theory set
within a system of restricted formal power.

Let us now look more closely at the kind of elementary trees the
CETM and θ-Criterion require us to posit. Consider first the case of a
simple clausal structure headed by a transitive verb such as *read*. By the
CETM, the heads and projections of such an elementary tree must together form the extended projection of this verb, hence either CP, TP, or
VP. If we assume that external θ-roles are assigned directly to the specifier of TP, a *read*-headed elementary tree that is rooted in VP will necessarily violate the θ-Criterion, as its verbal head will fail to assign all of its
θ-roles, leaving TP and CP as the only possibilities. If we assume instead
that external θ-roles are assigned within the projection of the verb, even a
VP elementary tree is possible. So as to leave open the greatest number of
structural options, let us assume the latter, predicate-internal view of external θ-role assignment. Supposing that root clauses are TPs, the *read*-
headed structure in (37) satisfies both the CETM and the θ-Criterion.

(37)

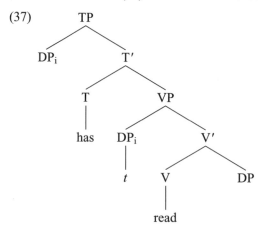

There are a number of things to observe about this elementary tree. First is the presence of the auxiliary *has* within the elementary tree. We assume that auxiliary verbs, including modals, are uniformly generated as the heads of a perhaps substantially expanded, though fixed, hierarchy of functional projections (Cinque 1999) and consequently form part of the same elementary tree as a lexical predicate. A second noteworthy property of this elementary tree structure is that syntactic movement has taken place within it. Specifically, the DP external argument has moved from its base position to the surface subject position. As already noted in chapter 1, I assume that movement as a syntactic operation is substantially restricted so that it may apply only within the confines of an elementary tree. I also assume here that movement applies to the DP frontier nonterminal, leaving behind a trace in its base thematic position. I take such traces to lack structural content, much like frontier non-terminals, and therefore they can be present within a verbally headed elementary tree.[19] We will see throughout the remainder of the book that this elementary tree local view of movement provides substantial conceptual and empirical gains in the theory of syntactic dependencies. I also assume, following Chomsky (1995), that the raising of the subject is motivated by the so-called Extended Projection Principle (EPP). As a first attempt, let us formulate this as follows:

(38) *Extended Projection Principle (TAG version)*
   All TP projections within an elementary tree must have specifiers.

Failing to raise the DP to the specifier of TP will result in a structure that violates the EPP and is consequently an ill-formed elementary tree. Similarly, I assume that raising the object to the specifier of TP, leaving the subject in situ, will leave the subject DP in violation of Case requirements. Note that I am not assuming any sort of locality requirement (e.g., Shortest Move) constraining elementary-tree-internal movement, to ensure that subjects move to subject position and objects do not. Rather, I take such local applications of movement to be restricted only by the well-formedness requirements imposed on the resulting structure. For more discussion, see chapters 3 and 4 (especially section 4.3).

   As noted earlier, the CETM prohibits the slots for the DP subject and object in (37) from having lexically projected internal structure. Thus, these DPs are brought into the TAG derivation as separate elementary trees like those in (39) and substituted into the DP slots in (37) during the derivation.

(39) a.

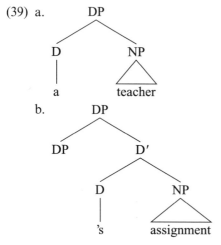

The DP elementary tree in (39b) also includes a slot for a possessive DP, which is filled via substitution of yet another DP elementary tree. In all of these cases, we will need to guarantee that the DP elementary trees are Case-marked in a fashion appropriate to the context in which they are substituted. For purposes of the current discussion, it is sufficient to assume that substitution nodes are annotated with a feature that specifies the Case assigned to the DP by the surrounding syntactic context.[20] Satisfaction of Case requirements will then follow from the need for the features of the root of a substituted structure to be compatible with those on the frontier nonterminal into which it substitutes.

Let us turn next to an elementary tree headed by *try*, a verb taking an infinitival CP complement. Again, since the extended projection of a verbal head can be either a VP, IP, or CP, a *try* elementary tree could project to any of these and still accord with the CETM. Let us consider the case of a CP-rooted elementary tree, as shown in (40).

(40)

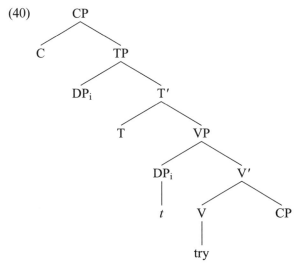

As before, the DP subject slot will be filled via substitution of a DP-rooted elementary tree. The same derivation is possible for the CP complement as well. But note that this complement node is labeled identically to the root. Consequently, this tree meets the definition of an auxiliary tree, as it is a recursive piece of structure. If we do take (40) to be an auxiliary tree, the complement to *try* can now be inserted by another derivation: adjoining this tree at the CP node of another elementary tree. Following Kroch (1989b), I will label such auxiliary trees *complement auxiliaries*.

For derivations involving the elementary tree in (40), there seems little reason to prefer the Substitution or the Adjoining derivation over the other, and I will assume that either is possible with this elementary tree. This is a different view from the one usually adopted in TAG-based work, where the nature of a particular node—whether it is a site for substitution or a foot node of an auxiliary tree—is fundamental in determining the nature of the elementary tree in question—specifically, whether or not it is an auxiliary tree. I believe that the distinction between auxiliary and nonauxiliary elementary trees, though important from the perspective of the formal characterization of well-formed derivations, is not linguistically central. Instead, I maintain that in the absence of any extrinsically imposed linguistic constraint, elementary trees like the one in (40), which meet the recursion requirement, are free to function either as auxiliary trees or as nonauxiliary trees, and either CP node is free to function as a foot node or substitution site.[21]

This lack of differentiation between foot nodes and substitution sites is supported by some French examples discussed by Abeillé (1988), in which the verb *préférer* 'prefer' selects for two CP complements.

(41)  Jean préfère [$_{CP}$ se   casser   une jambe] [$_{CP}$ plutôt que   d'aller à
      Jean prefers      self to break a   leg          more COMP to go   to
      New York].
      New York
      'Jean prefers breaking his leg to going to New York.'

Following what I have just said, if we consider an elementary tree headed by *préfère* that projects up to CP, as in (42), we should expect that either of the two CP complement slots could serve as the foot node for an auxiliary tree, as they are both categorially identical to the root.

(42)

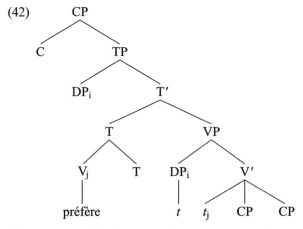

Given how Adjoining works, if one clausal complement to *préfère* is inserted by adjoining (42) into that embedded clause, the other must be inserted by Substitution into the other CP node in (42): Adjoining tolerates only a single foot node. Consequently, if we can show that there exist derivations in which each complement clause is introduced by Adjoining, we will have shown that either CP can function as a foot node. The problem we are faced with, then, is how to force an Adjoining derivation for one of the clausal complements. In order to do this, we will exploit a property of the TAG analysis of *wh*-extraction, already mentioned in chapter 1, and discussed at length in chapter 5: if a *wh*-element is extracted out of an embedded clause E into a matrix clause M, the elementary tree representing M must adjoin into E, since the *wh*-element must be generated within the same elementary tree in which it is assigned a θ-role. Thus, if we can show that extraction is permitted from a particular complement clause, we can conclude that the CP node representing that complement in the matrix elementary tree can function as a foot node, and if extraction from either is possible, then either CP can function as a foot node. In the case at hand, Abeillé observes that extraction from either CP complement to *préférer* is indeed possible.

(43) a. Où<sub>i</sub>   Jean préfère-t-il [aller *t*<sub>i</sub>] [plutôt que   de se   casser une
         where Jean prefers-he   to go     more  COMP to self break a
         jambe]?
         leg
         'Where does Jean prefer going to breaking his leg?'
    b. ?Où<sub>i</sub>   Jean préfère-t-il [se   casser   une jambe] [plutôt que
         where Jean prefers-he   self to break a   leg     more  COMP
         d'aller *t*<sub>i</sub>]?
         to go
         'Where does Jean prefer breaking his leg to going?'

These cases will be derivable if we assume the existence of elementary trees along the lines of those in (44), adjoining a structure like that in (42) at the lower CP. (For simplicity, I am abstracting away here from inversion in the matrix clause. Also, I take *wh*-elements to adjoin to CP, an assumption I revisit in chapter 5.)

(44) a.

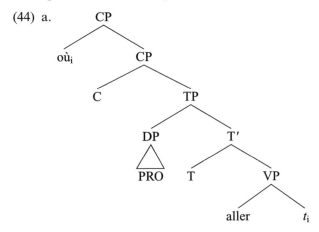

b.

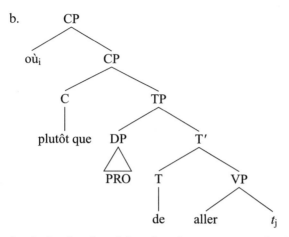

For the derivation involving the elementary tree in (44a), the first complement to *préférer* must serve as a foot node of an auxiliary tree, while for the derivation involving tree (44b), the second complement is the foot node.[22] Under Abeillé's analysis, this dual foot node possibility was an accidental fact about the verb *préférer* and required two separate auxiliary trees to be associated with its lexical entry. However, under the view I am advocating wherein the status of a particular frontier nonterminal as a foot node or as a substitution site is not determined by the structural representation itself, it is the cases where both extractions are *not* possible that must be explained by appeal to some additional grammatical constraint on what may serve as the foot node of an auxiliary tree. Thus, the proposal I am making forces us to face the question of why certain extraction possibilities fail to exist, and it does not permit us to stipulate away which nodes are possible foot nodes merely as a matter of lexical idiosyncrasy. I turn to possible constraints on foot nodes in chapter 5.

   Let us look at one last type of elementary tree, the one involved in modification structures, such as relative clauses and prepositional phrase adjuncts.

(45) a. I read the story [that Abigail recommended].
     b. The plane landed [near the house].

Note that such modifiers cannot be introduced into the derivation in a manner similar to arguments—for example, by substitution into a pre-existing frontier nonterminal. As modifiers are not assigned a θ-role by the lexical head H whose projection they modify, the TAG version of (the second half of) the θ-Criterion in (36) blocks the possibility of having a frontier nonterminal in an elementary tree headed by H into which the modifier could substitute. Instead, I assume that such modifiers themselves project auxiliary trees, complete with recursive root and foot nodes, like the one in (46).

(46)

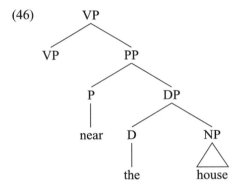

In this auxiliary tree, the recursive foot node is not a frontier nonterminal in the argument position of the tree's lexical head *house*, as was the case for complement auxiliaries (cf. (40)). Rather, the foot node represents the category of which the modifier is predicated. To distinguish this class of auxiliary trees from complement auxiliaries, I will refer to them as *modifier auxiliary trees*, following Schabes and Shieber (1994).[23]

While the PP–DP–NP sequence of projections within the auxiliary tree in (46) is unproblematic, under the assumption that P forms part of the extended projection of N, it is not obvious how to reconcile the presence of the VP projection with the requirement that elementary trees consist of a single extended projection. Furthermore, there is also the question of whether the VP foot node in this auxiliary tree is in accordance with the θ-Criterion: is it licensed in virtue of being assigned a θ-role? Concerning the first issue, the answer follows directly from the formulation of the CETM given in (34): the CETM requires only that syntactic heads and their projections form an extended projection. Since the root VP node is not projected from a V head present in the elementary tree, the CETM is blind to its presence, just as phrasal argument slots do not count for the purposes of the CETM since they are not the projections of heads present in the elementary tree. Concerning the question of licensing the VP foot node, note that in the framework of Higginbotham 1985, the adjunction configuration is one in which the process of θ-identification obtains between the external θ-role of the preposition and the sister of the preposition's maximal projection, the DP foot node in (46). I will assume that θ-identification is simply another species of θ-role assignment; hence, an argument slot so licensed will satisfy the θ-Criterion.

I have been assuming that once θ-roles are assigned to frontier nonterminals within elementary trees, it is the function of the TAG derivational machinery to insert argument content. However, I have not as yet shown that this will take place in a well-behaved fashion, so that θ-roles are assigned consistently and coherently. In other words, we have no guarantee that TAG derivations will obey a natural interpretation of the Projection Principle requiring that θ-roles, once assigned, remain assigned. In fact, we can show that so long as elementary trees satisfy the local version of the θ-Criterion, we can be guaranteed that the derived global structure will also satisfy more standard global formulations. For the first half of the θ-Criterion, requiring that all θ-roles be assigned, the reasoning is straightforward: any lexical predicate heading an elementary tree T will assign all of its θ-roles to frontier nonterminals within T. Since a TAG derivation is not complete if these nonterminals are not filled either by Substitution or by Adjoining, we can be certain that there will be some contentful element to which all the θ-roles are assigned in the final structure. Demonstrating that each argument must receive a θ-role is somewhat trickier. I will assume, following Grimshaw's (1991) Generalized θ-Criterion, that this requirement reduces to the claim that every extended projection must receive a θ-role.[24] Since each elementary tree is a separate extended projection, we need only show that as each combinatory operation takes place, a θ-role is assigned to one of the extended projections that is being combined. Substitution can take place only along the frontier of an elementary tree, and consequently only into one of the frontier nonterminals licensed by θ-role assignment. Thus, any extended projection that is substituted is assigned a θ-role. In the case of Adjoining, things are a bit more complex. Once again, we can be sure that an argument slot will be filled during the combination. This time, the "filled-in" node is the foot node of the adjoining elementary tree, which as a frontier nonterminal must be assigned a θ-role. Consequently, the structure that is inserted as the content of this foot node's argument slot is assigned a θ-role. Unlike in the Substitution case, however, the structure that is inserted does not exhaust the extended projection formed by the elementary tree into which adjoining takes place. Consider, for ex-

ample, the case of a complement auxiliary tree such as (47) that selects
for a TP complement.

(47)

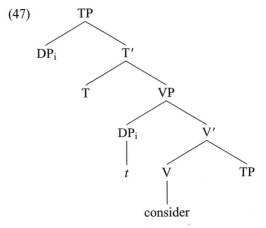

If such a tree adjoins into a verbally headed, CP-rooted elementary tree
like that in (48), as might occur in cases of *wh*-extraction from the sentential complement to *consider*, the TP projection in (48) is assigned a
θ-role, as it becomes *consider*'s complement under Adjoining.

(48)

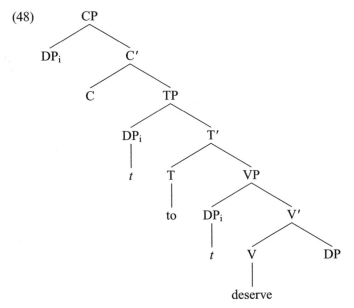

There remains, however, a residue of structure from this CP elementary
tree that is not assigned a θ-role, namely, that located above the TP at

which adjoining takes place. How, then, is this CP projection licensed? By the CETM, every elementary tree must consist of an extended projection. However, an auxiliary tree that adjoins within the body of another, leaving a residue, must be a nonmaximally extended projection, that is, one that could include "higher" functional projections. Indeed, the targeted elementary tree demonstrates the possibility of additional functional structure above the auxiliary's root in an elementary tree of the same lexical type. The recursive nature of auxiliary trees guarantees that the "bottom" of the residue will match the root of the adjoined auxiliary tree. Consequently, it is fair to assume that after Adjoining applies, the residue is reanalyzed as part of the extended projection of the lexical head of the adjoined auxiliary tree. The thematic licensing of this residue, then, will take place along with that of the rest of this auxiliary tree. Thus, we can conclude that TAG derivations using trees that accord with the local formulation of the θ-Criterion will have the effect of producing derived structures all of whose extended projections are licensed.[25]

Note finally that the local application of the θ-Criterion within the domain of an elementary tree has the interesting benefit of allowing us to sidestep the vexing problem of multiple θ-role assignment that occurs in modification. We have been assuming that a modified DP is both the external argument of the adjoined modifier and the argument of, say, some verbal predicate. Yet, under usual formulations, the θ-Criterion requires that each argument receive a unique θ-role, in apparent conflict with what is going on here. Under the TAG proposal made here, we can maintain the strong position that there exists a biunique relation between arguments and θ-roles within elementary trees, though as noted before the notion of argument is identified here with the frontier nonterminal elements. However, in the case of modification structures like that in (46), the semantic content of the VP at which adjoining takes place is identical to that of the resulting structure, since the root node of the adjoined structure is not projected. Thus, this outer VP (or its extended projection) is free to serve as an argument to some other predicate. Under the assumption that a phrase can be multiply modified (via adjoining of multiple modifier auxiliaries to the same node; see Schabes and Shieber 1994), arbitrarily severe violations of argument θ-role uniqueness can arise.

# Chapter 3

## A Case Study: Raising

In chapter 2, I began to develop a theory of the elementary objects of TAG derivations, elementary trees. In this chapter, I apply this theory to the detailed analysis of one construction, subject-to-subject raising. This analysis, I believe, demonstrates the explanatory power that follows from incorporating the TAG formalism into a theory of grammar. We will see that the view of elementary trees developed in chapter 2, coupled with the TAG derivational machinery, enables us to derive a wide range of the properties of the raising construction without resort to conditions on the locality of movement or on the well-formedness of empty categories.

### 3.1 The Displacement Phenomenon and Motivations for Movement

As is well known, predicates taking infinitival sentential complements split into two classes. On the one hand, raising predicates such as *seem*, *appear*, and *likely* are distinguished by the fact that certain aspects of the form of their subject DP are determined by the predicate within the infinitival complement clause. Thus, if the embedded predicate licenses a subject that is an expletive *there*, an idiom chunk, a weather or expletive *it*, or a quirky Case-marked subject (as in Icelandic, for example), then the raising predicate permits such a subject.

(1) a. There seems to be a problem.
    b. The shit seems to have finally hit the fan.
    c. It seems to be hailing outside.
    d. It seems to anger Felix that the bathroom is a mess.
    e. Henni   virðist hafa leiðst bókin. (Sigurðsson 1992)
       her.DAT seems have bored book
       'She seems to have found the book boring.'

In contrast, the second class of infinitival-complement-taking predicates, so-called Equi (or control) predicates such as *want*, *hope*, and *try*, impose their own restrictions on the form of the subject and do not allow subjects of the sort seen in (1).

(2) a. *There hoped to be a problem.
    b. *The shit hoped to hit the fan.
    c. *It hoped to be hailing outside.
    d. *It hoped to anger Felix that the bathroom is a mess.
    e. *Henni   vonast til  að leiðast ekki bókin. (Sigurðsson 1992)
       her.DAT hopes for to bore   not book
       'She hopes not to find the book boring.'

The fundamental difference between these two classes of predicates, from which all grammatical analyses of these contrasts have been taken to follow, concerns whether or not they stand in some kind of thematic relation to their subject: Equi predicates assign a θ-role to their subjects, while raising predicates do not. In transformational grammar, DPs are assumed to begin the derivation in the position in which they are assigned a θ-role. Consequently, the traditional transformational analysis of raising constructions involves the surface subject originating in the embedded infinitival clause and moving up to the matrix subject position. The post-movement representation of the sentence in (1a) is the following:

(3) There$_i$ seems [$t_i$ to be a problem].

The presence of a chain linking the subject positions of the matrix and embedded clauses is taken to explain why the form of the matrix subject depends on the embedded predicate, as such licensing is presumed to obtain in the position into which an argument is first inserted.[1]

On this account, Equi predicates differ in the fact that the matrix subject is initially inserted directly into its surface position (but see Hornstein 1999).[2] This means that there must be a separate phonologically null subject to satisfy the thematic requirements of the embedded clause, what has been called the empty category PRO. This yields a representation of the following sort:

(4) Eleanor tried [PRO to leave].

The fact that the matrix subject is coreferential with the embedded subject is explained not through membership in a single movement-derived chain but through an independent module of the grammar concerned with the control of PRO.

## 3.2   A TAG Analysis: Factoring Recursion

It is a straightforward task to translate the analysis of control just sketched into the TAG framework. Within the characterization of elementary trees offered by the CETM, we represent the matrix clause as the CP extended projection of the control verb selecting for a CP complement. This yields the elementary tree in (5).

(5)
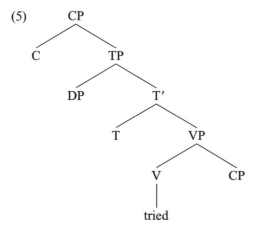

The embedded clause is also represented as a CP extended projection, this time with an untensed T, as in (6).

(6)
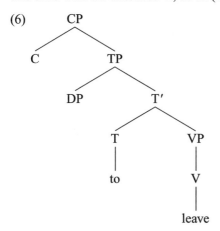

To force the insertion of PRO, the DP subject position in this tree might be annotated with contextually determined featural information, related perhaps to Case assignment or whatever is taken to govern the distribution of PRO. The derivation of example (4) can now proceed either by adjoining the auxiliary in (5) into the root node of the initial tree in (6), or by substituting the tree in (6) into the CP node on the frontier of the tree in (5). In either case, the resulting representation is identical to that standardly assumed, and it therefore provides an equivalent structural basis for determining control relations.

As noted in chapter 2, the TAG formalism does not allow movement operations to apply across clauses, or more precisely, across elementary trees. Consequently, there is no way to translate the movement-based analysis into this context. How then can we preserve the insight that underlies this analysis, the existence of a selectional dependency between the raised subject and the lower clause, without making recourse to interclausal movement? The answer that I suggest here and return to again throughout this book derives from the application of Adjoining. In the raising case, as proposed in Kroch and Joshi 1985 and Frank 1992, the raised subject is generated in the elementary tree of the embedded clause and is "raised" into the higher clause by the adjoining of a subjectless elementary tree headed by a raising predicate. To see how this works in detail, let us consider the derivation of example (7).

(7) Eleanor seemed to know the answer.

Recall that the TAG version of the θ-Criterion demands that all of the θ-roles of a predicate be assigned within its elementary tree. This has the immediate consequence, noted just above, that all arguments to the embedded predicate *know* in (7), including the raised subject DP *Eleanor*, must be syntactically realized within the elementary tree that it heads. Thus, a TP infinitival elementary tree headed by *know* will be as in (8).[3]

(8)

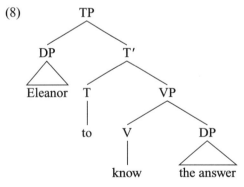

As noted, raising predicates like *seem* are distinguished by their failure to assign a θ-role to their subject. Hence, the θ-Criterion does not require the existence of a subject position in an elementary tree headed by such a predicate. Thus, the tree in (9) is a well-formed elementary tree headed by the verb *seem*.[4]

(9)

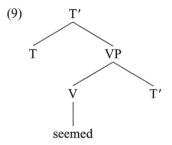

Note that as soon as we permit projections at the top of elementary trees that lack specifiers, indicated as X′-level projections, we must also allow heads to select for X′-level arguments. Otherwise, there would be no way for such X′-rooted elementary trees to be embedded either by Substitution or by Adjoining. Embedding such a structure via Substitution would be blocked by the absence of X′-level frontier nonterminals into which the structure could substitute. Similarly, embedding via Adjoining would be blocked since there could not be any X′-level foot node in an elementary tree rooted in X′. In the case at hand, we assume that the lack of a specifier of TP in the raising structure in (9) implies that *seem* must take a T′ complement.

We can now apply Adjoining, inserting the auxiliary in (9) at the T′ node in the elementary tree in (8). This results in the structure shown in (10).

(10)

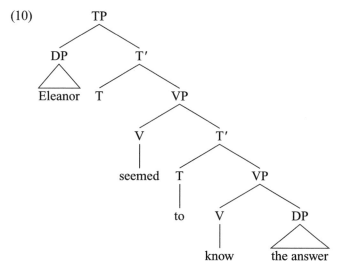

This application of Adjoining interposes *seem* and its clausal structure between the subject *Eleanor* and the rest of its thematically related clause, stretching the originally local relation between the subject and the verb on which it is thematically dependent. Thus, Adjoining has the effect of displacing the embedded DP from its base position in the embedded clause to a position in the matrix, without invoking transformational movement.[5]

This same style of derivation can be applied to produce cases involving multiple raising predicates, such as (11).

(11) Eleanor seemed to appear (to be certain ...) to know the answer.

The usual transformational derivation of examples like this involves the successive-cyclic movement of the subject *Eleanor* from the subject of one clause to the next higher one. The structure resulting from such a derivation includes a trace in each of the nonfinal subject positions.

(12) [TP Eleanor$_i$ seemed [TP $t_i$ to appear [TP $t_i$ to know the answer]]].

Generating examples like this one in TAG requires the use of additional raising auxiliary trees, like that in (9), but with nonfinite T, as shown in (13).

(13)

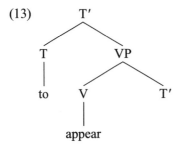

The derivation proceeds by first adjoining the original auxiliary tree in (9) into the auxiliary tree in (13) at the root node, to form the complex auxiliary tree shown in (14).[6]

(14)

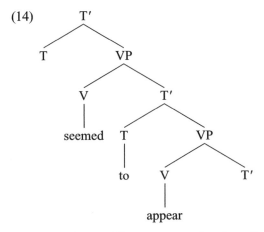

This complex auxiliary tree can then be adjoined between the subject and the rest of the embedded clause at the T' node, yielding the effect of iterated applications of raising. Note that nothing would have prevented us from combining even more raising auxiliary trees via Adjoining prior to the final derivational step of adjoining into the embedded clause. The fact that such derived auxiliary trees may grow without bound yields the desirable result that raising dependencies may be unbounded.

This Adjoining-based analysis of raising differs from movement-based analyses in denying the existence of a trace in the subject position of the clause from which the DP raises, as well as in all intervening subject positions. Such traces have been exploited for a variety of purposes, from accounting for the selectional effects discussed in section 3.1, to capturing the locality constraints on the relation between the derived and base positions of the DP, to specifying the possibilities of scope interpretation for the raised DP. One might wonder, then, whether the absence of these traces in the TAG context has negative consequences for analyses of these phenomena. In the next section, I turn to the locality issue. In section 3.4, I consider other implications of the absence of traces in the TAG raising analysis.

### 3.3   Deriving Locality

Let me first address head on what is perhaps the main reason behind the assumption that raising proceeds via successive-cyclic movement: the need to ensure that the dependency between the subject positions is sufficiently local.[7] As is well known, raising into a position two clauses higher than the base position is only possible if the subject position of the intermediate clause is "empty."

(15) a.  Eleanor$_i$ seemed [to be certain [$t_i$ to know the answer]].
     b. *Eleanor$_i$ seemed [it was certain [$t_i$ to know the answer]].

In movement-based analyses, the necessity of this empty subject position has been tied to the necessity of an intermediate landing site for movement.

(16) Eleanor$_i$ seems [$t_i$ to be certain [$t_i$ to know the answer]].

Example (15b) is blocked since the intermediate subject position, the necessary landing site, is filled. In much work of the 1980s, cases of "super-raising" like (15b) were ruled out via well-formedness conditions on the lower trace: traces of A-movement needed to be either antecedent governed (Rizzi 1990) or locally bound (Chomsky 1982). In either case, the presence of the intermediate subject *it* prevented such relations from obtaining, leading to ungrammaticality.

More recently, the ill-formedness of such sentences has been taken to derive from a condition on the application of movement itself, namely, Shortest Move. In the formulation in Chomsky 1995, movement, now conceived of as attraction of the moved element by some feature in a higher functional head, must proceed to the landing site from the closest possible position. In a derivation of (15b), we would have the following representation immediately prior to raising:

(17) [$_{T'}$ T seemed [it was certain [Eleanor to know the answer]]]

Chomsky assumes that the highest T, like all T heads, contains features that instantiate the Extended Projection Principle (EPP), the requirement that all subject positions be filled. In order to be properly checked, these features require, roughly speaking, a nominal element of some sort within their specifier position. Chomsky's conception of movement involves a search for the element c-commanded by and closest to T (where closeness is defined hierarchically in terms of c-command) that is capable of satisfying these EPP features. This closeness condition instantiates the Shortest Move requirement: only the closest checker for some feature is a possible candidate for attraction. In (17), the possible EPP satisfiers are *it* and *Eleanor*. The first of these, *it*, is chosen by Move since it is closer to T, as *it* c-commands *Eleanor*, but not conversely. Raising *Eleanor* is blocked, then, as this would not constitute a possible instance of Move, with the desired result that (15b) is ruled out.[8]

One can imagine an alternative derivation for (15b) that does not violate Shortest Move in the manner just discussed. Specifically, instead of proceeding from the representation in (17), we instead construct the structure in (18), differing from (17) only in the fact that the intermediate subject position has not yet been filled by *it*.

(18) [$_{T'}$ T seemed [was certain [Eleanor to know the answer]]]

Now, the closest element to T that can check the EPP features is the lower subject *Eleanor*, which could then be attracted by the matrix T. After this movement, the intermediate subject position could be filled by merging *it*. Chomsky (1993) suggests that this derivation violates the requirement that syntactic derivations proceed cyclically: once an operation is performed in a higher clause, the derivation cannot return to a lower clause. Chomsky instantiates this idea by the requirement that all applications of Merge, whether as part of a movement operation or not, must target the highest node in a phrase marker that is being constructed. In other words, Merge must "extend" the targeted phrase marker upward. We will henceforth refer to this as the *Extension Condition*. It is straightforward to observe that this condition is sufficient to block the alternative derivation for (15b): once *Eleanor* has moved, the expletive *it* cannot be inserted, as this insertion would take place internal to the previously constructed phrase marker.[9]

One welcome result of the TAG-based analysis of raising constructions is that locality properties, and more specifically the impossibility of superraising constructions like (15b), follow directly from the way in which Adjoining composes elementary trees. Thus, the effects of Shortest Move and the Extension Condition, or an antecedent government condition on traces, follow without explicit stipulation. To see how this works, consider how we might derive the ungrammatical example (15b) in the TAG-based theory we are exploring. The representation of the subordinate infinitival clause must remain as in (8), as this structure was dictated by the combination of the CETM and the θ-Criterion. To accomplish the effects of "moving" the subject *Eleanor* to the front of this sentence, we will need to adjoin an auxiliary structure that realizes the lexical material *seemed it was certain* appearing between *Eleanor* and *to* in the sentence. Such a structure would be as in (19).

(19)

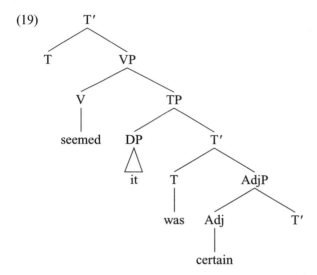

Under the conception of elementary trees that the CETM provides, this structure must be composed of two separate elementary trees, as the lexical predicates *seemed* and *certain* must head distinct extended projections. Suppose that the auxiliary tree representing the clause headed by *seemed* is as in (9). To derive (15b), this structure must be combined with the elementary tree for the *certain* clause, and the result must then adjoin to the T′ node of the elementary tree in (8). Note, however, that the representation of the *certain* clause must be rooted in TP, since this clause must include a position for the expletive subject *it*.[10] Thus, we cannot simply adjoin the *seem* T′ auxiliary tree to the root of a *certain* TP auxiliary tree, as shown in (20), even if we allow *certain* to take TP complements, since the labels do not match: one is a TP, the other is a T′.

(20)

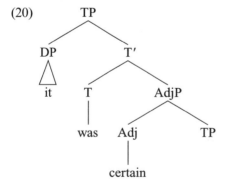

Furthermore, there is no way to insert the expletive *it* into the specifier of TP position of a composite T′ structure, like that derived in (14). Adjoining can only introduce recursive structures, and since *it* is in a specifier position, its mother and sister have distinct labels.

One other way we might try to derive the superraising structure would combine the *seemed* and *certain* clauses using Substitution and then adjoin the result into the infinitival complement clause. Doing this would necessitate the elementary trees in (21).

(21) a.

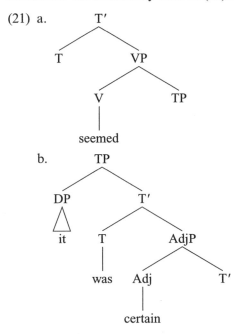

b.

The elementary tree in (21b) could substitute into the TP node on the frontier of (21a), yielding precisely the structure in (19). This structure has a T′ root node and a T′ node on the frontier, and we therefore might try to adjoin it to the T′ node in (8) to derive example (15b).

This derivation is, however, blocked by the "Markovian" or "context-freeness" condition on TAG derivations mentioned in chapter 1, requiring that each derivational step be insensitive to the previous derivational history. What this means in the TAG context is that the combinability of two structures $\alpha$ and $\beta$ is determined entirely by the properties of the elementary trees $\alpha_0$ and $\beta_0$ that served as the basis for constructing $\alpha$ and $\beta$. Recall that TAG derivations are represented by derivation structures, each of whose nodes $\eta$ represents an elementary tree $\tau$, and where the

daughters of η correspond to other elementary trees τ′ that have been adjoined or substituted into τ. Of course, such τ′ may themselves have been
the target of Substitution or Adjoining and consequently their corresponding nodes in the derivation tree may have daughters. However, the Markovian condition on derivations demands that the well-formedness of a
derivation structure be determinable on the basis of whether the elementary trees that stand in mother-daughter relationships are combinable. In
cases of Substitution, this amounts to the requirement that the root of the
derivation structure for the substituted phrase structure object must be an
elementary tree whose root matches the label of the site of substitution.
In cases of Adjoining, however, something more is required, as the possibility of Adjoining demands the presence of an auxiliary tree, that is, one
in which there is a recursive pair of root and foot nodes. Thus, in order to
satisfy the Markovian condition, a derivation that implicates adjoining of
a phrase structure object β will only be possible when the elementary tree
that is at the root of the derivation structure for β is an auxiliary tree.
Somewhat more prosaically, we can restate this conclusion as "Auxiliary
trees must be born and not made."

Returning to the alternative derivation of superraising we are investigating, consider what the derivation structure would look like. As noted
above, the structure that is adjoined into the elementary tree in (8)—
namely, the structure in (19)—is composed by substituting the elementary tree in (21b) into (21a). Thus, the derivation structure is as follows:

(22)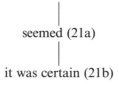

Does this derivation structure satisfy the Markovian local well-formedness
property? At the lowest level, the answer is yes: substituting the TP-
rooted *it was certain* tree into the TP complement position of the *seemed*
tree is licit. At the higher level, things break down: adjoining the *seemed*
tree into the T′ node of the *Eleanor to know the answer* tree is not possible for the simple reason that the *seemed* tree lacks recursive root
and foot T′ nodes and hence is not an auxiliary tree of the appropriate type (or, for that matter, of any type since it is not recursive).
Detecting that the composite structure formed by substitution of *it was*

*certain* into *seemed* constitutes a structure of the appropriate type for Adjoining would require us to go beyond local detection of derivational well-formedness, and indeed cases could be constructed that would require arbitrarily large searches through a derivational history to determine well-formedness. Following our Markovian local well-formedness assumption, then, leads us to the conclusion that all such derivations are ruled out.

Crucially, this local well-formedness property of TAG derivations does not prevent us from adjoining additional structure into an elementary auxiliary tree $\alpha$ prior to adjoining $\alpha$ into some other elementary tree. Indeed, as we have already seen, such a sequence of operations is needed in deriving examples involving iterated successive-cyclic subject-to-subject raising, like (11). Here, however, the derivation proceeds by adjoining one $T'$ auxiliary tree into the root of another, the result then being adjoined into the infinitival TP elementary tree. This is represented by the following derivation structure:

(23)  Eleanor to know the answer (8)

to appear (13)

seemed (9)

Here, the derivation structure is entirely locally well formed, as adjoining the *to appear* elementary tree to the $T'$ node of the *Eleanor to know the answer* tree is possible independently of the other combination that has taken place.

We see, then, that the principles of elementary tree well-formedness prevent us from forming a derived auxiliary tree of the appropriate size to derive the ungrammatical (15b). The auxiliary tree must be recursive on $T'$, but the embedded clause must be a full TP. This, coupled with the restrictive TAG conception of structure composition, prevents instances of superraising from being derived. Thus, the effects of Chomsky's cyclicity constraint, at least in this case, are captured without explicit stipulation.

In general, the CETM, combined with the use of Adjoining to accomplish long-distance movement, enforces a restriction on long-distance dependencies very similar to Rizzi's (1990) Relativized Minimality condition. The reason for this is the following: in order to create unbounded dependencies, the process of adjoining one auxiliary tree into another must be repeated for all of the intervening clauses, and the resulting derived auxiliary structure must adjoin between the antecedent and its base position. By the CETM, all of the constituent auxiliary trees in this derived auxiliary tree must form extended projections, and since each adjoins into another, none of these extended projections can project any higher than the ultimately derived auxiliary tree. It is exactly this that kept us from incorporating a TP (or CP) extended projection into a T′ auxiliary tree in the superraising example just discussed. Now, let us suppose that in an extended projection, specifiers of distinct projections are distinct position types, in the sense relevant for Relativized Minimality. Then, any instance of Adjoining that places material between an antecedent and its trace is guaranteed not to introduce any specifiers of the same type as the antecedent. So, for example, if the antecedent is in a specifier of TP position and the trace is within the VP, any auxiliary tree that adjoins at the T′ or VP level is guaranteed not to introduce an intervening TP specifier so long as the CETM is obeyed.

Raising is but one example of a construction in which an element is moved successive cyclically from one clause to the next, occupying the same structural position in each clause.[11] Using Adjoining in a manner similar to that already discussed, we can analyze all instances of putative successive-cyclic movement without transformational movement, but rather through the adjoining of intervening material. Thus, to handle cases of successive-cyclic *wh*-movement, we will, following proposals in Kroch 1987, 1989b, and Frank 1992, use a derivation similar to the one given above for raising, but where Adjoining stretches the relation between an element in the specifier of CP position and its base-generated clause. This case will be discussed in detail in chapter 5. The general point is that so long as elementary trees are constrained to have at most one landing site of a given type, an Adjoining-based derivation of successive-cyclic constructions will have the same empirical coverage as one involving a movement operation that is restricted through stipulated constraints on possible representations (e.g., chain well-formedness) or on the movement operation (e.g., Shortest Move and the Extension Condition).[12]

This raises the question of whether any constraints on elementary tree local movement are necessary at all. Clearly, it would be most appealing if the perspective on locality afforded by TAG allowed us to answer this question in the negative. Past analyses have exploited combinations of conditions like Subjacency and Relativized Minimality/Shortest Move, with overlapping though distinct roles in restricting movement. I would like to suggest that in fact the TAG derivational architecture allows us to unify these different aspects of locality and thereby eliminate the need for explicitly stated restrictions on movement. As we will see in chapters 4 and 5, the implications of both Subjacency and Relativized Minimality/ Shortest Move can be derived from the fact that Move must apply over the domain of an elementary tree.

## 3.4   Getting By without Traces

We have seen that the TAG analysis of raising allows us to derive the locality properties of the construction without reference to traces of movement. Let us now turn to other empirical consequences of the absence of such traces in the context of this analysis. For a number of these cases, I will simply show that the TAG-based, trace-free analysis of raising does no worse at explaining phenomena whose explanations have been tied to the presence of traces. In other cases, however, I will show that the absence of traces is indeed advantageous, extending the explanatory force of the analysis.

### 3.4.1   Nonlocal Licensing and Thematic Assignment

Consider once again the raising examples from (1).

(1)  a.  There seems to be a problem.
     b.  The shit seems to have finally hit the fan.
     c.  It seems to be hailing outside.
     d.  It seems to anger Felix that the bathroom is a mess.
     e.  Henni    virðist hafa leiðst bókin. (Sigurðsson 1992)
         her.DAT seems  have bored book
         'She seems to have found the book boring.'

In each of these cases, some property of the embedded predicate licenses a subject having "unusual" properties, be it an expletive, an idiom chunk, a quirky Case-marked NP, or the like. It is usually assumed that selection is a local process, as witnessed by the inability of the same predicates to license "unusual" matrix subjects when selected by a matrix control predicate (as in the cases in (2)). Consequently, the apparent cases of nonlocal selection in (1) have been argued to be possible only because of the presence of a trace in the subject position of the embedded clause, where local selection can take place. A similar argument can be made on the basis of the need to recover or interpret the thematic relation between the embedded predicate and matrix subject of raising constructions at LF.

Both of these arguments depend, of course, on the assumption that thematic relations are established and various properties of "unusual" subjects are licensed over the representation that results after the derivation is completed, that is to say, LF. If we instead assume that these processes can occur at some earlier point in the derivation, beyond that point there will be no need to preserve any sort of explicit representational vestige of the link between the subject and its licensing predicate.

In the context of the TAG-based theory we are exploring, it is natural to assume that unusual subjects are licensed and thematic relations are established within the confines of an elementary tree. Since the relevant subject-predicate relations are local within the elementary tree, no trace is necessary to check whether the subject is licensed or thematically interpretable. As discussed in section 2.4, thematic combination mirrors the syntactic composition of elementary trees. Hence, relations—once locally established—will continue to hold. Since the force of the TAG version of the θ-Criterion is precisely to establish such linkages within elementary trees, it would only introduce redundancy and imperfection into the grammatical architecture if we require that these links be preserved through some representational device like a trace after Adjoining has applied, as their well-formedness has already been assured at the elementary tree representational level.

### 3.4.2  Scope Reconstruction

The representational device of a trace of a raised DP has also been invoked in explaining the multiple possibilities for scope interpretation in examples like (24) (May 1985).

(24)  Many unicorns are likely to be in the garden.

The interpretation of this sentence in which it is a statement about the properties of a sizable group of unicorns, each being a frequent garden-goer, has been tied to the possibility of interpreting the moved DP *many unicorns* in the matrix subject position, outside the scope of *likely*. In contrast, the interpretation in which the sentence is a statement about the great attractiveness of the garden to unicorns, so that it is in general likely that many unspecified unicorns will be there, has been related to the possibility of interpreting the DP in the position of the trace in the embedded subject position (via some process of reconstruction or quantifier lowering). In this position, the quantifier can be interpreted within the scope of the predicate *likely* and hence does not introduce any entailments of unicorn existence. As there is no trace in the lower subject position in the TAG-based analysis, it is not possible to link these two interpretations to two distinct subject positions. Indeed, the DP subject remains in a single position throughout the TAG derivation. How, then, can we account for these two readings? Recall that in the infinitival elementary tree that represents the clausal complement of the raising verb (that of *many unicorns to be in the garden*), the subject, already in its specifier of TP position, c-commands and hence takes scope over the T′ at which adjoining takes place. As part of this T′ node dominates the raising predicate after Adjoining, in a sense that can be made more precise, this relationship can be taken to capture the wide scope interpretation of *many unicorns* within this elementary tree.[13] Turning to the narrow scope interpretation, it is sufficient to assume that the subject starts out in a VP-internal subject position and then moves to a specifier of TP position within its own elementary tree. The trace of this movement in predicate-internal position then provides a structural locus for the narrow scope reading, as this position is ultimately c-commanded by the raising predicate.[14]

This analysis of the scope ambiguity in (24) leads to a prediction concerning the effects of negation on the scope ambiguity under discussion. In monoclausal sentences, quantifiers of a certain class including *some*, *many*, and *several* (perhaps the weak quantifiers) that occur in subject position are unable to take scope inside sentential negation.

(25) a. Many/Several unicorns are not in the garden.
       (Interpretation: OK many/several > not, * not > many/several)
     b. Many/Several machines are not working.
       (Interpretation: OK many/several > not, * not > many/several)

The impossibility of interpreting the quantifier narrowly with respect to negation is especially clear for the cases in (25a): there is no interpretation for these examples that does not imply unicorn existence. If the quantifier were interpreted within the negation, as in (26), such an implication would be lacking.

(26) There are not many/several unicorns in the garden.
     (Interpretation: * many/several > not, OK not > many/several)

Without worrying about the basis for the interpretive asymmetries in (25), let us simply assume that *not* somehow interrupts the relation between the subject quantifier and its predicate-internal trace, thereby rendering scope reconstruction impossible. Now, given that our analysis of the narrow scope reading of a raised quantifier with respect to the raising predicate depends crucially on the possibility of scopal interpretation in such a predicate-internal position, we should expect that when the lower clause of a raising structure contains *not*, not only should narrow scope interpretation of the quantifier with respect to negation be blocked, but also narrow scope interpretation with respect to the raising predicate. As the following examples demonstrate, this prediction is borne out:[15]

(27) a. Many/Several unicorns seem not to be in the garden.
        (Interpretation: OK many/several > seem,
        * seem > many/several)
     b. Many/Several machines seem not to be working.
        (Interpretation: OK many/several > seem,
        * seem > many/several)

Interestingly, the sentences in (27) contrast with the similar examples in (28) where the semantic force of the negation is embedded within the lexical predicate and does not block lower scope interpretation.

(28) a. Many/Several unicorns seem to be missing from the garden.
        (Interpretation: OK many/several > seem,
        OK seem > many/several)
     b. Many/Several machines seem to be malfunctioning.
        (Interpretation: OK many/several > seem,
        OK seem > many/several)

This contrast would be inexplicable if we took raising to leave a trace in the lower subject position. Under a view of scope reconstruction that derived narrow scope via reconstruction of the quantifier to the position of a trace in the embedded specifier of TP, there would be no reason to expect the presence of negation in the embedded clause to have an effect, as it does not intervene between the matrix and subject positions. Hence, we see not only that traces of raising to subject are not necessary to account for scope reconstruction effects, but also that an analysis without them is simpler.[16]

### 3.4.3 Contraction

The transformational analysis of raising as involving successive-cyclic movement, though empirically quite successful, suffers theoretical embarrassment in syntactically conditioned cases of phonological reduction, such as *wanna*-contraction.

(29) a. They want to meet Daniel.
     b. They wanna meet Daniel.

One fairly well established generalization concerning such cases is that traces of *wh*-movement block the otherwise possible contraction of phonologically adjacent *want* and *to* (see, e.g., Postal and Pullum 1978; Jaeggli 1980).

(30) a.  Who do they want *t* to meet Daniel?
     b. *Who do they wanna meet Daniel?

Traces of NP-movement, however, do not block contraction.

(31) a. Hugh seems *t* to have left.
     b. Hugh seemsta have left.

(32) a. Janet was supposed *t* to be here.
     b. Janet was sposta be here.

This contrast has forced a complication in the specification of one of the conditions that determine when contraction is possible, so that only Case-marked empty categories block contraction.[17] As Kroch and Joshi (1985) note, however, there is no need for such a complication in the context of the TAG raising analysis, as it does not posit a trace in the embedded subject position in cases of raising. As we shall see in chapter 5, the TAG analysis of *wh*-movement I propose does posit a trace in the embedded subject position in examples like (30). Consequently, the maximally simple statement of one condition on contraction—namely, that it is blocked by traces—can be maintained.[18]

### 3.4.4  *There*-Insertion

Another dilemma posed by the usual successive-cyclic analysis of raising derives from the distribution of the so-called expletive *there*, seen in constructions like the following:

(33) There was a spy at the meeting.

A rough generalization concerning this construction is that the element *there* can appear in the subject position of *be* (and perhaps unaccusative predicates generally) whenever there is a local postverbal indefinite DP, the so-called associate of *there*. This DP, which ordinarily moves to subject position, does not raise when *there* is present.

(34) [A spy] was *t* at the meeting.

Assuming that the motivation for such movement into subject position derives from the EPP, the complementarity of *there*-insertion and movement to subject position suggests that the insertion of *there* provides an alternative method for satisfying the EPP.[19] Now, if the EPP requirement holds for all clauses, it is a straightforward inference from the examples in (35) and (36) that *there* can undergo raising: it is first inserted into subject position of the lowest clause and then raised to satisfy the EPP requirements of higher clauses.

(35) a. There seemed *t* to be a spy at the meeting.

   b. [A spy] seemed *t* to be *t* at the meeting.

(36) a. There was likely *t* to seem *t* to be a spy at the meeting.

   b. [A spy] was likely *t* to seem *t* to be *t* at the meeting.

This simple and elegant analysis of *there*, essentially that of Chomsky (1995), suffers from one simple defect. It fails to explain why we never see partial raising of an indefinite DP to an intermediate subject position, followed by insertion of *there* into a still higher subject position.

(37) a. *There seemed [a spy] to be *t* at the meeting.

   b. *There was likely [a spy] to seem *t* to be *t* at the meeting.

To explain the impossibility of such cases, Chomsky (2000) puts forward a novel principle of derivational economy: at a point in the derivation when both operations are possible, Merge is preferred to Move. Consider the implications of this principle in the (bottom-up) derivation of (37a) at the point depicted in (38).

(38) [$_{T'}$ to be [a spy] at the meeting]

The next derivational step must check infinitival T's EPP feature. This can be done by moving the already incorporated DP *a spy* to the specifier of TP. However, if *there* is present in the lexical array associated with the derivation, this gives rise to an alternative way to check the EPP, by merging the expletive. By the Merge-over-Move preference, the latter option must be chosen, blocking the possibility of moving *a spy* to even the lowest subject position.

   Considering this puzzle in the TAG context, let us start by assuming that the relationship between *there* and the postverbal DP associate, the one underlying Case transmission perhaps, is established within an elementary tree.[20] As soon as we do this, it is no longer even clear how to translate the problematic "partial movement" derivation into TAG terms. If the associate DP is raised to the specifier of TP position in its (infinitival) elementary tree, as will be necessary to generate the examples in (37), adjoining a *seem*-headed T' auxiliary tree will necessarily raise this DP, occupying the specifier of TP, into the matrix clause. On this view, then, this range of empirical data requires that we resort neither to a stipulated preference for Merge over Move during the process of elementary tree creation nor to some other notion of derivational economy that might apply during the composition of elementary trees.[21]

The success of this explanation of the impossibility of cases of partial raising like (37a) depends on little beyond the mechanisms required for the basic TAG-based analysis of raising. However, there is also a sense in which it is too successful, since it leaves us in a bit of a quandary about why analogous examples are possible in Icelandic (Jonas 1996).

(39) Það  virðast margir menn vera  í  herberginu.
       there seem   many  men   to be in the room

I would like to suggest that this quandary is only apparent, since we have overlooked one way in which examples like those in (37), as well as the one in (39), might be generated in the TAG-based analysis. This alternative derivation involves an elementary tree containing both the expletive and the subject DP, perhaps of the form in (40).[22]

(40)

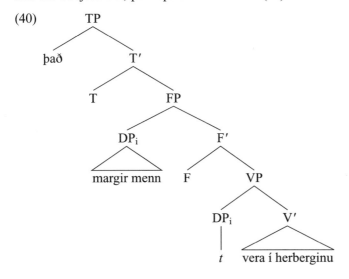

In this structure, which adopts in essential respects the analysis of
Bobaljik and Thráinsson (1998), the structure of a simple clause includes
an additional functional projection, labeled here FP, in whose specifier the
external argument appears. Example (39) can now be derived by adjoining the *virðast* 'seems' headed auxiliary tree in (41) to the T′ in (40).

(41)

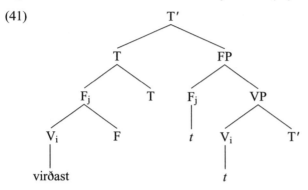

Why should such a derivation be allowed in Icelandic, but not in
English? The answer derives from an independently necessary difference
between the languages, relating to the licensing of so-called transitive expletive constructions (TECs), in which both an expletive and a lexical DP
appear in VP-external specifier positions. TECs are possible in Icelandic,
though not in English (example (42b) from Bobaljik and Thráinsson
1998).

(42) a. *There has some cat eaten the mice.
     b. Það   hefur einhver köttur étið   mýsnar.
        there has   some    cat    eaten the mice

If we assume that external arguments must always appear in a position
external to VP, the presence of the additional functional projection FP is
crucial in licensing TECs. Bobaljik and Thráinsson (1998) argue that
only languages with rich verbal inflectional morphology permit the requisite additional functional projection. The relative richness of Icelandic
verbal morphology as compared with that of English, then, implies that
the grammar of Icelandic permits elementary structures like the one in
(40), but the grammar of English does not.[23]

An alternative to this analysis might take the expletive and DP subjects
to be generated in multiple specifier positions of the lower clause's TP
projection, giving rise to the elementary tree in (43).

(43)

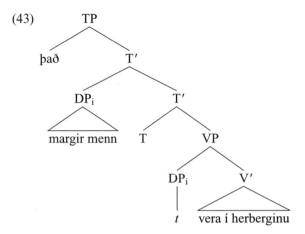

By adjoining a T' raising auxiliary headed by *virðast* to the higher T', we derive (39). On this alternative, one might expect it to be possible to adjoin raising auxiliaries not only at the upper T', but also at the lower T' (subject to the verb-second constraint; see note 23).[24] If this is so, it would provide a means for deriving examples like the English (37b), which appear to be ill formed in Icelandic as well (Halldór Sigurðsson, personal communication). I therefore tentatively adopt the structure for TECs in (40), with the expletive and subject in specifiers of distinct functional projections.

### 3.5   Nonraising in Nominals and Gerunds

Chomsky (1970) notes a striking contrast in acceptability between raising out of the complements to nominal predicates and raising out of the complements to verbal predicates: raising of the sort we have been discussing is impossible with nouns.[25]

(44) a.   Leon appears to have left.
     b.   *Leon's appearance to have left surprised me.

(45) a.   Leon is likely to have left.
     b.   *Leon's likelihood to have left was not doubted by anyone.

Chomsky explains this contrast by stipulating that certain grammatical transformations, including subject-to-subject raising, apply only to sentences and not to noun phrases. Kayne (1984, chap. 3) provides a more principled solution and aims to link this contrast to the Empty Category

Principle (ECP). As evidenced by their inability to assign Case, Kayne suggests that nouns are unable to properly govern the traces of raising within their complements, leading to an ECP violation. Verbs, in contrast, are capable of properly governing the trace of raising, and therefore such movement does not run afoul of the ECP.

More recent discussions of raising have said little about this contrast.[26] Interestingly, as Kroch and Joshi (1985) point out, the line of analysis given above accounts for the nominal/verbal raising contrast without any additional stipulations. Let us continue to assume that all cases of apparent raising involve only stretching of a dependency preexisting within a single elementary tree. By the CETM, the lexical heads *appearance* and *left* of example (44b) must head separate elementary trees. Consequently, any derivation of (44b) will need to involve the adjoining of an *appearance*-headed auxiliary tree into an elementary tree that includes both the derived position of the raised DP and its base position, in other words, one that realizes the lexical material *Leon's to have left*. For the moment, assume that the structure involved in this construction is as shown in (46).

(46)

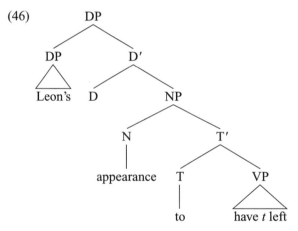

Here, the derived position of the raised DP lies in the specifier of the higher DP position. The base position of this DP, in contrast, presumably lies somewhere within the projection of the verbal head *left* that assigns it a θ-role. Decomposing this structure in accordance with the CETM, then, produces the pair of structures in (47).

(47) a.

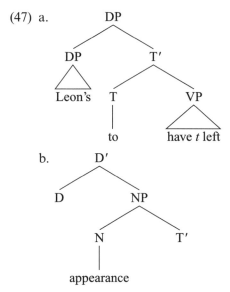

However, there are a number of problems with taking these structures to be elementary trees involved in TAG derivations. First, it is plausible to assume that the tree in (47a), though meeting the formulation of the CETM given in chapter 2, could not have been the result of a derivation along the lines envisioned in chapter 1 (see figure 1.4): when the DP frontier nonterminal that is moved from its base position within the projection of *left* is merged with T′, the DP cannot itself project further (Chomsky 1995). Furthermore, although the structure in (47b) is a possible elementary tree, it is of no use in deriving (46) via Adjoining, as it fails the formal requirements on auxiliary trees, not having recursive root and foot nodes. Thus, there is no way to derive the structure in (46).

If we consider alternative structures to the one in (46) for raising nominals, we can in fact come up with well-formed TAG derivations that produce them. Specifically, suppose that the derived structure for (44b) is as shown in (48).

(48)

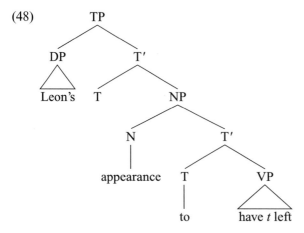

Here, the derived position of the raised DP is in a specifier of TP. As shown in (49), this structure can be decomposed into a well-formed auxiliary tree, recursive on T′, and a TP elementary tree.

(49) a.

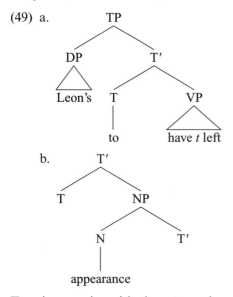

Two issues arise with these trees, however. The first concerns the compatibility of tense projections with nominal extended projections. Such an incompatibility has in fact been suggested by Alexiadou (1999), offering as evidence the impossibility of using "high" adverbs (e.g., manner adverbs, which have been associated with T and projections above it) to modify process nominals. Alexiadou takes the EPP features of T to be implicated in driving the movement underlying raising and consequently derives the conclusion that raising in nominals cannot be triggered. In essence, this is what the TAG analysis forces us to, though for reasons unrelated to the feature content of T.[27] A second issue relates to the assignment/checking of genitive Case of the prenominal genitive *Leon's*. If we assume that genitive Case is checked in a specifier of DP position, it is not clear what licenses the genitive Case on the raised DP, as it never proceeds through such a position. One possibility might stem from the presence of a D projection between T and N, with this D adjoining to the higher T, checking its Case features in its derived position in the specifier of TP.[28]

As we have seen, the proposed analysis derives the absence of raising nominals from the lack of recursion between the projection of the nominal and the projection of the clausal complement. If recursion is what is at issue, we ought to expect that a nominal taking another nominal as its complement would be able to license raising, as the resulting elementary trees would be unproblematic under the CETM. Thus, we would predict (incorrectly) that examples like the following are allowed:

(50)  *the city's appearance the destruction
       (intended meaning: the appearance of the city's destruction)

There is, however, an independent means of deriving the impossibility of examples like this, as nouns are in general prohibited from taking DP complements. Grimshaw (1990) attributes this to the inability of nouns to directly θ-mark their complements without mediation by a preposition. Alternatively, we might relate such impossibility to the inability of nouns to assign Case to their complements. If either of these suggestions were correct, we might (again incorrectly) expect examples like the following to be acceptable:

(51)  *the city's appearance of the destruction

The presence of the preposition in the elementary tree headed by the embedded nominal, however, will block the possibility of a raising derivation in a manner exactly analogous to those discussed above in the verbal domain, as the necessary elementary trees will not be well formed.

There do, however, exist cases of prepositional complements to nominals that at least superficially look like cases of raising. The following example is cited by Kayne (1984):

(52)  ?John's likelihood of winning

Kayne suggests that this case does not involve raising at all, but instead is a case of control. As seen in (53), control into the complements of nominals is unproblematic, and it is predicted to be so on a TAG analysis whereby control involves Substitution.

(53) a. John's desire [PRO to win]
     b. Alice's attempt [PRO to leave]

In support of this suggestion, Kroch and Joshi (1985) note that the construction in (52) does not exhibit any of the diagnostic properties of raising.

(54) a. *There's likelihood of being a depression is difficult to estimate.
     b. *Headway's likelihood of being made is uncertain.
     c. *Its likelihood of raining is practically zero.

Consequently, this sort of case is not a real counterexample to the TAG analysis prediction that recursion is necessary for raising.

If we change our focus from nominalizations to gerunds, the empirical situation changes. Once again, we can construct examples like (52) that on the surface look like cases of raising out of the clausal complement of a gerund.

(55) a. I was astonished at John's appearing to have won.
     b. I was astonished at John appearing to have won.

If we apply standard raising diagnostics, however, the two types of gerunds, so-called poss-*ing* gerunds (like (55a)) with genitive subjects and acc-*ing* gerunds (like (55b)) with accusative subjects, behave differently.[29]

(56) a. *I was astonished at there's appearing to be a riot.
     b.  I was astonished at there appearing to be a riot.

(57) a. *I was astonished at headway's appearing to have been made on
        the problem.
     b. ?I was astonished at headway appearing to have been made on
        the problem.

These contrasts suggest that poss-*ing* gerunds head nominal extended projections and therefore lack the recursive structure that would allow them to head auxiliary trees of the sort necessary to participate in an Adjoining-based derivation. This proposal is in line with the analysis of Abney (1987), who suggests that these gerunds should be analyzed as verbal heads embedded within DP projections. This would mean that the apparent instance of raising in (55a) is better analyzed as a case of control along the lines suggested for (52) with the structure in (58).

(58)

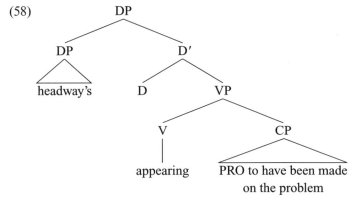

Following Frank and Kroch (1994), I suggest that acc-*ing* gerunds differ from their poss-*ing* counterparts in that the former possess verbal functional structure—more specifically, that they are TP projections, as shown in (59).

(59)

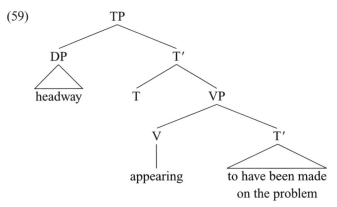

As such, there is no impediment to constructing an auxiliary tree of the sort necessary to derive this structure by adjoining the gerund between the DP *headway* and the rest of its clause. Indeed, the derivation of these cases proceeds exactly like that of the standard verbal cases discussed at the outset.

Note that if this analysis of raising is correct, it suggests that Kayne's (1984) proposal that the impossibility of raising is due to government properties is not correct. Both poss-*ing* and acc-*ing* gerunds are internally verbal, being distinguished only by their external structural context. This external context is crucial in creating the recursive structural context that determines the possibility of an Adjoining-based derivation.

## 3.6   Raising Passives

Let me turn briefly to another example of a raising construction, that which occurs when exceptional-case-marking (ECM) verbs are passivized. ECM verbs are so named because of their ability to exceptionally assign accusative Case to the subject of their (infinitival) complement clause, as in (60).

(60)  Myrna expects [him to be late].

For some time, the possibility of exceptionally assigning Case in this way has been tied to the assumption that the clausal complement to the ECM verb is in some sense defective and hence tolerates the assignment of Case across its boundary. One common view takes the defective property of this clause to be its categorial status, a TP rather than a CP.

Now consider what happens under passivization. In general, passivized verbs lose their ability to assign either an external θ-role or structural accusative Case. In the context of transformational analyses, this forces the embedded subject of the ECM verb's clausal complement to raise to the subject position of the (finite) ECM verb. This position, in which the raised DP can be assigned nominative Case, is available because the external argument is suppressed under passivization. This derivation is, in essential respects, identical to that assumed for raising sentences.

Let us now apply the same logic in the TAG context. Within a TAG-based theory, the effects of passivizing a verb, like all lexicosyntactic operations, must be realized within the elementary tree headed by that verb. As before, we assume that the passivized matrix verb no longer assigns an external θ-role. By the θ-Criterion, this means that the elementary tree headed by this verb can no longer include a frontier non-terminal corresponding to an external argument. As in the case of raising predicates, then, the elementary tree will project only as high as T′, meaning that it must tolerate T′ complements if it is to participate in well-formed derivations. This results in an auxiliary tree of the form in (61).

(61)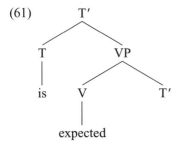

Given the geometry and labeling of this tree, it should be clear that it will play precisely the same derivational role as the auxiliary trees headed by *seem* considered above. As in the transformational analysis, then, we are led to conclude that passivization of ECM verbs produces structures identical to those involved in raising.

In this analysis, the filling of the matrix subject position with the lower subject is rendered possible by the fact that the syntactic category of the clausal complement was the same as that of the root, namely, T′. This was necessary for the matrix clause elementary tree to meet the definition of auxiliary tree and to participate in Adjoining. If the complement of the ECM predicate were of a different category, the situation would be just like the one that arises with nominal raising structures like (47b): the absence of recursion leads to the impossibility of Adjoining, and hence raising. With such a predicate, then, we would expect that passivization would be impossible, as there would be no way to raise the embedded subject. In fact, there is a class of ECM predicates that exhibit precisely this pattern, namely, causative and perception verbs. As seen in (62), the infinitival complement clauses to these ECM verbs differ from those to verbs like *expect* and *believe* in lacking the element *to*, which I have been taking to be a T head.

(62) a. I saw [her leave the party].
    b. I made [her leave the party].

For this reason, it has often been assumed that the "naked infinitive" complements to such verbs are best represented as bare VPs (Kroch, Santorini, and Heycock 1988). Adopting this view, the derivation for the examples in (62) will involve the substitution of the elementary tree in (63a) into (63b).

(63) a.

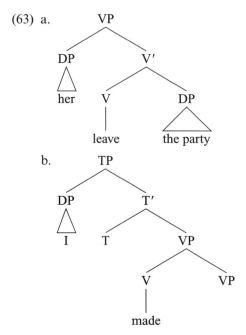

As is well known, the passive counterparts of sentences like those in (62) are ungrammatical.

(64) a. *She was seen leave the party.
     b. *She was made leave the party.

This curious contrast follows directly from the assumptions we have made concerning passivization and the TAG machinery. In order to passivize the elementary tree in (63b) headed by the causative verb, we suppress its external argument and hence project only as high as T'. Let us assume that since passivization also deprives *made* of its ability to assign accusative Case, substitution of a bare VP into the complement position will not allow the embedded subject to be Case marked. However, even if we modify the level of projection of the complement as we did earlier— say, from VP to V'—we cannot produce the effects of raising via Adjoining in this case: the complement is of category VP, while the root is of category T. Thus, the resulting elementary structure, shown in (65), will not constitute a possible auxiliary tree.[30]

(65)

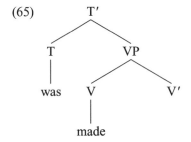

Interestingly, causative and perception verbs can appear in passive forms, but only when they take clausal complements containing a T projection, as indicated by the presence of *to*.

(66) a.  John was seen to leave.
     b.  John was made to leave.

Such structures are, of course, derivable in exactly the fashion discussed above for passives of verbs like *expect*.[31] The fact that the change from a bare VP to a TP complement is sufficient to render these sentences grammatical suggests that it is indeed the presence of a recursive T' structure, as demanded by Adjoining, that allows raising to take place, thereby supporting the TAG-based analysis of this construction that we have been pursuing.[32]

### 3.7  Raising from Small Clauses

One case of raising that does not appear to fit in with the conclusion that raising demands T' complementation involves raising from small clause complements, that is, from predications that do not involve any sort of verbal material, finite or otherwise. Small clauses show up as complements to verbs like *consider*.

(67)  Henry considers [Fay a hero].

When *consider* passivizes, the small clause subject is realized in the matrix subject position, as in (68).

(68)  Fay is considered a hero (by all who know her).

Raising out of small clauses has also been implicated in the analysis of sentences like those in (69) involving raising predicates, as well as copular sentences like those in (70) (traces indicate the position from which raising would occur in a transformational analysis).

(69) a. Arnold appears [*t* anxious about the upcoming exam].
      b. Lucy seems [*t* happy about her good fortune].

(70) a. Lucy is [*t* happy about her good fortune].
      b. Arnold is [*t* my favorite actor].

To derive examples like those in (68)–(70) using the type of TAG analysis we have been exploring, we must assume that small clauses are less small than has often been thought. Rather, small clauses must contain structure beyond the projection of the predicative head, as has sometimes been suggested (Moro 1988; Bowers 1993; Cardinaletti and Guasti 1995). Some evidence for additional structure is provided by small clauses in which a DP predicate includes a prenominal genitive.

(71) Henry considers [his sister Alice's best friend].

Under the assumption that the genitive DP occupies the outermost specifier of the predicate DP, there is no position within the DP that could host the subject of the small clause. I suggest that in example (71), the small clause subject *his sister* in fact occupies the specifier of the projection of a covert functional head that I will label F. This head F is present, I would like to suggest, as a result of an inability of nonverbal predicates to host their external arguments within their own projection (Baker and Stewart 1997). Instead, I claim that such subject-predicate relations must be mediated by the functional element F.[33]

How does the presence of the functional head F resolve the dilemma posed by such cases of raising? Let us take F to be underspecified in its categorial features, and let us also suppose that Adjoining requires not categorial identity between the label of the site of adjoining and the root and foot of the auxiliary tree, as we have assumed thus far, but categorial nondistinctness. The derivation of (68) can now proceed, with the auxiliary tree in (72a) adjoining at the F′ node in the small clause tree in (72b).

(72) a.

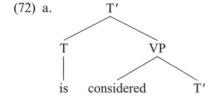

b.

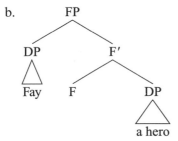

Trees analogous to the one in (72a), but headed by *seem*, *appear*, and the copula, would allow the examples in (69) and (70) to be generated.

One potential argument against taking these cases to involve raising comes from facts noted by Williams (1983) concerning scopal interpretation.

(73) a. Some unicorns seemed to be white.

b. Some unicorns seemed white.

In (73a), we see the familiar ambiguity of the scope of the indefinite DP *some unicorns* with respect to the raising predicate *seemed*. On the narrow scope reading of *some unicorns*, no unicorns need exist for the sentence to be true, while on the wide scope reading, unicorns must exist. In the small clause example in (73b), the former reading is unavailable, as the truth of the sentence entails the existence of unicorns. Given the parallelism in the derivations we are assigning to these sentences, how can we explain this difference in their range of interpretations? Recall our earlier hypothesis concerning the structural basis of the narrow scope interpretation in raising-from-TP complements: the trace of the raised subject inside VP. I have suggested that subjects of small clause structures are assigned their θ-role by the small clause predicate in the specifier of F position, the F head being necessary to mediate the subject-predicate relation (Baker and Stewart 1997). Consequently, there will be no elementary-tree-internal movement, and thus no trace below the raising passive verb to allow narrow scope. Thus, the scopal contrast presents no problem for the "traceless" TAG analysis.

**3.8   Raising and Inversion**

Though I suspect the line of analysis we have been pursuing is correct for raising with *seem*-type predicates and ECM passives, I believe there are important reasons to doubt that the copula cases work the same way.

In this section, I describe one major reason, relating to contrasts in the acceptability of a certain type of inversion, and I demonstrate how the TAG conception of derivations, coupled with the characterization of elementary trees I have proposed, predicts these contrasts in a principled way.

In addition to the canonical form in (74a), copular constructions admit an "inverse" form, following Moro's (1990, 1997) terminology, as exemplified in (74b).[34]

(74) a. The assassination of the king was the cause of the war.
     b. The cause of the war was the assassination of the king.

In (74b), it is the semantic predicate rather than the subject of the predication that occupies the surface subject position. One analysis, advocated by Stowell (1978) and Couquaux (1982), takes this alternation to derive from differences in the underlying syntactic subject-predicate relation. Under such an analysis, the DP *the cause of the war* would be the small clause predicate in (74a), but the small clause subject in (74b). However, a variety of facts argue against such a syntactically uniform treatment of the two types of copular sentences. Moro (1990, 1997) notes that extraction from the postcopular DP is possible only in canonical copular sentences, being strictly forbidden in inverse copular sentences.

(75) a.   Which war was the assassination of the king the cause of?
     b. *Which king was the cause of the war the assassination of?

In addition, Moro observes that only one order of the two DPs is possible in coherent small clause complements to verbs like *consider*.

(76) a.   I consider the assassination of the king the cause of the war.
     b. *I consider the cause of the war the assassination of the king.

Finally, a syntactically uniform analysis of the cases in (74) runs afoul of attempts to render semantic relations in a syntactically consistent manner, such as Baker's (1988) Uniformity of θ-Assignment Hypothesis (UTAH). As pointed out by Dan Hardt (personal communication), the DPs in the examples in (74) function the same way semantically, whether in the canonical or the inverse order: the DP *the assassination of the king* is interpreted referentially, while the DP *the cause of the war* is interpreted attributively. For either of the sentences in (77), then, only the sentence in (78a) is a felicitous continuation, indicating that *the president of the Soviet Union* is consistently understood referentially regardless of the order in the copular sentence.

(77) a. A: The president of the Soviet Union was the cause of the riot.
     b. A: The cause of the riot was the president of the Soviet Union.

(78) a. B:   Well, he's actually the president of Russia, but you're right.
     b. B:   #He was actually the cause of the coup, but you're right.

Moro (1990, 1997) proposes an alternative analysis of copular constructions in which the structure of the small clause is identical across both canonical and inverse constructions, as in (74) (see also Heycock 1991). What differs across these sentence types is which element raises out of the copula's small clause complement to subject position. In inverse copular constructions, it is the small clause predicate rather than the small clause subject that raises to become the subject of the sentence. The derivations for the examples in (74a) and (74b) are thus depicted in (79a) and (79b), respectively.

(79) a. [$_{TP}$[The assassination of the king]$_i$ was [$_{SC}$ $t_i$ [the cause of the war]]].
     b. [$_{TP}$[The cause of the war]$_i$ was [$_{SC}$[the assassination of the king] $t_i$]].

This analysis allows the assignment of semantic subject-predicate relations to be performed in a syntactically uniform manner. Additionally, it explains the existence of the extraction asymmetry shown in (75) by an appeal to the Subject Condition: the postcopular DP in (75b) is a small clause subject and consequently counts as a barrier to movement. Finally, the ordering facts in (76) follow from the assumption that the complement to *consider* contains no position into which the predicate could invert.[35]

Moro's analysis treats copular constructions as identical to raising constructions involving predicates like *seem* or *be considered*. There is, however, an important distributional difference between these two. Unlike their copular cousins, constructions with raising predicates do not permit an inverse form, as demonstrated by the contrast between the following examples and those in (74):

(80) a.   [The assassination of the king]$_i$ is often considered [$_{SC}$ $t_i$ the cause of the war].
     b.   *[The cause of the war]$_i$ is often considered [$_{SC}$ the assassination of the king $t_i$]

The examples in (80) use a raising passive rather than a simple raising predicate because in my dialect and that of most American English speakers, such predicates do not tolerate DP-headed small clauses as their complements. Those (British English) speakers who do accept such sentences as (81a) uniformly reject the corresponding inverse sentences (cf. Ruwet 1982 for French).[36]

(81)  a.  (?*)John seems/appears the obvious choice.
       b.      *The obvious choice seems/appears John.

Moro (1997, chap. 4) in fact argues that inversion of the sort found in inverse copular cases does occur with *seem*, in sentences of the following form:

(82)  It$_i$ seems [[that John read that book] $t_i$].

Here, Moro analyzes the *it* subject as a propredicate that is raised past the CP subject of the small clause. Leaving aside the puzzle of why such inversion with *seem* should be impossible in cases like (81b), there is evidence that examples like (82) should not be analyzed as involving inversion of the inverse copula sort. As noted earlier, Moro derives the impossibility of extracting out of a postcopula small clause subject as seen in (75b) from its structural context: as a subject, it functions as an island for extraction. We should therefore expect that the putative CP small clause subject in (82) will similarly block extraction. However, as Moro himself notes (pp. 187–188), this post-*seem* CP tolerates extraction quite freely, permitting both arguments and adverbials to move out.

(83)  a.  Why does it seem [that John left $t$]?
       b.  How does it seem [that John left $t$]?
       c.  Which book does it seem [that John read $t$]?

I take the sharp contrast between these examples and those in (75) to argue against taking these examples to be cases of inversion of the type found in copular constructions.

However appealing, Moro's analysis of copular constructions leaves us with a significant puzzle. If the copula is taken to be a raising predicate and the derivations in (79b) and (80b) are otherwise identical, why is it only the copula that tolerates inverse raising? It turns out that the TAG-based analysis of raising developed here provides a solution. Recall that under this analysis, raising predicates head elementary trees that do not include any structural representation of the complement clause. The fact that a *seem*-headed elementary tree would have such a limited domain follows directly from the CETM. Raising predicates like *seem* or *be considered* assign a θ-role to their complements and are thus properly categorized as lexical heads. This means that although they may form extended projections with functional projections above them, their complements must be part of distinct extended projections and hence distinct elementary trees. In contrast, it is plausible to assume that the copula *be* does not assign any θ-role, instead playing a more purely grammatical role of realizing some complex of grammatical features. Evidence in favor of this is provided by languages like Russian and Hebrew that allow predications to be expressed without the copula. As such copula-free sentences are synonymous with their English counterparts, we are led to the conclusion that the copula, when it occurs, does not add any lexical meaning to the sentence. That is to say, the copula does not assign any θ-role. If we understand the notion of lexical head as one that does assign a θ-role, the copula does not qualify as a lexical head. Consequently, it does not head its own extended projection, and it need not form an elementary tree distinct from that of its complement. Instead, since the CETM requires the presence of some lexical head within every elementary tree, an elementary tree containing the copula must also include some of the additional, lower structure of its small clause complement.

This conclusion brings to the fore the question of the categorial status of the copula. In certain respects, the distribution of the copula patterns with that of (auxiliary) verbs, and indeed Heycock (1991) suggests that it is a V element. However, if V is necessarily a lexical head, then this is at odds with our conclusion that the copula is not lexical (at least for the purposes of the CETM). Under one potential reconciliation, we might extend the typology of functional and lexical heads, allowing for the possibility of a "functional verb": an element that is categorially verbal, but is nonetheless regarded as functional since it lacks a θ-grid.[37] Alternatively, we can follow Moro in assuming that the copula is generated as the head of some functional projection, which takes a small clause as its complement.

Whichever view we adopt on the categorial nature of the copula, we are left with the result that the copula is invariably generated as part of an elementary tree headed by some lower lexical predicate.[38] Assuming the copula to be generated in some projection CopP between TP and the small clause, simple canonical copular sentences like those in (70) are generated using elementary trees of the form shown in (84).[39]

(84)

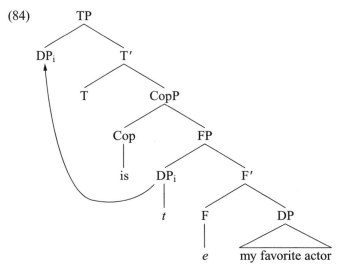

Notice that the raising of the subject DP from its base position within the small clause to its surface position in the specifier of TP takes place completely within the confines of this elementary tree.[40] This is in sharp contrast to the way in which raising was accomplished in constructions involving *seem* and the like, where the "raising" of the subject was accomplished via Adjoining.

Now consider how we might generate the inverse raising constructions. In the copular case, we need only make use of an alternative elementary tree in which the predicate DP rather than the subject DP has been raised to the specifier of TP position.

(85)

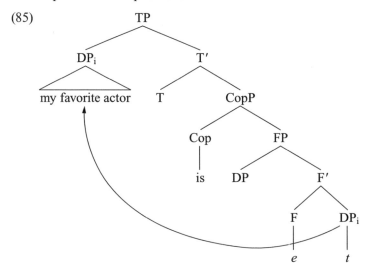

Under the assumption that this movement is possible within the elementary tree, there is nothing blocking this derivation. In the case of raising with a lexical verb, the same line of analysis cannot be pursued, since such an instance of "raising" involves the interpolation of the lexical predicate between portions of the small clause structure using Adjoining. Transformational movement from the small clause predicate position to the matrix subject position would cross two elementary trees and is therefore forbidden. Consequently, whatever relative hierarchy and ordering the small clause's elementary tree fixes between the subject and the predicate are condemned to be maintained throughout the derivation. To have a small clause's predicate raise past a lexical raising verb, then, will require that the predicate have already raised past the small clause subject within the raising verb's complement.

A quick inspection of the small clause elementary tree in (72b) reveals that there is no position to which the small clause predicate could move so that it could precede the small clause subject. The specifier of the highest projection, FP, is already filled by the small clause subject in its base position. What is needed is some additional structure that could serve as a "pivot" around which the subject and predicate of the small clause could invert. Such structure could come in the form of one more functional projection, call it *PivotP*, at the top of the extended projection in (72b), one whose specifier was a possible landing site for the raising of the small clause predicate.

(86)

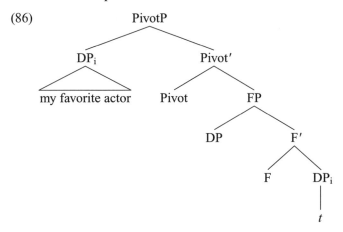

If we assume that the selectional properties of lexical raising predicates like *seem* prohibit the projection of such an additional pivoting head within their complement, instead demanding a small clause complement that is categorially FP, we derive the impossibility of inversion around these types of predicates.

Comparing the structure in (86) with the one in (79b), it becomes clear that the hypothetical functional head I have labeled as *Pivot* is playing exactly the role of the T-copula combination. Indeed, when a copula is added to the complement of a lexical raising predicate, inversion becomes well formed.

(87) The obvious choice seems *(to be) John.

(88) The cause of the war is considered *(to be) the assassination of the king.

This follows immediately under our current assumptions. These well-formed examples of inversion can be derived by adjoining a typical raising auxiliary tree of the sort given in (9) at the T′ node of an elementary tree of the form in (89).

(89)

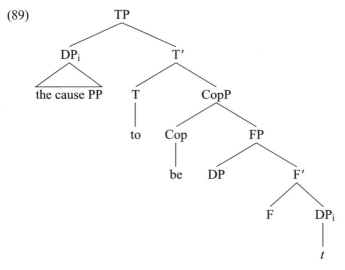

The presence of the higher specifier allows the predicate to be fronted, yielding the inverted order even prior to Adjoining.

Data from Hebrew, a language that does not uniformly require the presence of an overt copula in predicative constructions, provide further support for the view of the copula as a "pivot" element. As discussed by Rapoport (1987), present tense predicative sentences in Hebrew do not require the presence of any copula-like element.

(90) a. Ha-yeled student.
the-boy   student
'The boy is a student.'
    b. Ha-yalda pikxit.
the-girl   smart-F
'The girl is smart.'

Similarly, constructions in which the predicate DP is definite (i.e., those that are capable of entering into an inverse copular construction) do not require the presence of the overt copula.

(91) Dani ha-more.
Dani the-teacher
'Dani is the teacher.'

In contrast, when this construction exhibits its inverse form, an H element (to use Rapoport's term) must appear.

(92) Ha-more *(hu) Dani.

The character of this H element has been a subject of considerable debate. Rapoport argues that it is the morphological realization of Agr. This is certainly consonant with the view of English *be* as heading a functional projection, what I have labeled *CopP*. Hebrew differs from English, then, in not requiring a morphosyntactic realization of present tense. However, both languages require the presence of some overt functional head to serve as a pivot in the case of inverse copular constructions.

   Thus far, I have suggested that the distinction between predicates that tolerate inversion and those that do not (at least not without the benefit of any additional pivot structure) mirrors the functional versus lexical dichotomy. However, Heycock (1995) notes the existence of a class of lexical raising predicates that do exhibit inversion without the need for a copula.

(93) a. The real problem remains what to do next.
    b. The best solution remains instant retreat.

(94) a. At this point our real problem becomes John.
    b. The critical problem now becomes how to set the parameters.

Claiming that *remain* and *become* are non-θ-role-assigning functional verbs is considerably less plausible than was the case for the copula.[41] Thus, we cannot easily assimilate such cases to the copula. Interestingly,

Heycock suggests that the structure of the small clause complements to *remain* and *become* differs from that of the small clause complements to *seem*-type lexical raising predicates in that the former includes the projection of an additional aspectual head. I will take the specifier of this aspectual projection to be functioning as the crucial landing site for the small clause predicate. Thus, these cases become an instance of the empty copula cases just discussed and dismissed for *seem*-type predicates, where the aspectual head that is selected by this other class of raising predicates plays the crucial pivot role.[42] Thus, the small clause elementary trees into which *become* and *remain* will adjoin will have the structure in (95) as opposed to the one in (72b).

(95)

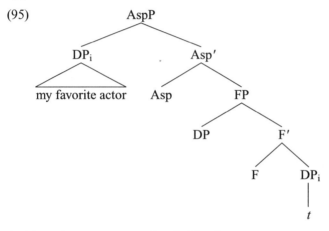

Raising elementary trees headed by *become* or *remain* can now adjoin at the Asp' node in (95), producing the inverted order, assuming that like the F head, Asp is potentially nondistinct from T. This kind of adjoining will not be possible with *seem*-type predicates, I assume, because of a conflict in selectional requirements: the foot node of a *seem*-headed auxiliary tree will include features that are incompatible with those specified on the Asp' node in (95).

Before concluding this section, I would like to comment on the distinction I have drawn between the two types of raising, involving on the one hand lexical raising predicates and on the other the copula. In both cases, the surface subject appears in a position distinct from the one in which it is generated. However, the manner in which this displacement takes place differs significantly. With copular constructions, the derived subject is "raised" within the elementary tree and occupies its derived position prior to any application of Adjoining. In contrast, with lexical raising predicates, it is Adjoining that brings about the displacement of the subject.

We see, then, that the grammatical process of movement, which was treated as a unified operation within transformational frameworks, is broken into two distinct processes in the TAG-based framework I am developing. Some of what have been treated as the effects of movement I continue to view as falling within the purview of such a transformational operation, one that must, however, apply within the domain of an elementary tree. The requirement that movement be elementary tree internal has an interesting effect on what such local movements may look like. As a simple nonrecursive structure, an elementary tree will never contain more than one position of a particular type. Hence, movement within an elementary tree will necessarily affect the type of position in which a phrase appears. Thus, elementary-tree-internal movements often have the effect of altering the grammatical function of a phrase. The inverse copular constructions we have been discussing are one example of this: the predicate DP begins its derivational life as the predicate of a small clause FP projection; but after movement, it occupies a subject position. Similarly, passivization takes DPs from object to subject position. *Wh*-movement, to be discussed at length in chapter 5, also has this property, as it takes an element from a position in which it receives a θ-role to one in which it functions as an operator.

The other class of transformational movements, those that I attribute to Adjoining, are ones in which position type and grammatical function remain constant. As an operation, Adjoining obeys a form of structure preservation: it cannot disturb the categories that stand in local relations with some element. That is to say, any sister and mother relations that are specified between nodes in an elementary tree will remain fixed throughout a TAG derivation. Consequently, cases of movement that are assimilated to Adjoining must have the property of maintaining position type as well as grammatical function. The lexical predicate raising case discussed above is a prime example of such a case. In transformational derivations, this movement always goes from one TP specifier position to another. Here, Adjoining alters which clause a particular DP is the subject of, but it is powerless to alter the fact that that DP is indeed the subject of a TP. It is precisely this structure preservation property that blocks the possibility of inverse raising with *seem*: if there has been no change in the grammatical functions of the subject and predicate DPs within the elementary tree, raising in its Adjoining guise cannot invert the two.

I would like to suggest that the distinction between these two types of raising provides an argument not only against models that treat both as transformationally derived, but also against any model in which both are derived in a uniform manner. In LFG and HPSG, for example, the link between subject and predicate in both raising and copular constructions is established via feature unification of the semantic content of the DP subject of the raising predicate with the external argument slot of the embedded predicate. This unification is driven by properties of the lexical entries of raising predicates and the copula. The difference in inversion possibilities between these two types of raising could of course be captured through explicitly stipulated differences in the application of lexical rules to the lexical entries. However, such stipulations do not constitute an explanation for the possibility of inversion in the intraclausal case analogous to the one provided by the TAG analysis developed here. Note that this type of objection applies also to TAG-based models in which elementary trees are taken to be less structurally rich than envisioned here, perhaps including only the projection of a single head (Hegarty 1993a). Under such a model, the incorporation of either a copula or a raising predicate to a lower predication would necessarily involve Adjoining. Consequently, any inversion that occurs would need to take place within the elementary tree of the lower predicate, presumably identical in the two cases.

# Chapter 4

## Local Constraints and Local Economy

### 4.1 A Local Version of the EPP

In the discussion of *there*-insertion in chapter 3, I assumed that *there*-associate relations are established within an elementary tree in order to derive the impossibility of "partial raising" in English, as in (1).

(1) *There seemed a man from the CIA to be at the meeting.

Given such a strict locality condition on the expletive-associate relation, the only derivation for (1) necessitates a transitive expletive elementary tree into which a raising auxiliary tree could adjoin, a structure that is not permitted in English (but is in Icelandic). This analysis of the ill-formedness of (1) does not go through without the locality assumption, however, since one could derive such an example by adjoining the TP auxiliary tree in (2) to the root of the tree in (3) (or alternatively by substituting the elementary tree in (3) into the TP node in the tree in (2)).[1]

(2)

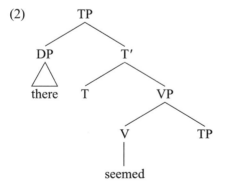

(3)

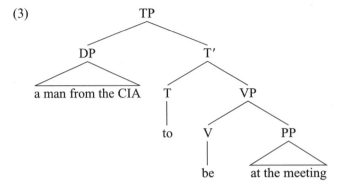

In these trees, the expletive-associate relation does not obtain within a single elementary tree, and therefore this alternative derivation is blocked by our assumption.

One might fairly ask why the expletive-associate relation must be established within the confines of the elementary tree. One standard approach to the locality of the expletive-associate relation connects it with the need for the associate to receive Case. Supposing that Case assigned to an expletive is transmitted to an associate within the same chain, one might take the locality of the expletive-associate relation to reduce to the need for Case to be assigned within an elementary tree, essentially an elementary-tree-local application of the Case Filter. The problem with this line of reasoning in the context of the thematically based conception of elementary trees we are exploring is that (structural) Case assignment does not apparently need to take place within an elementary tree.[2] In the raising analysis presented in chapter 3, for example, the embedded subject does not receive nominative Case within its infinitival elementary tree (see (3)), instead receiving it only once a raising auxiliary tree with a finite T head, like that in (4), adjoins in.[3]

(4)

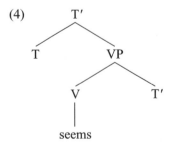

Another line of explanation for the locality of the expletive-associate relation might appeal to the formulation of the θ-Criterion in chapter 2, according to which only thematic arguments of an elementary tree's lexical head can adorn its extended projection spine. As an expletive, *there* will never be assigned a θ-role and therefore should never be possible within any elementary tree at all. To avoid this problem, we might reformulate the θ-Criterion, as suggested in note 10 of chapter 3, so that it applies to chains.

(5) *θ-Criterion (part 2)*

If A is a frontier nonterminal node of elementary tree T, A must be a member of a chain that is assigned a θ-role in T.

Under this formulation, an expletive could be present in an elementary tree, but only if it is a member of a chain with some other element that receives a θ-role. Since this is not the case in the putative elementary tree in (2), it would be ruled out. Unfortunately, this simple analysis cannot be the entire story. If (5) were adopted, we should expect that elementary trees headed by verbs that take no arguments, such as weather verbs and impersonal passives, could never include any frontier nonterminals, expletive or otherwise, since such predicates have no θ-role to assign to any nonterminal chain. This would lead to one of two incorrect predictions: either that simple sentences involving such verbs will altogether lack subjects in the specifier of TP position, or, if one assumes that the EPP constrains elementary trees, that elementary trees headed by such argumentless predicates will be impossible, as the EPP and θ-Criterion would impose conflicting demands. The English, Dutch, and French examples in (6) show that both of these predictions are incorrect.

(6) a. *(It) is raining.
   b. *(Er) wordt hier (door de jonge lui)   vell gedanst.
      it   was   here (by   the young people) a lot danced
      'There was a lot of dancing here (by the young people).'
   c. *(Il) a  été  tiré  sur  le  bateau.
      it  has been fired upon the boat
      'The boat was fired upon.'

One way of resolving this dilemma is to restrict the application of the θ-Criterion to semantically contentful DPs, arguments, as is standard. This means minimally that frontier nonterminals in which semantically contentful material is inserted, argument frontier nonterminals, will need to be distinguished from those into which expletives are inserted, something that can be expressed in the features on these nonterminals.

(7) *θ-Criterion (part 2)*
    If A is an argument frontier nonterminal node of elementary tree T, A must be a member of a chain that is assigned a θ-role in T.

As soon as we do this, however, we lose our potential explanation for the ill-formedness of (2): *there*, or more properly the DP nonterminal into which it substitutes, does not violate (7) since it is not an argument. Furthermore, it would seem that the same principle that forces the insertion of expletives in the elementary trees underlying the examples in (6)—say, the EPP—would force the insertion of an expletive here as well.[4]

Let us try a different tack, then. Under Chomsky's (1995) analysis of expletive sentences, *there* is inserted simply to satisfy the EPP requirements of the clause into which it is inserted. From this perspective, it is the failure of an indefinite DP to raise to the specifier of TP that forces *there* to be inserted. However, this reasoning is problematic in the TAG context: there are elementary trees that the TAG raising analysis requires—namely, auxiliary trees headed by raising verbs, as in (8)—that do not in any apparent way satisfy the EPP.

(8)

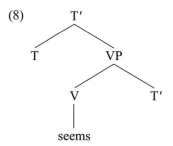

Note, however, that we cannot simply do away with the EPP as a constraint on elementary trees. As noted above, the EPP is needed to force the presence of a position for the expletive subject in the elementary trees underlying the examples in (6). Furthermore, without the EPP, it is at least not clear what would block the existence of a T′ auxiliary tree of the form in (9).

(9)

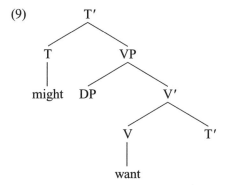

In this tree, the DP external argument has failed to raise to the specifier of TP, remaining in its base position. By adjoining such an auxiliary tree into a TP infinitival elementary tree like (3) at T′, anomalous sentences like the following could be generated:

(10)  A man from the CIA might Bill want to be at the meeting.
      (meaning 'Bill might want a man from the CIA to be at the
      meeting')

This leaves us with a problem even bigger than the one we started this chapter out with. Why are apparently EPP-violating trees like (8) allowed by the grammar, while others like (9) are not? And what does all of this have to do with the locality requirement on the expletive-associate relation?

Let us begin exploring these questions by focusing on the contrast between the trees in (8) and (9). One salient difference concerns the presence or absence of an external argument of the verb heading the elementary tree. Typically, it is just such an external argument that raises to the specifier of TP to satisfy the EPP. Since we want to force the presence of a TP specifier in (9) but not in (8), this suggests a conception of the EPP in which it is satisfied to the maximum extent possible given the structure of the elementary tree. That is, TP projections in an elementary tree must have specifiers exactly when there are independently available elements that can fill them—for example, external arguments thematically licensed by the verbal head. This requirement can be stated as follows:

(11)  *Extended Projection Principle*
      A TP projection in an elementary tree τ must have a specifier if and only if there is some otherwise licensed element within τ that can be moved to the specifier of TP.

It is straightforward to see how this formulation of the EPP blocks the elementary tree in (9). Since the external argument of *want* can be moved to the specifier of TP, this means that the specifier of TP in an elementary tree headed by *want* that satisfies the θ-Criterion cannot remain empty. In contrast, the elementary tree in (8) is well formed despite lacking a TP specifier: there is no element within the tree that can be moved to fill this position.

Let us consider for a moment the phrase "can be moved to the specifier of TP" appearing in the formulation of the EPP in (11). Above, I mentioned external arguments as one type of phrase possessing this property. Clearly, we will want to allow the objects of unaccusatives or passivized transitives to have the relevant property as well. Though I will for the moment refrain from making more precise what unifies these types of phrases, we will clearly need to distinguish cases like (9) from cases like (12).

(12)

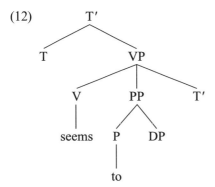

Let us suppose that (12) is the correct structure for an auxiliary tree in which the raising predicate assigns an experiencer θ-role to a dative DP.[5] Such an auxiliary tree will be necessary in deriving examples like the following:

(13) A man from the CIA seems to me to be at the meeting.

We need to ensure that the presence of the experiencer does not "trigger" the EPP, forcing the presence of a specifier of TP. Otherwise, the auxiliary in (12) would no longer be well formed, leaving us unable to derive (13), as a TP-rooted auxiliary tree could not adjoin below the subject at the T′ node of the infinitival elementary tree. Since English never allows dative DPs to move to the specifier of TP and function as subjects, we can assume that the DP in the tree in (12) cannot be moved to the specifier of TP. Hence, the EPP as formulated in (11) requires no specifier of TP, and the auxiliary tree in (12) remains well formed.

This line of argument has the interesting consequence that if a language were to differ from English in allowing datives to move to the specifier of TP, then it would not permit the auxiliary tree in (12), since the EPP would require a filled specifier of TP. This would have the effect of rendering examples like (13) ungrammatical. This prediction is confirmed by data from Icelandic discussed by Sigurðsson (1996) and Chomsky (2000).[6] As noted earlier, Icelandic allows subjects bearing nonnominative or "quirky" Case. As seen in (14a), dative is among the possible quirky Cases. Furthermore, we see in (14b) that Icelandic possesses a raising construction analogous to the English one. What we see in (14c), then, is the expected result: the presence of a dative argument to *virðast* 'seem' renders raising of the lower subject impossible.

(14) a.  Strákunum   leiddist í  skólann.
         the boys.DAT lacked  in school
         'The boys were missing in school.'
     b.  Margir menn virðast   vera í  herberginu.
         many   men  seem.3PL to be in the room
     c. *Margir menn virðast   mér     vera í  herberginu.
         many   men  seem.3PL me.DAT to be in the room

For Icelandic, then, the presence of the dative experiencer argument evidently triggers the requirement that the specifier of TP be filled within the *seem*-headed elementary tree. Consequently, we expect the grammar to license auxiliary trees of the form in (15).

(15)

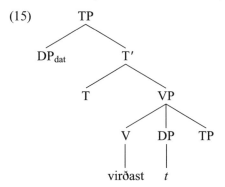

In fact, examples like the following constitute evidence that the grammar of Icelandic exploits elementary trees precisely like those in (15):

(16) Mér     virðast   margir menn vera í  herberginu.
     me.DAT seem.3PL many   men  to be in the room
     'It seems to me that many men are in the room.'

This example would be generated by adjoining the auxiliary in (15) at the TP root of an infinitival elementary tree. This derivation is similar to the one for raising, with the single difference that adjoining takes place at TP rather than T′, leaving the embedded subject in situ. Observe that in the resulting structure, the nominative DP *margir menn* 'many men' remains within the clausal complement of the raising verb. Under such a structure, we should expect that negation with matrix scope must precede the nominative DP, a prediction that is borne out.

(17) a. Mér     virðast   ekki lengur    margir menn vera í
       me.DAT seem.3PL not  any longer many  men   to be in
       herberginu.
       the room
       'It doesn't seem to me any longer that many men are in the room.'
     b. Mér     virðast   margir menn ekki lengur    vera í
       me.DAT seem.3PL many   men   not  any longer to be in
       herberginu.
       the room
       'It seems to me that many men are no longer in the room.'

Although the formulation of the EPP in (11) dictates when a specifier of TP must be present in an elementary tree, it does not determine which element must fill this position. So, in the case of an unaccusative verb like *arrive*, the fact that the object of this verb can be moved to subject position implies that the subject must be filled. One possible way for this to happen is that the object itself raises to subject position, as in the elementary tree in (18). However, it is also possible to fill the subject position with an expletive element, as in the elementary tree in (19).

(18)

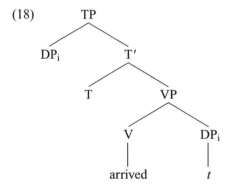

(19)

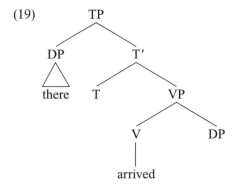

These two trees are both necessary to derive the examples in (20).[7]

(20) a. Three men from the CIA arrived.
     b. There arrived three men from the CIA.

This line of reasoning also extends to *it*-type expletives.

(21) a. [CP That Fred would be elected] was clear.
     b. [CP That Fermat's last theorem could not be proven] was
        believed.

(22) a. It was clear [CP that Fred would be elected].
     b. It was believed [CP that Fermat's last theorem could not be
        proven].

As seen in the examples in (21), the CP arguments to *clear* and *believed* can be moved to subject position. Consequently, the formulation of the EPP in (11) requires that the specifier of TP position of elementary trees headed by these predicates be filled. As before, we are not obliged to move the argument itself and can instead insert an expletive into subject position, as seen in (22).[8]

   Observe that when the expletive insertion option is taken, it is the unmoved "potential subject" that plays the role of associate. Under the formulation of the EPP in (11), expletive insertion is only an option when there is such a potential subject and hence associate for the expletive present in the elementary tree. A tree like (2) is ruled out since the EPP says that the specifier of TP is filled if and only if there is a phrase that can move to fill that position. Since there is no such movable phrase, the specifier of TP cannot be filled. We see, then, that the elementary tree locality requirement of the expletive-associate relation derives from the formulation of the EPP in (11).

Before concluding this section, let us return briefly to Icelandic. Our current line of reasoning leads us to expect that there should be an alternative to the auxiliary tree in (15), namely, one in which the subject position is filled by an expletive, as in (23).

(23)

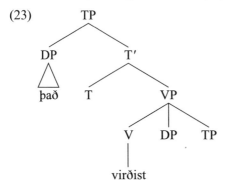

Adjoining such an auxiliary tree to a TP infinitival would produce the following sentence:

(24) Það virðist    mörgum stúdentum   þjófurinn      vera í
     there seems.3SG many       students.DAT the thief.NOM to be in
     herberginu.
     the room
     'It seems to many students that the thief is in the room.'

This example is indeed well formed. However, for it to count as support for our prediction, we need to ensure that it is not derived by adjoining a T′ auxiliary tree 'seems to many students' below an expletive that comes from the lower infinitival clause 'there the thief to be in the room'. From (14c), we know that this derivation is not possible when the "raised" element is a lexical subject of the lower clause, suggesting that it is unlikely to be possible here. Further evidence against this alternative analysis comes from definiteness effects. As with English *there* constructions, Icelandic *það* constructions show definiteness restrictions, requiring that the DP associate be indefinite/quantificationally weak. Assuming that the definiteness restriction arises from the expletive-associate relation, which as we have seen must obtain within an elementary tree, we can use the locus of the definiteness restriction as a means of determining the elementary tree in which the expletive is generated. In (24), the nominative subject in the embedded clause is definite, suggesting that this DP is not the associate of *það*. In contrast, the dative experiencer of the raising predicate in this example is indefinite. Making this DP definite renders the example ungrammatical.

(25) *Það virðist    þeim     þjófurinn     vera í herberginu.
     there seems.3SG them.DAT the thief.NOM to be in the room
     'It seems to them that the thief is in the room.'

The associate in this case, then, is the dative experiencer. On this basis, we conclude that the expletive *það* must be present in the elementary tree headed by the raising predicate.

## 4.2   Local Feature Checking and Local Economy

To recap the discussion of the last section, we have seen that elementary trees do not uniformly abide by the standard conception of the EPP, according to which every TP must have a specifier. By reformulating the EPP as in (11), however, we were able not only to retain the force of the traditional EPP in ruling out examples like (10), but also to derive the elementary tree locality of the expletive-associate relation. Unfortunately, this reformulation has complicated the statement of the EPP. This is at odds with what I suggested is one of the key motivations for adopting a TAG-based grammatical architecture: the potential for simpler and more natural grammatical principles. In this section, I argue that the added complexity in the statement of the EPP is only apparent. I will show that the need for the complex formulation of the EPP in (11) evaporates once this principle is taken to derive from more general processes of elementary-tree-local feature checking governed by principles of local derivational economy.

   The fundamental hypothesis guiding the application of TAG to syntactic theory is that all grammatical constraints should apply to elementary trees, the well-formedness of more complex structures being determined by the well-formedness of the constituent elementary trees. While it is generally possible to adhere to this guiding principle, there are some cases where different principles impose conflicting demands on what must be localized. In elementary trees like the raising auxiliary in (8), the thematic locality requirements imposed by the θ-Criterion are put in conflict with the demands of (a simple version of) the EPP that the specifier of TP always be filled. In this case, this conflict is resolved by allowing the EPP to be unsatisfied. Nonetheless, the formulation in (11) ensures that the EPP will be satisfied within an elementary tree to the greatest extent possible, and will only be left unsatisfied when satisfaction is impossible.[9]

We can recast this idea in the feature-checking framework of Chomsky 1995, 2000. Here, the effects of the EPP do not derive from a specifically stated principle but are subsumed under the more general requirement that uninterpretable syntactic features must be checked in the course of the syntactic derivation via the establishment of a certain sort of structural relation. Specifically, Chomsky takes the EPP to be the reflex of an uninterpretable selectional feature present on every T head. To check this feature, some element must be inserted into the specifier of TP, either by Merge or by Move. Let us assume, as already foreshadowed in chapter 1, that elementary trees are the result of a derivational process along the lines of Chomsky's system. In particular, suppose that an elementary tree derivation begins with a set of primitive structural resources, the numeration, and proceeds by combining these using the operations Merge and Move. Numerations in elementary tree derivations will differ from those in Chomsky's system in at least two respects. First, the numeration may include only as much structure as can produce a single elementary tree as determined by the CETM. This will have the effect of limiting the number of lexical heads in a numeration N to one, although N may include a larger number of functional heads so long as these all form a single extended projection with N's lexical head. This size limit on the numeration recalls Chomsky's (2000) notion of phase, in which numerations may include at most one $v$ or C head. Yet there remains a fundamental difference between Chomsky's proposal and mine. In the TAG context, there is a strict limit on how many lexical elements may appear within a numeration. In Chomsky's proposal, in contrast, a single numeration may include an unbounded amount of material, as in raising constructions. Such unboundedness is necessary in Chomsky's system to allow for, among other things, the possibility of long-distance agreement relations, a topic I take up in sections 4.5 and 4.6.[10] A second difference between my conception of numerations and Chomsky's relates to the fact that the numerations used here to build TAG elementary trees may include nonprojected nonterminals along with lexical and functional heads. These nonterminals, when merged into a structure, will become the frontier nonterminals into which arguments are inserted, other nonterminals in an elementary tree resulting from Merge. Because the TAG version of the θ-Criterion dictates that such nonterminals may appear in an elementary tree only if they are assigned a θ-role, the fact that lexical predicates never take more than three arguments means that the inclusion of these elements does not endanger the strict bound on the size of an elementary tree numeration.[11]

Now consider an elementary derivation that begins with the numeration in (26).[12]

(26)  {T, saw, DP, DP}

The derivation proceeds by merging *saw* with one DP, the resulting structure with the other DP, and then this result with T. This yields the structure in (27).

(27)

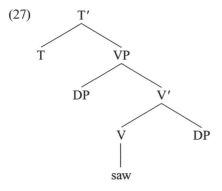

I assume, following Chomsky (2000), that applications of Merge require the existence of a selectional relation between the elements that are merged and also that it is this selectional relation that determines which of the merged elements projects its features to the resulting phrase: the selecting element projects. The need for such a selectional relation ensures that nonprojected nonterminals will be merged only in selected positions (i.e., ones in which they are assigned a θ-role), since, lacking a head, they cannot themselves select other elements. Consequently, we no longer need to explicitly impose the formulation of the θ-Criterion in (5) as a condition on elementary trees, since it is effectively enforced by the derivational machinery.[13] At the point in the derivation following the construction of (27), we need the DP nonterminal in the specifier of VP to raise to the specifier of TP, to produce the structure in (28).

(28)

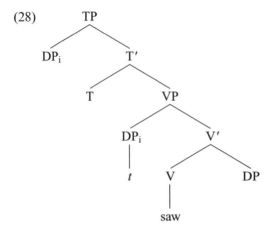

To drive this movement, we might adopt Chomsky's proposal that there is a point in the derivation at which all uninterpretable features (e.g., EPP features) must be checked. In the current context, it is natural to take this point to be that at which elementary trees are completely formed but have not yet entered into the TAG portion of the derivation. Assuming that the T head in this structure bears EPP features, failure of this DP to raise would result in unchecked uninterpretable features in the elementary tree, yielding ill-formedness.[14]

Unfortunately, this simple translation of Chomsky's system into the TAG context cannot be maintained. In raising auxiliary trees like the one in (8), there is no specifier of TP that can check the EPP feature of T, and hence this feature will remain unchecked within this elementary tree. Assuming that we want to maintain the analysis of raising we have been developing, we will need to relax the requirement on uninterpretable features within an elementary tree. Pursuing the idea that the structures of natural language are maximally economical (coupled with the assumption that uninterpretable features are uneconomical), a natural way to do this is as follows:

(29)  *Maximal Checking Principle (MCP)*
      The output of an elementary tree derivation from numeration N
      must contain as few uninterpretable features as possible.

I assume here that only those elementary tree derivations that begin from identical numerations are compared for the purposes of the MCP, following the line taken by Chomsky (2000).

It turns out that the MCP has the desired effect of distinguishing elementary trees like (8), in which we do not want unchecked EPP features to yield ill-formedness, from cases like (9), in which we do. Let us assume that every instance of finite T in a numeration includes an EPP feature. Now consider a derivation for the ill-formed elementary tree in (9). This derivation will begin with the numeration in (30a), and after a number of selectionally induced applications of Merge, it will produce the structure in (30b). (For simplicity, I assume here that the modal *might* heads the TP projection.)

(30) a. {might, DP, want, T′}

b.
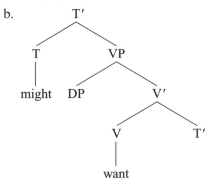

At this point in the derivation, the EPP feature of T remains unchecked. Having exhausted the numeration, we are faced with a derivational choice: either we can consider the structure in (30b) a completely formed elementary tree or we can continue the derivation, raising the DP to the specifier of TP, yielding the tree in (31), in which T's EPP feature has been checked.

(31)
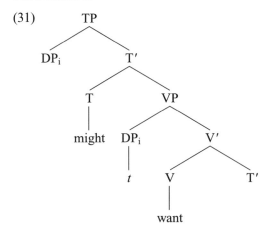

The MCP makes a clear choice between these two, favoring the derivation in which the DP raises to the specifier of TP, as this structure includes at least one fewer unchecked uninterpretable feature, namely, T's EPP feature. Contrast this situation with the case in which we are constructing an auxiliary tree headed by a raising predicate like that in (8). In this case, the numeration we will begin with is as follows:

(32)  {T, seems, T′}

Through a series of selectionally induced applications of Merge, the derivation produces the T′-rooted structure from (8), repeated here.

(8)

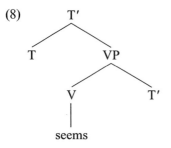

Once again, the EPP feature of T is unchecked. However, since the numeration is exhausted, there is no DP within this structure that could raise to the specifier of TP and there is no continuation to the derivation in which this feature is checked. As a result, the MCP permits this instance of an unchecked feature: it is the elementary tree that can be derived from the given numeration with the fewest unchecked features.[15]

Note that the MCP makes no distinction among different ways in which a particular uninterpretable feature is checked. Thus, for an elementary tree headed by an unaccusative verb like *arrive*, the MCP does not choose between derivations in which the specifier of TP is filled by raising of the single DP argument or by merger of an expletive *there*. These two structures would be derived from distinct numerations, one containing the expletive, the other lacking it, and by assumption, the MCP does not compare such derivations.[16]

## 4.3  Locality and the Maximal Checking Principle

As an economy constraint, the MCP shares something with the proposals made by Collins (1997) and Chomsky (2000) in that derivational economy is determined locally. That is, the choice among competing derivations can be made on the basis of properties that are determinable within the structural domain that constitutes an elementary tree.[17] Such a locality condition on economy means that syntactic derivations cannot trade off the checking of a feature F by an element X co-present in F's elementary tree $\tau$ for the (eventual) checking by an element Y outside $\tau$. For instance, consider a structural context like (33), with F an uninterpretable feature, and X and Y both potential checkers of F, and A an elementary tree boundary between X and Y. Here, if there are no elementary tree boundaries between F and X, the MCP dictates that X must always check F.

(33) [F ... X ... [$_A$ ... Y ...]]

In fact, we have already seen an instance of exactly this kind of structure in the case of Icelandic raising discussed in the last section (cf. examples (14c) and (16)). In that context, F is the EPP feature on the matrix T, X is the dative experiencer argument of the raising predicate, and Y is the embedded DP subject.

(34) T virðast DP$_{dat}$ [DP ...]

As we saw earlier, the result is just what the MCP leads us to expect: only the dative DP may raise to the specifier of TP to check T's EPP feature. In chapter 5, we will see another instance of this pattern in the case of superiority effects on *wh*-movement.

The MCP enforces a certain locality on the search for checkers (goals) for some uninterpretable feature (probe), so that elementary-tree-local checkers are preferred over all others.[18] Such locality is typically thought to derive from a condition like Shortest Move or Relativized Minimality. Since the MCP obviates the need for such conditions in this case, we might wonder whether they can be eliminated from the grammar entirely. I would like to suggest that they can.

To see how, we must consider cases in which the MCP does not supplant Shortest Move. These are of two sorts, depicted in (35), where F is the feature to be checked; X and Y are potential checkers, with X asymmetrically c-commanding Y; and A and B are extended projection boundaries.

(35) a. [F ... [$_A$ ... X ... [$_B$ ... Y ...]]]
     b. [F ... X ... Y ...]

Following any simple version of a Shortest Move–like constraint, X would be chosen to check F in both of these cases, since by assumption it c-commands Y and not vice versa. On the other hand, the MCP does not say anything about these cases. In (35a), the reason for this is that F will go unchecked in its elementary tree regardless of which of X or Y ultimately checks it, as F is separated from both by an elementary tree boundary. In (35b), in contrast, the movement of either X or Y will suffice to check F within its elementary tree, so that no unchecked features will remain in either case. If we are to rid the grammar of a Shortest Move–like constraint, then, we must say something about these cases.

In chapter 3, we have already seen a concrete case of the abstract situation depicted in (35a), in which Shortest Move is invoked to block the raising of Y to check X: superraising. In such a structure, F is the EPP feature of a matrix clause, and X and Y are the subjects of two recursively embedded TPs.

(36) T seems [it is likely [John to leave]]

Under a Shortest Move analysis, raising of *John* is blocked by the presence of *it*, a closer potential checker for T's EPP feature. As we saw in section 3.3, a TAG analysis of raising can instead derive the impossibility of raising *John* from the recursive nature of the TAG elementary trees and of Adjoining, which is implicated in the displacement of elements from one elementary tree domain to another. If superraising structures are indicative of all cases of the form in (35a), in the sense that the elements X and Y occupy identical structural positions in their distinct elementary trees, the effects of Shortest Move in this case will always be derivable in this way. I hypothesize that all cases in which the effects of Shortest Move are visible in fact have this form.

Let us turn next to the second type of Shortest Move effect not explained by the MCP, depicted in (35b). Structures falling under this case of Shortest Move include the raising of subject rather than object to the specifier of TP (37), Head Movement Constraint effects (38), (local cases of) superiority effects (39), and passivization in double object constructions (40).

(37) a. [$_{TP}$ Daniel$_i$ T [$_{VP}$ $t_i$ read a book]].
     b. *[$_{TP}$ A book$_i$ T [$_{VP}$ Daniel read $t_i$]].

(38) a. [$_{CP}$ Has$_i$ [$_{TP}$ Daniel $t_i$ [$_{VP}$ read a book]]]?
     b. *[$_{CP}$ Read$_i$ [$_{TP}$ Daniel has [$_{VP}$ $t_i$ a book]]]?

(39) a. (I wonder) [$_{CP}$ who$_i$ C [$_{TP}$ $t_i$ [$_{VP}$ read what]]].
     b. *(I wonder) [$_{CP}$ what$_i$ C [$_{TP}$ who [$_{VP}$ read $t_i$]]].

(40)  a.   [$_{TP}$ Gabriel$_i$ was [$_{VP}$ given $t_i$ a book]].
       b.   *[$_{TP}$ A book$_i$ was [$_{VP}$ given Gabriel $t_i$]].

In each of these pairs, ill-formedness results when a lower element raises to check some uninterpretable feature. This time, however, the TAG machinery does not explain the contrasts, as the relevant pair of possible checkers is within a single elementary tree, a domain too small to be affected by the TAG combinatory operations.

Instead, to account for local cases of Shortest Move, we can proceed in one of two ways. First, we might try to incorporate an explicit principle of Shortest Move into the system of elementary tree derivations. There is conceptual danger in such a move, however, as it threatens to introduce substantial redundancy into the derivational system, whereby many cases of ill-formedness are ruled out both by the nature of the TAG machinery and by Shortest Move. One might try to avoid such redundancy, by formulating a simplified version of Shortest Move that covers only the residue of cases within a single elementary tree. Past formulations of Shortest Move (e.g., Chomsky 1993) have incorporated complex notions like minimal domain and domain-extending head movement, so as to allow for certain apparent violations of the principle. It seems unlikely that restricting the domain of Shortest Move to an elementary tree domain will allow us to avoid this complexity, as it has been motivated largely on the basis of clause-internal phenomena.[19]

An alternative to adopting Shortest Move that avoids this redundancy denies the presupposition that it is the raising of the more distant element that leads to ill-formedness. This leaves us with the problem of explaining the patterns in (37)–(40). I will put off discussion of the superiority cases until the next chapter when I discuss *wh*-movement constructions in some detail. Let us examine the remaining cases in turn.

Concerning the contrast in (37) involving movement of the subject or object to the specifier of TP, we might argue that raising the object over the subject leads to a situation in which the subject is not assigned Case. This follows under Chomsky's (2000) adaptation of George and Kornfilt's (1981) proposal, according to which nominative Case assignment is a side effect of the checking of T's agreement features.[20] If the object, having been assigned accusative Case by the c-commanding verb, raises to the specifier of TP, in the process checking T's agreement features, there is no possibility for Case to be assigned to the in-situ subject.[21]

Turning next to the head movement cases in (38), it seems plausible that the participle may not raise because of some property of the feature in the C head that is driving the movement. Specifically, this feature might select for a finite verb. This line of argument leads to the expectation that there should be instances of head movement in which the closest head is not of the appropriate sort, resulting in the movement of a more distant head. In fact, such cases have been argued to exist: for example, Romance clitic climbing and aux-to-comp constructions (Roberts 1994), as well as so-called long head movement (Lema and Rivero 1990; Rivero 1991). I will suppose, then, that the degree to which head movement obeys the Head Movement Constraint is only the result of the existence of certain selectional relations and feature specificity and is not due to a locality condition on head movement.

Let us look finally at cases of passivization of double object verbs. Under the assumption that the indirect object asymmetrically c-commands the direct object, the examples in (40) seem to support the idea that raising to subject position is restricted to the higher of the two objects. However, closely related languages exhibit different patterns of passivization. British English, for example, differs from American English in that both examples in (40) are acceptable (judgments given above are for American English). Similarly, Swedish (41) patterns with British English, while closely related Danish (42) and Norwegian pattern with American English (Holmberg and Platzack 1995).

(41) a. Han blev erbjudet ett jobb.
        he   was offered   a  job
     b. Ett jobb blev erbjudet honom.
        a  job  was offered   him

(42) a. Han blev tilbudt en stilling.
        he   was offered a  job
     b. *En stilling blev tilbudt ham.
        a  job       was offered him

Furthermore, as discussed by McGinnis (1998), languages like Georgian and Albanian (43) show the reverse of the English pattern, allowing only the direct object to raise to subject position in such passives.

(43) a. Secili libër       iu kthye            autorit      të tij.
        each book.NOM CL returned-NACT author.DAT    its
        'Each book was returned to its author.'
     b. *Secilit djalë    iu dha         paga      i tij.
        each   boy.DAT CL gave-NACT pay.NOM  his
        'Each boy was given his pay.'

Under a view of movement that incorporates a Shortest Move–like requirement, the American English/Danish/Norwegian case is the expected pattern, with additional complications arising in the explanations of the other two patterns.[22] If we assume instead that elementary-tree-internal movement is not constrained by a Shortest Move–like requirement, the British English/Swedish pattern is the expected one, and additional complications are needed to explain the others. A straightforward way to do this is to adapt McGinnis's (1998) idea that DPs may bear "inert" Case, which renders them invisible to the process of feature checking. In languages showing the American English/Danish/Norwegian pattern, I assume that the direct object of a double object construction bears inert Case, while in languages showing the Georgian/Albanian pattern, the indirect object bears inert Case (as McGinnis assumes).

Let me close this section with a comment. My point in this refutation of the role of Shortest Move within elementary trees is not that we have gained significantly in explanatory force by abandoning Shortest Move, but that we have not lost any. It is no doubt true that certain elementary-tree-internal phenomena are naturally analyzable in terms of Shortest Move. However, it seems not unreasonable to conclude that this principle brings with it as many problems as it solves. I tentatively conclude, therefore, that there is no need to impose any explicit constraints on the locality of movement within an elementary tree.

## 4.4 Residues of the EPP

By ruling out candidate elementary trees containing potentially, but not actually, checked features, the MCP, coupled with the assumption that T contains an EPP feature, allows us to derive almost all of the consequences of the more complex formulation of the EPP in (11). Yet, there remains one residual issue that the MCP does not account for. Consider once again the derivation for an elementary tree headed by a raising predicate. This time, let us assume that the derivation proceeds from a different numeration, given in (44).[23]

(44) {there, T, seems, TP}

Once we reach the point in the derivation at which we have constructed the T′ depicted in (45), we are faced with the question of whether the elementary tree can tolerate the presence of an unchecked EPP feature.

(45)

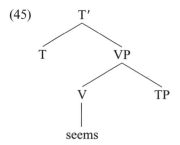

In the context of the derivation discussed earlier that proceeded from the numeration in (32) (like that in (44) but lacking *there*), the answer was yes: since the numeration was exhausted and no element within the structure was capable of checking the EPP feature, the derivation with the fewest unchecked features necessarily included an unchecked EPP feature. In the case we are currently considering, the situation is different. Here, the expletive *there* remains unselected from the numeration. Since *there* is capable of checking the EPP feature of T, the MCP dictates that it must do so. The result is the structure shown in (2), repeated here.

(2)

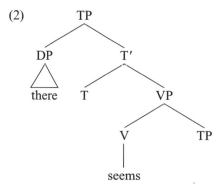

In earlier discussion, we noted that this elementary tree must be ruled out if we are to avoid deriving partial raising sentences like (1). The formulation of the EPP in (11) does this by making reference to elements that are independently licensed in an elementary tree. The MCP has no way of doing anything similar, and thus we are left without a way to block this structure.[24]

To see how we might prevent the MCP from yielding this unfortunate result, let us examine in further detail the range of uninterpretable features that occur within elementary trees and the processes by which they are checked. Let us begin with the elementary tree given in (18), repeated here, headed by the unaccusative verb *arrived*.

(18)

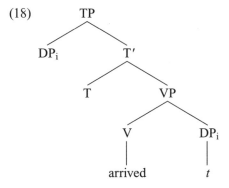

As discussed earlier, the finite T head in this elementary tree includes an EPP feature, checked by raising DP to the specifier of TP. I assume that finite T also includes a set of uninterpretable agreement features, so-called $\phi$-features. Furthermore, I take nonprojected argument DPs to possess uninterpretable Case features, which need to be checked, along with interpretable $\phi$-features, which do not.[25] As mentioned above, I follow Chomsky's adaptation of George and Kornfilt's proposal under which the assignment of structural (nominative) Case by T is the reflex of a $\phi$-feature checking relation. For the structure in (18), then, the raised DP also checks T's $\phi$-features, and in virtue of this relationship, the T checks the DP's Case features. In structures involving *there*-insertion, as in the elementary tree given in (19), repeated here, the situation is different.

(19)

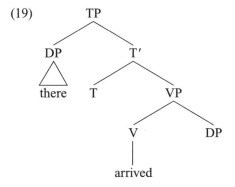

Although the insertion of *there* into subject position checks T's EPP features, it does not simultaneously check its $\phi$-features (perhaps because *there* lacks a full complement of $\phi$-features, following Chomsky (2000)). Instead, we see that the verb in such a configuration shows agreement with the in-situ DP object, suggesting that it is this element that checks T's $\phi$-features. Following Chomsky (see also Burzio 2000), I assume that the structural configuration required for the checking of $\phi$-features (and hence Case assignment) is distinct from that required for the checking of EPP features: the latter, involving selectional features, requires an application of Merge, thereby establishing a specifier-head relation, while the former demands only c-command. (Note that it is not possible to similarly relax the structural conditions on the checking of EPP features, if we are to prevent an unmoved DP from checking T's EPP features in situ.) In structures like (19), then, the uninterpretable features in T enter into separate checking relations with two distinct DPs: the EPP features with the expletive in the specifier position, and the $\phi$-features with the DP argument. Under this view, then, the existence of an expletive-associate relation that mediates the assignment of structural Case to the DP associate is only apparent, as the T itself enters into relations with both expletive and associate.

In light of this discussion, we can observe a notable property of the problematic elementary tree in (2): while the EPP feature of T is checked within the elementary tree (through merger of *there*), T's $\phi$-features remain unchecked. In all of the other cases we discussed in connection with the MCP, either both the EPP and $\phi$-features were checked or neither was. We can thus exploit this property to rule out the elementary tree in (2), adopting the following:

(46) *All-or-Nothing Checking Regimen (ANCR)*
     In an elementary tree, if some of the uninterpretable features of a
     lexical item are checked, they must all be checked.

Thinking of the two-stage derivational system we are adopting, in which movement and feature checking of the sort we have been discussing cease once the TAG operations begin to apply, we can understand the ANCR as deriving from the assumption that the TAG operations cannot manipulate the internal feature composition of lexical items.[26] If no uninterpretable features remain, a lexical item will be syntactically inert, whereas if all uninterpretable features remain, the lexical item will be syntactically active (in a sense to be made precise) in the TAG derivation. What is not possible is for only some of the uninterpretable features of a lexical item to remain, as it would not be clear whether this item should or should not be syntactically active.

The ANCR might seem like an ad hoc solution to the problem raised by the elementary tree in (2). However, the ANCR's explanatory force goes considerably beyond this case. First of all, it explains the distinctive distributions of *there*- and *it*-type expletives. Following Chomsky (2000), let us suppose that expletive *it* differs from *there* in possessing $\phi$-features (see McCloskey 1991), with the effect that when merged into the specifier of TP position, *it* can check the $\phi$-features of T. Let us now ask why only *it*, and not *there*, can occur in the subject position of elementary trees whose lexical heads lack arguments entirely—for example, those under-lying the sentences in (6). In such cases, merging *it* with T' checks both EPP and $\phi$-features of T. Merger of *there* with T', in contrast, could check only the EPP features. Since by hypothesis there is nothing else within the elementary tree that can check T's $\phi$-features, these features will necessarily remain unchecked at the conclusion of the elementary tree derivation, in violation of the ANCR. Now consider the derivation of an elementary tree like those representing the main clause in examples like (22a) and (22b), involving expletive *it* subjects and CP complements. As before, merger of *it* with T' checks both EPP and $\phi$-features on T, leaving no features unchecked. In contrast, a variant of this derivation that attempted to merge *there* rather than *it* with T' would leave T's $\phi$-features unchecked, assuming that in-situ CP cannot check T's $\phi$-features.[27]

From this discussion, it follows that unlike trees like (2), which are ill formed, analogous trees with *it*-expletive subjects should be possible. This is indeed correct, as the elementary tree in (47a) must be available to underlie the derivation of an example like (47b) (cf. (1)).

(47) a.

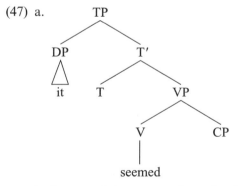

b. It seemed that a man from the CIA would be at the meeting.

In allowing (47a), the MCP and ANCR resolve a significant problem with the formulation of the EPP in (11) that I have thus far ignored.

Recall how this version of the EPP ruled out elementary trees like (2): since there is no independently licensed element within the tree that can move to the specifier of TP, this specifier position cannot be filled in the elementary tree. Note that precisely the same reasoning applies in cases where *seem* takes a CP rather than T' or TP complement. As shown by (48), this CP complement cannot move to subject position.

(48)  *[That a man from the CIA would be at the meeting] seemed.

Since the version of the EPP in (11) does not distinguish between *it*-type and *there*-type expletives, it incorrectly predicts that nothing could ever fill the specifier of TP position in a *seem*-headed elementary tree.

The MCP and ANCR also resolve another similarly problematic consequence of the formulation of the EPP in (11) related to elementary trees headed by non-argument-taking predicates, such as impersonal passives or perhaps weather verbs. Once again, since elementary trees headed by such predicates do not include an independently licensed element that can move to the specifier of TP, the EPP forbids the presence of such a specifier in the elementary tree. In contrast, as we have seen, the MCP and ANCR permit the presence of *it*-type expletive subjects.[28] The move from a complex formulation of the EPP to the economy constraints instantiated in the MCP and ANCR, then, yields not only a conceptual simplification, but also empirical benefits.

**4.5   Quirky Subjects, Agreement, and Nominative Case Assignment**

Given that the ANCR forces EPP and nominative Case checking to take place together (or not at all) within an elementary tree, one might take the existence of the Icelandic elementary tree depicted in (15), repeated here, to be problematic.

(15)

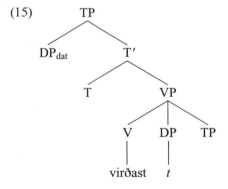

Recall that I argued above that this elementary tree is necessary for the derivation of the example in (16), repeated here, in which the dative experiencer argument of the raising predicate raises to the matrix specifier of TP and the lower (nominative) subject remains in place.

(16) Mér    virðast   margir menn vera í  herberginu.
     me.DAT seem.3PL many   men   to be in the room

In the earlier discussion, I suggested that the possibility of dative subjects in Icelandic renders impossible a T′ raising auxiliary tree that includes a dative experiencer argument. We can now understand this in terms of the MCP: by moving the dative to the specifier of TP, we end up with an elementary tree having at least one fewer uninterpretable feature, namely, T's EPP feature. Note, however, that if this elementary tree is also to satisfy the ANCR, T's φ-features must be checked as well. Otherwise, this tree should have the same status as the ill-formed (2), in which an expletive *there* checks T's EPP feature but leaves its φ-features unchecked. Under the view of Case assignment I am adopting, in which checking of T's φ-features by a DP triggers assignment of nominative Case to that DP, it is not clear how such φ-features can be checked within (15), given the absence of a DP within this tree bearing nominative Case. Instead, the nominative DP with which matrix T agrees is located in a separate elementary tree, shown in (49), that of the embedded infinitival complement to whose root (15) is adjoined (or alternatively that is substituted into the TP frontier nonterminal in (15)).

(49)

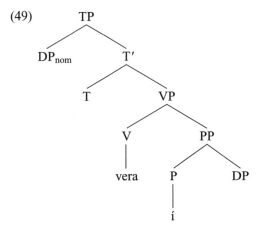

Must we then modify or abandon the ANCR in the face of elementary trees like (15)? In this section, I will demonstrate that the answer to this question is no. Once we better understand the processes of φ-feature checking and Case assignment, we will see not only that (15) fully conforms with the ANCR, but also that the MCP/ANCR combination yields novel and correct predictions concerning the locality of verbal agreement relations.

The first part of my strategy for resolving this apparent contradiction will be to assume the existence of an agreement relation between the dative DP subject and T, which can check T's φ-features. On the face of it, there seems to be little evidence for such an agreement relation. In (16), for instance, the verb shares neither number nor person with the first person singular dative subject. Similarly, in monoclausal quirky subject constructions, the verb apparently agrees only with the φ-features of the nominative object.

(50) Mér      mistókust allar tilarunirnar.
     me.DAT failed.3PL all    the attempts.NOM
     'I failed in all the attempts.'

Let us assume that such facts show what they appear to, namely, that there is an agreement relation between T and the nominative object in such cases. What then of the putative agreement with the dative subject?

It has been noted in numerous places in the literature that the presence of a dative subject, whether in monoclausal or biclausal structures, restricts the nominative object to third person (examples from Sigurðsson 1996 and Taraldsen 1995).

(51) a. *Henni   leiddust   þið.
         her.DAT bored.2PL you.PL.NOM
     b. *Henni   leiddumst við.
         her.DAT bored.1SG we.NOM

(52) a. *Henni   þóttir    þú       vera dugleg.
         her.DAT thought.2SG you.SG.NOM to be industrious
     b. *Henni   virtumst  við      vera duglegar.
         her.DAT thought.1PL we.NOM to be industrious
     c. *Mér     þykið     þið      vera gáfaðir.
         me.DAT think.2PL you.PL.NOM to be gifted

If T's φ-features stand in an agreement relation only with the nominative object in such structures, it is mysterious why T should be unable to agree with a first person nominative object. Burzio (2000) argues that this mystery is resolved if we take T to agree not only with the nominative object, but also with the dative subject.[29] Before we see how this suggestion unravels the mystery, let us turn to two problems that arise immediately. First, we must ask why in an example like (16), the verb apparently shows neither person nor number agreement with the features of the dative subject. Second, given the assumption that nominative Case assignment is parasitic on agreement, we must explain why the dative subject does not bear nominative Case. Burzio suggests that the second puzzle stems from a faulty presupposition; he argues that the subject does in fact bear abstract nominative Case, along with dative. The simultaneous presence of these two Cases is possible, Burzio proposes, only in a structure in which the structurally assigned nominative Case is superimposed or stacked atop the inherently assigned dative.[30] On Burzio's analysis, Case superimposition also provides a resolution to the first question. He suggests that nominative Case is assigned to an outer shell of the DP, which insulates the DP's lexically determined φ-features from the external context, with the result that these features are not externally visible. Thus, when the T agrees with the subject, this agreement relation is not with the DP's lexically determined φ-features, but with those in its outer shell, which he suggests are like those in other elements that lack explicit person and number specification. Burzio (1991) characterizes the process of agreement, which he labels *pseudo-agreement* (PA), as one in which one of the elements in the agreement relation lacks person and number specification. Romance reflexive pronouns, such as Italian *si/sé*, instantiate such a zero feature form, being unspecified for number, gender, and person.[31] As Burzio notes, the range of verbal forms with which such featureless elements may enter into PA is restricted. In impersonal constructions involving *si*, for example, the verbal form that agrees with *si* must be third person.

(53) Si    mangia/*mangio/*mangi bene in questo ristorante.
     REFL eats.3SG/eat.1SG/eat.2SG  well in this    restaurant
     'One eats well in this restaurant.'

Note that when such impersonals include a nominative object with which the verb agrees, this object may only be third person.

(54) a.  Si   inviteranno    anche loro.
         REFL will invite.3PL also   they
         'They will also be invited.'
     b. *Si    inviteremo    anche noi.
         REFL will invite.2PL also   we

Burzio argues that the Italian pattern as well as that in Icelandic quirky subject constructions follows if T must simultaneously enter into (a) PA with featureless *si* or the outer shell of a quirky dative subject, forcing T to be third person, and (b) true agreement with the nominative object.[32] The existence of the former PA relation thus has the effect of (indirectly) restricting the nominative object to third person.

Supposing this analysis to be on the right track, there remains the problem of how it is possible for T to enter into multiple agreement relations. So far, I have been assuming that T's uninterpretable φ-features, once checked, are eliminated from the phrase marker. Such a view, however, rules out the possibility that they could be checked a second time. But now suppose that checking of features does not necessarily entail their elimination.[33]

(55) φ-features need not delete when checked against pseudo-agreeing forms.

As it is the deletion of uninterpretable features (for the purposes of Full Interpretation) that motivates checking in the first place, what (55) says is that there are situations in which feature checking fails to accomplish its goal of deleting uninterpretable features. In the derivation of (50), then, T first checks its EPP and φ-features against the dative subject, the former deleting, the latter not, under (55). These φ-features then enter into another relation with the postverbal DP, this time resulting in their deletion as well as the deletion of the Case features on the nominative object. Since T enters into two separate agreement relations, it is bound to respect both of them. By the first one (with the dative) it must be third person, and by the second one (with the nominative object) it must be plural as well.

Note that (55) is formulated as "need not delete" rather than "do not delete." This is not accidental, being necessary to allow for sentences with quirky subjects but no corresponding nominative.[34]

(56) Strákunum   leiddist/*leiddust.
     the boys.DAT bored.3SG/bored.3PL
     'The boys were bored.'

To derive such a case, T's φ-features will delete immediately upon checking with the pseudo-agreeing dative subject, resulting in default (third singular) agreement. Had these features not deleted after checking, a possibility consistent with (55), we would have been left with a tree in which T's EPP but not φ-features were deleted, in violation of the ANCR. In contrast, such "eager" deletion of T's φ-features would not be possible in the derivation of an example like (50), as it would have led to an elementary tree containing a frontier nonterminal DP, the object, with unchecked Case features. Though this would not violate the ANCR, such a tree would not be usable in any TAG derivation, since, for reasons to be discussed in the next section, these Case features could never be checked. This unavailability of "eager" deletion is a welcome result, as it allows us to correctly predict the impossibility of default agreement in cases like (50).[35]

(57) *Henni   mistókst   allar tilraunirnar.
     her.DAT failed.3SG all    the attempts.NOM
     'She failed all the attempts.'

In this context, let us return to the Icelandic raising examples like (16) with which this section began. Interestingly, Sigurðsson (1996) notes that examples of this form are generally possible not only with agreement with the lower nominative, as we have already seen, but also with default agreement.

(58) Mér      virtust/virtist          þær        vinna    vel.
     me.DAT seemed.3PL/seemed.3SG they.NOM to work well
     'It seemed to me that they work well.'

On the analysis we are pursuing, this default agreement would result if T's φ-features delete immediately upon checking by the quirky subject. In the absence of an agreement relation between matrix T and the embedded nominative subject, we should expect the person restriction on the nominative to disappear. This is correct, as noted by Sigurðsson (1996, 36) (cf. (52)).[36]

(59) Henni   þótti         þú/við              vera dugleg.
     her.DAT thought.3SG you.SG.NOM/we.NOM to be industrious
     'She thought you/we are industrious.'

Unlike in (50), eager checking of T's φ-features in these cases does not result in an elementary structure with an unchecked and uncheckable Case feature: since there is no DP other than the quirky dative in the relevant elementary tree in (15), all local DPs are assigned Case.

This proposal leaves open two issues. First, when there is no agreement with matrix T, as in (59), how is nominative Case assigned/checked on the embedded subject? Second, in cases like (16), where matrix T does agree with the embedded subject, how does such agreement (i.e., the checking of T's φ-features) take place, given that the embedded subject is generated in a different elementary tree from the one that includes the agreeing T head and the dative experiencer? I turn to these questions next.[37]

Consider the first of our two puzzles, concerning the assignment of nominative Case to an embedded subject in the absence of agreement with matrix T. Maling and Sprouse (1995) note that nominative Case in Icelandic does not always depend on finite T: it can occur in (control) infinitivals, both adjuncts and sentential subjects, where there is no finite T that could serve as the assigner of nominative Case, assuming that only one overtly marked nominative DP can be checked by a single finite T (see note 33; examples from Maling and Sprouse 1995, 179, and Freidin and Sprouse 1991, 409).

(60) a. Það  komu margir strákar    í  skólann án þess að    hafa
        there came many  boys.NOM to school  without COMP to have
        batnað          hálsbógan.
        recovered from sore throat.NOM
        'Many boys came to school without having recovered from a
        sore throat.'

   b. Að    batna          veikin          er venjulegt.
      COMP to recover from the disease.NOM is  unusual
      'Recovering from the disease is unusual.'

Additionally, Sigurðsson (1991) convincingly demonstrates that PRO subjects of nonfinite control clauses in Icelandic can bear nominative Case, and suggests that such nominative Case can be assigned by the nonfinite T heading such clauses. Maling and Sprouse argue that examples like those in (60) show that such a nonfinite T is also capable of assigning nominative Case to overt postverbal DPs in clauses having quirky Case-marked PRO subjects. To account for nominative Case in the TP complements to (nonagreeing) raising verbs, then, requires only the small step of assuming that the nonfinite T heads of these infinitival complements as well may assign nominative Case, a proposal made by Schütze (1997). We can express this proposal in our current terms by allowing nonfinite T to contain φ-features, which assign nominative Case to the DP whose φ-features check them. I assume that φ-features are only optionally generated on the T head of infinitival complements to raising verbs, though perhaps obligatorily in complements to control verbs. When infinitival T contains φ-features, the nominative Case features on some DP, whether in subject or object position, will be checked internally to the infinitival clause. As a result, agreement with the matrix (finite) T is no longer necessary in order for nominative Case to be assigned to this lower DP.

European Portuguese provides compelling morphological evidence for the optional generation of φ-features on nonfinite T, and moreover for the connection of such φ-features with nominative Case assignment (Quicoli 1996). As the following examples show, a subject of the clausal complement of the verb *ver* 'see' bears ECM accusative Case when the infinitival verb shows no agreement, but bears nominative Case when the infinitival verb agrees with the subject (examples from Napoli 1993, 227–230, 347–348).

(61) a.  Vi-os                assaltar      a velha.
         saw.1SG-them.ACC to assault.∅ the old lady
         'I saw them assault the old lady.'
     b. *Vi-os               assaltarem    a velha.
         saw.1SG-them.ACC to assault.3PL the old lady

(62) a.  Vi      eles      assaltarem    a velha.
         saw.1SG they.NOM to assault.3PL the old lady
     b. *Vi      eles      assaltar      a velha.
         saw.1SG they.NOM to assault.∅ the old lady

This is just what we expect if agreement morphology on a verbal form indicates the presence of φ-features, which assign nominative Case to the DP with which they agree.[38] I suggest, then, that the possibility of agreement on infinitivals that is expressed overtly in Portuguese is present in Icelandic as well, though covertly expressed, and allows nominative Case to be assigned within the infinitival complements to raising verbs.

Let us turn next to the second puzzle, concerning how agreement is ever possible between the matrix T in a raising auxiliary tree and the embedded nominative DP, given that the T and DP reside in distinct elementary trees. Under our current line of analysis, we might expect this to be the case when matrix T's φ-features fail to delete after being checked by the dative subject, a possibility licensed by (55) (cf. Chomsky 2000, 128). Unlike in the monoclausal case in (50), however, where there is another DP within this elementary tree to check these φ-features, there is

no such additional DP in a raising elementary tree like (15). Consequently, noneager checking of T's φ-features leads directly to a violation
of the ANCR, as only T's EPP features have been checked. Assuming
that we want to maintain both the ANCR and the view that nominative
Case assignment is parasitic on agreement, there are at least two paths we
might pursue. One possibility maintains that neither EPP nor φ-features
on T have deleted in the elementary tree, while another holds that T's φ-
features have actually been checked within this tree. I reject the former
possibility, as it would leave us without an explanation for why the dative
experiencer moves to the specifier of TP in the first place.[39]

Pursuing the hypothesis that T's φ-features are checked and deleted in
the elementary tree in (15), we are faced with the question of which element does the checking if not the dative experiencer. I propose that this
element is the raising predicate's TP complement. It is usually assumed
that such verbal projections are incapable of checking the φ-features of
another verbal head. Let us suppose that this impossibility is the result of
some property of verbally headed phrases, which I will refer to as π.
Now, it is also commonly assumed that TP complements to raising (and
ECM) verbs are deficient in some sense, and it is this deficiency that
allows raising out of (or ECM into) them. I will make the minimal assumption that the deficiency of such TPs is characterized by the absence
of π. This will give the desired result that any π-less TP may enter into
agreement relations. Thus, in (15), T may check and delete its φ-features
on its TP complement.

This proposal leaves open three related questions. First, if matrix T
agrees with the embedded TP, why does the morphology actually reflect
agreement with the embedded nominative DP? Second, assuming that
nominative Case assignment is parasitic on agreement, why is it the embedded DP subject that bears nominative Case, rather than the TP itself?
Third, what exactly characterizes property π? I will take up the last question first, proposing that property π is characterized by the presence of
uninterpretable φ-features on a verbal head (and its projections). I assume that uninterpretable φ-features are uniformly present on finite T.[40]
Now, suppose that uninterpretable φ-features, and perhaps uninterpretable features in general, may only be checked and deleted by interpretable features of the same sort; that is, uninterpretable φ-features must be
checked by interpretable φ-features. This would render the φ-features on
finite TP complements, projected from finite T, incapable of checking the

φ-features on a higher (finite) T head, as both sets of features are uninterpretable.[41] What about the TP projections of nonfinite T, then? As mentioned in the preceding discussion of nominative Case assignment in infinitival clauses, I am assuming that nonfinite T can lack φ-features entirely. Does this mean that the TP projections of φ-featureless T heads will similarly lack φ-features? I suggest that the answer is no. Suppose that something like Williams's (1982, 1994) notion of relativized head is operative in determining the content of phrasal projections, so that features that are absent from the "absolute" head of a phrase can instead be projected by the nonhead. In the case at hand, this would mean that the (interpretable) φ-features of a DP could project to TP so long as the T′ with which it merges lacked φ-features. Since the resulting TP will then contain interpretable φ-features, these φ-features can exceptionally check the uninterpretable φ-features in the higher T.

Returning to the discussion of the dative subject elementary tree in (15), I will n( w assume that the TP nonterminal that is the complement to the raising ve. b in this elementary tree may bear interpretable φ-features. These features will be subject to a compatibility check when the nonterminal is filled, whether by Substitution or Adjoining. It is only because TPs of the type selected by raising verbs permit the exceptional appearance of interpretable φ-features, as just discussed, that this compatibility check can ever be satisfied. Within the elementary tree in (15), then, the φ-features on the finite T can be checked by this TP complement nonterminal, ensuring agreement with the embedded subject, as the features on this TP must be identical with those on the embedded subject if the compatibility check is to succeed.

We now have the makings of an answer to the question of why agreement on T reflects the features of the embedded subject: the subject's φ-features project to the TP, and thus agreement with this TP will reflect apparent agreement with the embedded subject. Concerning the remaining question, relating to the assignment of nominative Case to the embedded subject, we can say that its Case features are checked in virtue of the establishment of a checking relation between its features (residing in TP) and the higher T. I postpone until the next section the mechanics of how this might work.

There is an interesting interaction between the proposals I have made concerning the possibility of "long-distance agreement" and nominative Case assignment by nonfinite T. In earlier discussion, I suggested that

nonfinite T in Icelandic can optionally bear (uninterpretable) φ-features
—features that, when checked by the interpretable φ-features of a DP
argument within the infinitival clause, will assign nominative Case. Observe, though, that if such (uninterpretable) φ-features are present on
nonfinite T, it is no longer possible for the interpretable φ-features of the
DP in the specifier of TP to project to TP. This leads to the prediction
that whenever nonfinite T bears φ-features, there should be no agreement
between an embedded DP subject and matrix T. Unfortunately, Icelandic
verbal morphology provides no independent way to determine whether a
given nonfinite T possesses uninterpretable φ-features. Consequently, we
cannot test whether the predicted interaction obtains. Recall, however,
that Portuguese infinitivals exhibit a morphological alternation between
agreeing and nonagreeing forms. Assuming that this is an overt analogue
of what I propose to be occurring in Icelandic, as I argued earlier, we can
use Portuguese as a testing ground for the prediction.

Note first of all that Portuguese permits a raising construction much
like the one seen in English, in which the infinitival complement obligatorily lacks agreement.[42]

(63) a. *As coisas parecem estarem   quentes em Belfast.
        the things seem.3PL to be.3PL hot       in Belfast
        'Things seem to be hot in Belfast.'
     b.  As coisas parecem estar   quentes em Belfast.
        the things seem.3PL to be.∅ hot       in Belfast

Like Icelandic, Portuguese also permits the embedded subject to remain
within the lower clause. And as in the Icelandic case, agreement between
the raising predicate and the embedded subject is optional (Eduardo
Raposo, personal communication).

(64) a. Parece     estarem   as coisas quentes em Belfast.
        seems.3SG to be.3PL the things hot       in Belfast
        'It seems that things are hot in Belfast.'
     b. Parecem estar   as coisas quentes em Belfast.
        seem.3PL to be.∅ the things hot       in Belfast

Strikingly, the possibility of agreement on the infinitival correlates in-
versely with agreement on the raising predicate: when the raising verb
agrees, the infinitival does not and conversely. If agreement is present
in both or neither of these clauses, the result is anomalous (Eduardo
Raposo, personal communication).

(65) a. *Parecem estarem   as coisas quentes em Belfast.
         seem.3PL to be.3PL the things hot        in  Belfast
     b. *Parece     estar   as coisas quentes em Belfast.
         seems.3SG to be.∅ the things hot        in  Belfast

Assuming again that morphological agreement is an indication of un-interpretable φ-features on T, this is just the sort of interaction the current analysis predicts: uninterpretable φ-features on the infinitival T lead to the impossibility of agreement between the embedded subject and the matrix T.[43]

It is interesting to observe that the MCP and ANCR, coupled with the CETM conception of elementary trees, enforce a severe locality restriction on the distance between elements that enter into checking relations with a single head: they must all reside within the same elementary tree. The mechanism suggested above by which the features of a TP's specifier can project to the TP itself provides a way to extend this domain slightly, but there is evidence that this extension exhausts the limit on the separation of the two checkers. Taraldsen (1995) (citing Höskuldur Thráinsson, personal communication) notes that if the infinitival TP complement to a raising verb is itself headed by a quirky subject verb with a nominative complement, agreement with the embedded nominative is impossible (examples from Taraldsen 1995, 317, and Schütze 1997, 108).

(66) a. Mér      fannst/*fundust          henni  leiðast    þeir.
         me.DAT seemed.3SG/*seemed.3PL she.DAT to be bored they.NOM
         'I thought she was bored with them.'
     b. Mér      hefur/*hafa            alltaf virst    honom   líka
         me.DAT has.3SG/*have.3PL often seemed him.DAT to like
         bækur.
         books.NOM
         'It has often seemed to me that he likes books.'

This follows on my proposed analysis, since there is no way for the φ-features of the object nominative in these sentences to be projected on the embedded TP, as would be necessary for agreement with matrix T, since they are too deeply embedded to project to TP. Thus, the only possibility is checking and deletion of T's φ-features by the quirky subject, with default agreement resulting.[44] Examples like those in (66) contrast with those in (67), where the matrix dative subject has raised from the embedded clause, and agreement between a finite T and the embedded clause's nominative object is possible, and perhaps obligatory (cf. Schütze

1997, 108n. 16; examples from Freidin and Sprouse 1991, 407, and Schütze 1997, 108).

(67) a. Henni  eru    taldir  hafa   verið sýndir bilarnir.
        her.DAT are.3PL believed to have been shown cars.NOM
        'She is believed to have been shown the cars.'
     b. Jóni    virðast/?*virðist    vera taldir  líka  héstarnir.
        Jon.DAT seem.3PL/seems.3SG to be believed to like horses.NOM
        'Jon seems to be believed to like horses.'

The possibility of such long-distance agreement is predicted on the analysis proposed here, since neither EPP nor ɸ-features are checked within the raising auxiliary tree, the dative having raised from the lower clause.

Schütze (1997) suggests an account of the patterns of agreement in (66) and (67) rooted in a Relativized Minimality–like condition on ɸ-feature checking (see also Chomsky 2000). On this analysis, the dative DP in the former class of cases intervenes between finite T and the embedded nominative, with a minimality condition blocking the possibility of agreement with the more distant DP. In the latter cases, the DP, having raised past T, no longer intervenes between T and the nominative, leading to the possibility of agreement, under the assumption that only heads of chains induce intervention effects.

Though both my analysis and Schütze's correctly predict the status of agreement with embedded nominative for the cases considered thus far, they diverge in examples of the following sort:

(68) Það  hefur/(?)hafa    einhverjum  þótt   þeir    leiðinlegir.
     there has.3SG/have.3PL someone.DAT thought they.NOM boring
     'Someone found them boring.'

If verb-second in Icelandic involves raising the verb only as high as T (Thráinsson 1985; Rögnvaldsson and Thráinsson 1990), leaving the matrix verb's dative experiencer between T and the embedded nominative, this configuration should, on Schütze's account, induce a minimality effect whereby T is unable to agree with the embedded nominative, just as in the cases in (66). Under the TAG analysis, in contrast, the nonraising of the experiencer leaves unaffected the fact that the infinitival TP complement node (with the embedded nominative's interpretable ɸ-features) remains within the same elementary tree as the finite T, leaving intact the possibility of ɸ-feature checking.[45] As we see from the judgments given for (68), the predictions of the TAG analysis are correct.

This difference in prediction between my analysis and Schütze's rests crucially on the analysis of verb-second, as Carson Schütze (personal communication) has pointed out to me. If verb-second involves raising of V (together with T) to a higher head—say, C or Agr$_S$ (Vikner 1995; Bobaljik and Jonas 1996)—it is possible that the dative experiencer in (68) occupies the specifier of TP. If this is so, the T head could establish an agreement relation with the embedded nominative without any intervening elements at the point in the derivation after which the experiencer has moved to the specifier of TP, but before T has raised to C/Agr$_S$. There is, however, another type of example on which Schütze's proposal and mine make different predictions, even allowing for this alternative conception of verb-second.

(69) Það ??virðist/(?)virðast    mörgum stúdentum    líka    þessir
     there   seems.3SG/seem.3PL   many      students.DAT  to like  these
     bílar.
     cars.NOM
     'It seems that many students like these cars.'

In this case, the dative DP that intervenes between the matrix verb and the embedded nominative is the quirky subject of the embedded clause, just as in (66), though this time the matrix subject position is filled by an expletive. Once again, agreement with the nominative is at least marginally possible across the dative and is, for some speakers, preferred to default agreement. It might be suggested that the dative subject in this example has raised to the matrix specifier of TP position and as a result does not intervene between T and the embedded nominative, just as might be claimed for (68). In this case, however, there is evidence that the embedded dative need not raise in order for agreement with the nominative to be (at least marginally) possible.[46]

(70) Það virðast    ekki (lengur)    mörgum stúdentum    líka    þessir
     there seem.3PL  not (anymore) many      students.DAT  to like  these
     bílar.
     cars.NOM
     'It doesn't seem (anymore) that many students like these cars.'

Under the assumption that the negative marker *ekki* occupies a position below TP, the dative subject of the embedded clause in (70) cannot have raised to TP's specifier. Consequently, Schütze's analysis predicts that this DP should induce an intervention effect between the raising verb and the embedded nominative, blocking the possibility of agreement, incorrectly it seems. In contrast, this pattern fits into my proposed TAG analysis if we assume that the expletive is merged into an outer subject position in the infinitival elementary tree representing the lower clause, a plausible assumption given the existence of a definiteness effect on the embedded dative subject.[47]

(71) *Það virðist/virðast      Joní     líka     þessir bílar.
      there seems.3SG/seem.3PL Jon.DAT to like these cars.NOM

In the *virðast*-headed auxiliary tree underlying (70), then, neither EPP nor ϕ-features are checked. Consistent with the ANCR, this is a context where the controller of agreement need not be within this elementary tree. Instead, the observed agreement pattern is analogous to that of a transitive expletive construction headed by a verb with a dative subject and nominative object, where agreement with the nominative is obligatory.

(72) Það  *mistókst/mistókust  mörgum stúdentum   allar
      there  failed.3SG/failed.3PL many     students.DAT all the
      tilraunirnar.
      attempts.NOM

I put off until section 4.6 the mechanism by which such agreement takes place across elementary trees.

   Before concluding this section, let us reconsider one of the problems with which this chapter began in light of the machinery we have built up, namely, the impossibility of elementary trees like (2), repeated here.

(2)

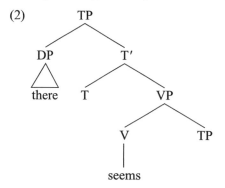

Earlier, I suggested that the ill-formedness of this structure derives from the ANCR: only T's EPP features have been checked. However, now that we have allowed for the possibility that T can check its ϕ-features on a

TP complement (at least in Icelandic), why isn't such a structure possible (see note 47)? The generalization seems to be that T can only establish an agreement relation with TP as a secondary agreement relation, that is, once it has already established a relation with a quirky subject (or object; see (68)). Since neither *there* nor its Icelandic counterpart *það* bears φ-features and therefore neither may enter into an agreement relation, the TP complement in (2) would be the only element agreeing with T in such a case.[48] I have nothing enlightening to offer about why this restriction on agreement with TP ought to hold.

### 4.6   Constraints on Adjoining: Feature Checking across Elementary Trees

To this point, we have focused on the issue of what features can and must be checked within an elementary tree. Let us now consider what happens when, in accordance with the MCP and ANCR, certain features remain unchecked within the confines of an elementary tree. In this section, I will argue that there is reason to maintain Chomsky's (1995) basic insight that the syntactic representations that are passed to the grammar-external systems of interpretation and production are subject to a principle of Full Interpretation: they may not be polluted by uninterpretable features. In the derivational architecture I am advocating, these interface representations are the product of the TAG derivations that combine elementary trees. Consequently, uninterpretable features that are not checked within an elementary tree T must be checked during any derivation involving T. As we have seen, feature checking during the derivation of an elementary tree can drive movement or force merger of a lexical item. During the portion of the derivation in which elementary trees are combined, however, neither of these operations is allowed. Hence, we must somehow allow feature checking to take place in conjunction with the TAG combinatory operations. Once this is done, we will see that the presence of unchecked features in elementary trees has the effect of driving certain instances of structural composition.

To begin to understand the process of feature checking during the TAG derivation, let us return once again to the TAG derivation for simple raising sentences like the following:

(73) Daniel seems to adore his brother.

As already discussed at length, this derivation involves adjoining a T′ auxiliary tree headed by *seems* into an elementary tree consisting of an

infinitival extended projection of *adore*. Nearly all of the properties of
this derivation and the elementary trees involved follow from the nature
of Adjoining and the constraints that are imposed on elementary trees.
By the TAG θ-Criterion, the matrix subject must be generated in the elementary tree headed by *adore*, which by the CETM may not also include
the projection of *seems*. As a result, the insertion of *seems* below the subject must be accomplished via adjoining at T′, forcing the *seems*-headed
elementary tree to take on the characteristic recursive shape of an auxiliary tree. Since this means that the T head of the *seems* tree will lack a
specifier, the EPP features of this head will necessarily remain unchecked,
a situation the MCP tolerates as a result of the absence of any potential
checkers for these features. There is, however, one property of this derivation that we have not yet derived, namely, the requirement that the tree
into which the *seems* auxiliary adjoins must be infinitival. Thus, nothing
in what we have said rules out an example like (74), where raising proceeds out of a finite clause.

(74) *Daniel seems adores his brother.

This example could be derived by an exactly analogous derivation, with
the same *seems*-headed T′ auxiliary adjoining into an elementary tree like
(75), built around the finite extended projection of *adores*.

(75)

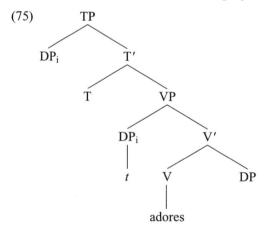

Given that the elementary trees involved in the derivation of the ungrammatical (74) are independently necessary, both to generate grammatical
instances of raising and to generate simple finite clauses, it does not seem
that we can account for the contrast between (73) and (74) by appealing

to some as yet unspecified principle of elementary tree well-formedness. Instead, the ill-formedness of (74) must come from a restriction on TAG derivations that blocks the *seems*-headed auxiliary tree from adjoining at the T' node of a finite elementary tree like (75).

There are a number of conceivable sources for such a derivational restriction. Perhaps the most straightforward of these relates to the selectional properties of the raising predication: *seem* selects for nonfinite complements. The illicit adjoining involved in the generation of (74) would then be blocked as a result of the failure of the feature compatibility check between the selectionally determined features on the [−finite] T' foot node of the *seems* auxiliary and those of the [+finite] T' node at which it adjoins. However, this proposal runs into immediate problems in the face of the nonraising variant of *seem*, which allows, and in fact requires, a finite complement.

(76) It seems (that) Daniel adores his brother.

The complement to nonraising *seem* in (76) contrasts with raising *seem* as in (74) on another dimension besides finiteness, namely, its categorial identity: it is a projection of T in the raising case, and a projection of C in the nonraising case (assuming a phonologically empty C head is present in the absence of overt *that*). We could rescue our selectional account by allowing *seem* to select complements having either [C, +finite] or [T, −finite] feature specifications. This proposal introduces an unfortunate redundancy, however: the single difference between the raising and nonraising forms of *seem* brings with it two independent changes in the feature make-up of the selected complement. Obviously, it would be preferable to avoid such a redundancy.

In this connection, it is interesting to note that under the TAG analysis, it follows that there can never be raising to subject out of a CP complement, as the predicate taking such a CP could not head the T'-recursive auxiliary tree necessary to adjoin below the subject of the embedded clause. Consequently, it is tempting to take the fundamental selectional difference between the raising and nonraising variants of *seem* to be the category, rather than the finiteness, of its complement: C-headed versus T-headed. In fact, there is evidence from Romanian that this is the right path to pursue. As noted by Grosu and Horvath (1984), Romanian has a number of predicates like English *seem* that have both raising and nonraising variants.[49]

(77) a. Se   poate   ca   bombele   să   explodeze in orice moment.
        REFL can.3SG that the bombs SUBJ explode   in any   moment
        'It is possible that the bombs will go off any minute.'

   b. Bombele   pot   (*ca) să   explodeze in orice moment.
      the bombs can.3PL  that SUBJ explode   in any   moment
      'The bombs can go off any minute.'

(78) a. S-a            nimerit   ca toţi băieţii   să   fie      bolnavi.
        REFL-has.3SG happened that all the boys SUBJ be.3PL sick
        'It happened that all the boys were sick.'

   b. Toţi băieţii   s-au            nimerit   (*ca) să   fie
      all   the boys REFL-have.3PL happened   that SUBJ be.3PL
      bolnavi.
      sick
      'All the boys happened to be sick.'

The fronting of the lower subject in these cases triggers agreement on the
finite verb, indicating that we are dealing with the same sort of movement
to an A-position as in the corresponding English construction.[50] Grosu
and Horvath observe that the raising and nonraising variants differ
sharply with respect to whether the complementizer *ca* may appear at the
front of the embedded clause. In raising cases, it may not appear, while in
nonraising cases, it is essentially obligatory.[51] Grosu and Horvath take
the impossibility of the complementizer in raising cases to suggest that
Romanian raising predicates may take a defective clausal complement,
lacking the projection of a complementizer, what I will assume to be a
projection of T.[52] In this respect, then, these Romanian constructions
parallel the corresponding English ones: raising occurrs only with T-
headed complements, not with C-headed complements. At the same time,
Grosu and Horvath note that these Romanian cases differ from the corresponding English ones in one significant respect: in both raising and
nonraising variants, the clausal complement remains finite (subjunctive).
This state of affairs suggests that the basic split between raising and nonraising is tied to category and not to finiteness. Italian constructions with
the verb *sembrare* 'seem' argue for a similar result. As noted by Rizzi
(1981) (see also Kayne 1984, 119n.7), *sembrare* may take infinitival complements both with and without the element *di*.

(79) a. Mi      sembrava   di lavorare troppo.
        me.DAT seemed.3SG DI to work  too much
        'It seemed to me that I worked too much.'

    b. Mario sembrava    lavorare troppo.
       Mario seemed.3sɢ to work  too much

Following Kayne's (1984, sec. 5.1) suggestion that *di* is a complementizer, these two cases correspond to nonfinite CP and TP complements, respectively. It is interesting to note, then, that in the examples above, only the one lacking *di*, by hypothesis a case of TP complementation, involves raising from the lower clause. If we try to raise out of an infinitival complement with *di*, a CP, the result is ungrammatical.[53]

(80) *Mario sembrava di lavorare troppo.

Once again, the crucial factor determining the possibility of raising is the category of the complement and not its (non)finiteness. Assuming that there should be only a single difference in the selectional properties of *seem* in the English examples (73) and (76), we can then conclude that this difference relates to category.[54]

If the preceding discussion is on the right track, the selection-based account of the contrast between (73) and (74) cannot be correct, as both could involve T' complementation. What, then, is wrong with (74)? One possible line of analysis might try to tie the ill-formedness of (74) to an illicit multiple assignment of nominative Case to the raised subject *Daniel*, under the assumptions that an element appearing in the specifier of a finite TP at any point in the derivation is assigned nominative Case by that T head and that a DP may be assigned at most one Case. Yet, in the face of the previous discussion of expletive and quirky-subject constructions, both of these assumptions seem too strong: *there* can appear in the specifier of TP but is not assigned Case (or so I have assumed), and quirky subjects seem to be able to bear both their quirky inherent Case and the nominative Case they receive in subject position. Suppose we reject the idea that elements in the specifier of finite TP must be assigned Case, but retain the restriction to a single Case for nonquirky DPs. Under these assumptions, we can avoid multiple nominative Case assignment in (74) so long as only one of the finite T heads assigns nominative Case to *Daniel*. Consider first the possibility that it is the matrix T that assigns nominative Case. Thinking in feature-checking terms, this will mean that the Case features of the subject DP in the embedded-clause elementary tree in (75) are not checked until the *seems*-headed auxiliary tree adjoins at the T' node, putting aside for the moment the mechanism by which such inter-elementary-tree feature checking takes place. Now, given the connection I have been assuming between the checking of Case features on DP and the checking of φ-features on T, this will mean that the φ-features on the T head in (75) will not have been checked within this elementary tree. This is in violation of the MCP, however, as these features could have been checked within this elementary tree. Furthermore, assuming that T's EPP features were checked when the DP subject raised to the specifier of TP, this elementary tree also violates the ANCR, as only some of T's uninterpretable features have been checked.

This leaves open an alternative derivation for (74) in which the raised DP's Case features are checked within the subordinate elementary tree in (75). What goes wrong in this case? Here, I would like to pursue the intuition, proposed in various forms by Chomsky (1993, 1995, 2000) and Lasnik (1995), that such a derivation would be uneconomical, or overly complex. Chomsky (1993), for instance, puts forward a principle of Greed that allows an element E to undergo movement only if some feature of E is checked in the process. Examples like (74) are blocked, then, since raising the DP *Daniel* out of the embedded clause would violate Greed, its Case features having already been checked by the lower T head.[55] This idea can be directly recast into TAG terms as a restriction on Adjoining.

(81) *Greed*
     Adjoining may apply at some node of an elementary tree T only if
     it results in the elimination of uninterpretable features in T.

Stated another way, if some application of Adjoining does not achieve any reduction in the number of uninterpretable features present in an elementary tree, it is regarded as unnecessary and hence is prohibited.[56] To apply this condition, we need to say something about how feature checking can take place across elementary tree boundaries. Let us assume that features on two elements $E_1$ and $E_2$ from distinct elementary trees enter into a checking relation, so long as $E_1$ and $E_2$ stand in the appropriate structural configuration in the derived structure. In well-formed raising derivations, the two elements of interest are the T head of the *seems*-headed raising auxiliary, with unchecked EPP and φ-features, and the DP in the specifier of TP in the elementary tree into which adjoining takes place, with unchecked Case features. After Adjoining, these two stand in a specifier-head relation. Supposing this to be an appropriate configuration for inter-elementary-tree feature checking, T's EPP and φ-features can now be checked by DP and DP's Case features are checked by T. Note that this derivation satisfies the formulation of Greed in (81), since uninterpretable features of the targeted elementary tree, specifically DP's Case features, are checked after Adjoining. Now consider derivations of ill-formed cases of raising like (74), where the same raising auxiliary adjoins at the T' node of a finite elementary tree, like that in (75). This elementary tree differs from its nonfinite counterpart in that its DP specifier lacks Case features, these having already been checked elementary-tree-internally. Consequently, adjoining a raising auxiliary at the T' node of (75) cannot result in the checking of uninterpretable features in this elementary tree, and it is ruled out by (81).[57]

It is interesting to observe that by assuming that Adjoining is greedy in the sense of (81), a formal similarity emerges between Adjoining and Chomsky's (2000) characterization of Move: both must involve an instance of feature checking coupled with the satisfaction of selectional requirements.[58] Recall that in Chomsky's proposal, feature checking takes place when the feature to be checked (the probe) identifies a c-commanded checking element (the goal), through the operation Agree. In contrast, satisfying selectional requirements necessitates applying Merge to the selecting head and the selected element. Chomsky suggests that Move is simply the successive application of Agree and Merge to the same pair of elements, simultaneously satisfying the selectional and feature-checking requirements imposed by so-called selectional features, such as the EPP. In the raising case, Agree first establishes a relation between the probe EPP feature in T and the goal (the closest DP with unchecked Case features), in the process checking T's EPP feature. This DP is then merged with (a projection of) T, thereby satisfying the selectional requirements imposed by its EPP feature. Under the TAG formulation of Greed, instances of Adjoining must also induce feature checking. Moreover, since a foot node of a (complement) auxiliary tree A will necessarily be a selected argument of the lexical head of A, adjoining of A into another tree will also satisfy the selectional properties of A (see section 2.4). There is one significant difference between Adjoining and Move, however. In Move, it is a single element that imposes the selectional and feature-checking requirements and a single element that satisfies both of these. In Adjoining, though, selectional requirements are imposed on an auxiliary tree's foot node by the lexical head of the auxiliary tree, while feature checking is obliged to take place on some element within the elementary tree targeted by Adjoining.[59] Similarly, the element satisfying the selectional requirement will be necessarily distinct from the one that checks the uninterpretable feature.

In light of the current discussion, let us reconsider the derivation of instances of successive-cyclic raising.

(82) Daniel is likely to seem to adore his brother.

As discussed in chapter 3, the derivation of this example will first combine the two raising auxiliary trees in (83a), one finite and one nonfinite. The resulting derived auxiliary tree in (83b) then adjoins at the T′ node of an infinitival elementary tree headed by *adore*.

(83) a.

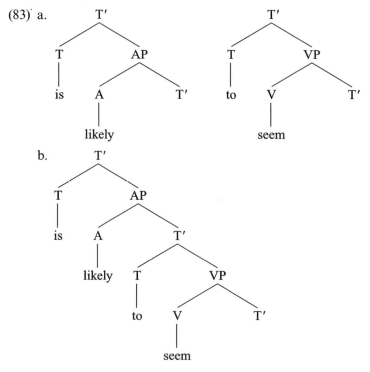

b.

Both T heads in the raising auxiliary trees in (83a) will contain unchecked EPP features in T, and the finite T head will also include ϕ-features. Now, does adjoining of one of these trees into the other satisfy the formulation of Greed in (81)? Before we answer this question, recall that there are two ways in which these trees may be combined by Adjoining: either the finite auxiliary may adjoin to the T′ root of the infinitival auxiliary, or the infinitival auxiliary may adjoin to the T′ foot of the finite auxiliary. Nonetheless, if we assume that inter-elementary-tree feature checking may take place only under a specifier-head configuration, it is clear that neither of these derivational paths will result in features being checked in the targeted elementary tree, as no specifier-head relations are ever produced.

To render this case compatible with the formulation of Greed in (81), I would like to pursue an idea inspired by Higginbotham's (1985) proposals concerning the satisfaction of thematic requirements during syntactic combination. It is often assumed that "thematically active" syntactic combination always involves an unsaturated predicate P and a saturated element E, where P assigns one of its lexically specified roles to E through a process of θ-role assignment. Higginbotham observes, however, that this view is incompatible with examples like (84), in which two unsaturated predicates, the nominal predicate *animals* and the adjectival predicate *green*, combine to produce an unsaturated predicate that is semantically the conjunction of *green* and *animals*.

(84) Frogs are green animals.

To accommodate such combinations, Higginbotham suggests that the calculus of syntactic combination be enriched with an additional mechanism, which he labels *θ-identification*. In this operation, the single unsaturated argument positions of two distinct predicates are conflated to produce a new predicate with a single unsaturated argument position.[60] By means of this mechanism, the unsaturated predicates *animals* and *green* can combine, with the variables representing their arguments being conflated. When θ-role assignment finally takes place to the DP subject by the T′, the DP saturates both *animals* and *green* as a result of the previous identification of these predicates' unassigned θ-roles. These combinations are depicted in (85).

(85)

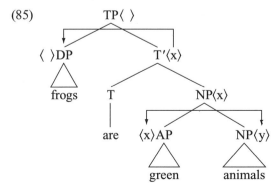

Recent conceptions of the calculus of feature combination assume the presence of a single operation, feature checking, that is analogous to θ-role assignment: when an unchecked uninterpretable feature, the probe, enters into a relation with some other feature, the goal, the probe is deleted and has no further effects on the derivation, just as in the case of a θ-role that undergoes θ-role assignment. I suggest that the derivations of examples like (82) include an additional operation for feature combination analogous to θ-identification, which I will call *feature identification*. During the first stage in the derivation of this example, the unchecked EPP features of the T heads of the raising auxiliary trees undergo feature identification during Adjoining and effectively combine, thereby producing the auxiliary tree in (83b) with a single unchecked EPP feature. When this derived auxiliary tree is adjoined at the T′ node of an infinitival elementary tree, this feature is checked.

To clarify the conditions under which such feature identification may obtain, we will first need to understand more precisely the mechanism by which features may interact across elementary tree boundaries. Under (81), inter-elementary-tree feature checking serves to limit the class of possible TAG derivations. It is therefore natural to adapt one of the existing proposals for imposing constraints on TAG derivations (Joshi 1985; Vijay-Shanker and Joshi 1985, 1988; Vijay-Shanker 1987). One promising candidate is Vijay-Shanker's (1987) and Vijay-Shanker and Joshi's (1988) proposal whereby the nodes of an elementary tree are associated with pairs of sets of features, called the *top* and *bottom* features of the node. The idea underlying the use of pairs of feature sets derives from one way of conceiving Adjoining, namely, as the splitting of a node (the site of adjoining) in two, the auxiliary tree being inserted in the separation that is created. The two feature sets associated with a node N correspond to the two halves of N after Adjoining. When an auxiliary tree A with root R and foot F adjoins at N, N's top feature set combines (via feature unification in Vijay-Shanker and Joshi's proposal) with R's top feature set, while N's bottom feature set combines with F's bottom feature set. This is depicted in (86).

(86)

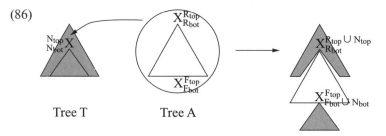

Tree T                    Tree A

The distinction between top and bottom feature sets has a natural application in grammatical description. The top feature set is used to encode the properties of a node that are determined by the structural context above it, as this is what remains local to the top feature set after Adjoining. In contrast, the bottom features encode properties that derive from the structural context below a node, as these will remain local to the bottom feature set after Adjoining. At the conclusion of a derivation, when no more nodes will be split, we will require that the top and bottom feature sets associated with each node combine with one another (again, via feature unification in Vijay-Shanker and Joshi's proposal). This ensures that the top and bottom structural contexts of a node impose compatible demands.

To see how such feature sets can be used to constrain derivations, consider the derivation of the following example:

(87) Which of those books had you hoped that they would read?

Leaving aside the substitution of DPs, this example will derive from two elementary trees, one headed by the matrix verb *hoped* and the other headed by the embedded verb *read*. Since the *wh*-phrase is an argument of the embedded verb, fronting must occur within the *read*-headed elementary tree, as in (88).

(88)

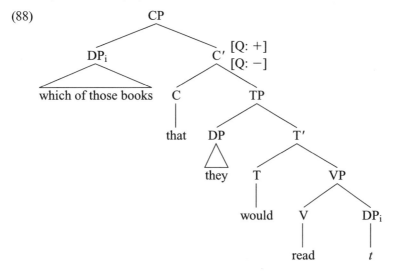

In this structure, I have assigned features to the top and bottom feature sets of the C' node: I have taken the presence of the *wh*-DP in the specifier of CP (part of the external context of C') to indicate the presence of a [+Q] feature, and the lexical specification of *that* (part of the internal context of C') to impose a [−Q] feature. Assuming that these two feature specifications are incompatible, any well-formed derivation involving this tree will necessarily involve Adjoining at this node, so as to resolve the feature conflict. We see, then, that a feature conflict at a node of an elementary tree renders that node a site at which Adjoining is obligatory. Now consider the auxiliary tree (89) representing the matrix clause.

(89)

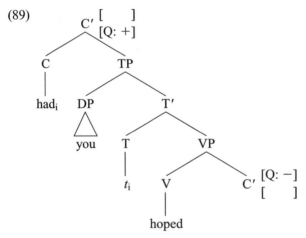

Since *hoped* selects for a [−Q] complement, I assign a [−Q] specification to the top feature set of the C' foot node. If we take the fronting of the auxiliary tree to indicate that the C head of this tree is specified as [+Q], we will assign a [+Q] specification in the bottom feature set of the C' root. Now, by adjoining (89) to the C' node of (88), we split up the conflicting feature specifications in that tree, placing the originally conflicting feature sets adjacent to ones with which they are compatible, as in (90).

(90)

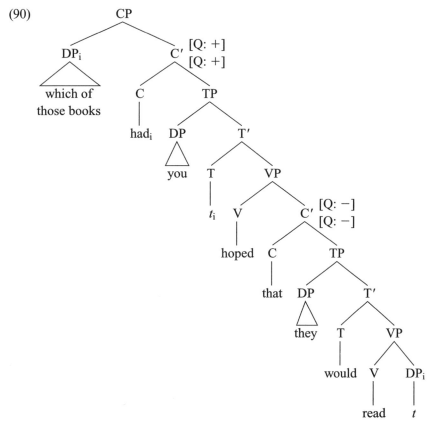

Since no feature conflicts remain, all pairs of feature sets can now combine, yielding a well-formed derivation. Observe, however, that not just any auxiliary tree would have achieved this result. For example, had the C head of the auxiliary tree in (89) been specified as [−Q], yielding a [−Q] specification in the auxiliary tree's C′ root, the structure resulting from Adjoining would have continued to exhibit a feature conflict. As a result, we would correctly rule out the following variant of (87):

(91) *Which of those books that you had hoped that they would read?

Thus, the particular constellation of features present in an elementary tree imposes a certain degree of selectivity on what instances of Adjoining are possible.

    As already noted, Vijay-Shanker and Joshi's original proposal combines feature sets via unification, an operation that ensures feature compatibility. Since I am assuming that during the TAG derivation any uninterpretable features that have not been checked within an elementary tree not only must be checked for compatibility, but also must be deleted, the feature unification operation is not sufficient. Fortunately, there is nothing inherent in Vijay-Shanker and Joshi's idea of using paired feature sets that prevents the use of different operations for feature set combination. I will assume, then, that when feature sets combine, the features present in these sets may undergo checking and identification. I will take feature checking to apply when a feature set $S_1$ containing an uninterpretable feature F is combined with a feature set $S_2$ containing an interpretable feature $F'$ that can check F. For example, if a feature set containing uninterpretable $\phi$-features is combined with one containing interpretable $\phi$-features, the former are deleted. In contrast, feature identification applies when feature sets $S_1$ and $S_2$ are combined and both contain an instance of some particular uninterpretable feature F. Additionally, I will make use of the schema for feature set combination depicted in (92).

(92)

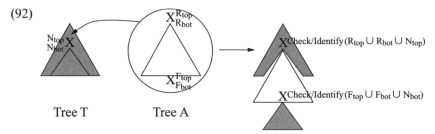

Tree T                    Tree A

This schema differs from the earlier one in a number of respects. First, feature sets are combined via set union rather than unification. Second, according to this schema, feature set combination is a bit more eager than before: Adjoining collapses the top and bottom features at both the root and the foot nodes of the auxiliary tree immediately, blocking any further adjoining at a node once adjoining has already taken place there. If the root or foot of an auxiliary tree has served as the locus of adjoining at some earlier stage in the derivation, so that the top and bottom feature sets of such a node have already been combined into a single feature, Adjoining combines just this set with the appropriate feature set at the site of adjoining. The final and most important difference concerns what happens after the feature sets are combined: the combined set is given as input to the operations of feature checking and identification.

To illustrate how this operation works, let us return once again to a raising derivation, where a finite *seem*-headed auxiliary tree adjoins at the T′ node of some infinitival TP elementary tree. As already discussed, the Case features on the DP node in the specifier of TP of the infinitival clause will not have been checked. In order for these features to be checked by an element with which this DP enters into a (derived) specifier-head configuration, it is sufficient to percolate the specifier's Case features (as well as the interpretable D and φ-features, the latter annotated as $φ^I$) to the top feature set of the T′ node of this elementary tree, as shown in (93).

(93)

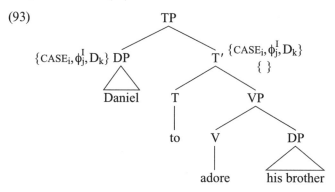

In this representation, I indicate percolated features via cosubscripting. I take such cosubscripted features to be token identical, so that their deletion from one feature set suffices to delete them from all feature sets in which they occur. In the raising auxiliary tree, the T head will contain unchecked EPP and uninterpretable φ-features (the latter annotated as $φ^U$). I assume that such features will percolate to the T′ node, as in (94).

(94)

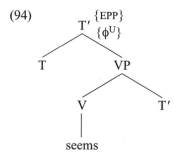

Although T's EPP and φ-features have both percolated to T′, I have placed them in distinct feature sets of T′, EPP in the top set and φ-features in the bottom set. Though not crucial for the current derivation, this difference becomes significant immediately below. Now, by following the feature set combination regimen depicted in (92), adjoining of this auxiliary tree into the infinitival TP produces the result shown in (95).

(95)

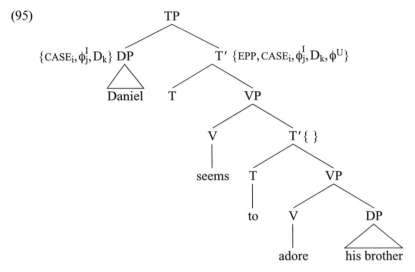

After these feature sets have been combined, the feature-checking operation applies to eliminate some of the features in the resulting set on $T'$. I assume, first of all, that EPP features are checked against interpretable D features present in the same feature set. Further, the presence of interpretable $\phi$-features in a feature set licenses the deletion of uninterpretable $\phi$-features in the same set. Finally, deletion of Case features will be licensed as a corollary of $\phi$-feature checking in the same feature set. As a result of feature checking, then, the feature set associated with the $T'$ node is reduced to $\{\phi_j^I, D_k\}$. Because this instance of Adjoining results in the deletion of features, it satisfies Greed. Further, because the feature sets in the resulting structure contain only interpretable features, the derivation converges.

Let us now return to the case of successive-cyclic raising. As noted above, this derivation begins with the combination via Adjoining of the auxiliary trees in (83a), repeated here with feature set annotations.

(96)

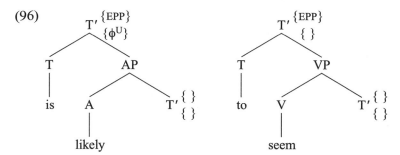

Earlier, we observed that these trees can combine either by adjoining the finite auxiliary tree at the root of the nonfinite auxiliary tree or by adjoining the nonfinite auxiliary tree at the foot of the finite auxiliary tree. Though these derivations produce identical results from the point of view of the structure, the resulting feature sets are distinct: the first derivational option yields the representation in (97a), while the second yields the one in (97b).

(97) a.

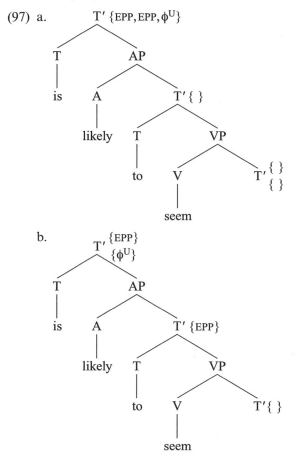

b.

In (97a), the feature set on T′ can be reduced by feature identification: the two instances of an EPP feature can be combined to yield a feature set with a single EPP feature. If we take such cases of feature identification to have eliminated a feature on the auxiliary tree that has adjoined in, this case of Adjoining satisfies the formulation of Greed in (81). By contrast, in (97b) there is no way to reduce the number of features, either by feature checking or by feature identification. Correspondingly, this derivation is ruled out.

To complete the derivation of (82), it suffices to adjoin the derived auxiliary tree in (97a) into the T′ node of (93), producing the representation in (98).

(98)

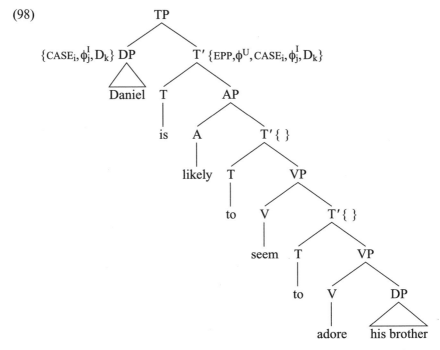

As before, all of the uninterpretable features in the feature set of T′ can be eliminated through feature checking, producing a convergent representation.

I already pointed out that I am assuming that T's EPP and ϕ-features project to different feature sets on T′. This difference plays a crucial role in ruling out cases of successive-cyclic raising that pass through the specifier of TP of a finite clause.

(99) *Daniel seems is likely to adore his brother.

To derive such a case, we first adjoin the finite *seems*-headed auxiliary in (94) to the T′ root of the *is likely* auxiliary tree depicted in (96). This results in the derived auxiliary tree in (100).

(100)

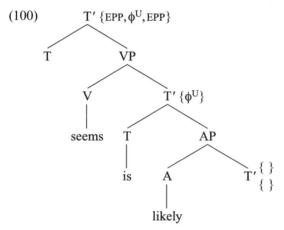

This application of Adjoining satisfies Greed, as the two instances of EPP features may be combined through feature identification, just as in the case discussed above. Note though that since the $\phi$-features of the lower T head were percolated to the lower feature set of T′, they end up stranded inside this auxiliary tree. In this position, they cannot be checked by further applications of Adjoining, since this T′ node no longer includes a pair of feature sets and as a result cannot serve as the locus of adjoining. Consequently, even if we adjoin this derived auxiliary at the T′ node of a nonfinite TP, thereby checking the EPP and $\phi$-features at the root, uninterpretable $\phi$-features will remain at this internal T′ node, leading to an ill-formed derivation. Observe, however, that if the $\phi$-features of T had been percolated to the top feature set of T′, the two instances of $\phi$-features from the raising auxiliary tree could have undergone feature identification just like the EPP features. The derivation for (99) would therefore have converged, improperly. Why should different features project in these different ways? At present, I do not have much to say about this, except to observe that the difference might be tied to the distinction between features that induce movement (i.e., selectional features) and those that do not.[61]

The assumption that inter-elementary-tree feature checking takes place uniformly under specifier-head agreement poses an apparent problem in cases involving raising of an element like *there* that does not check T's φ-features.

(101) There seems to be a unicorn in the garden.

Rather, under the framework of Chomsky 2000 that we are largely following, it is the postcopular DP *a unicorn* that checks T's φ-features. There are two possible solutions to this problem. One would be to allow inter-elementary-tree feature checking to take place under c-command, by permitting the percolation of unchecked features to c-commanded frontier nonterminals, the $T'$ foot node in the case of raising. This would still leave open the question of how the postcopular DP's Case and φ-features percolate to (the bottom feature set of) the $T'$ node within their own elementary tree, so as to allow feature checking.[62] A second possibility, which I tentatively adopt, retains the idea that inter-elementary-tree feature checking uniformly takes place in a specifier-head relation, though with the notion of specifier reinterpreted to be the top feature set of an $X'$ projection. I do this by allowing any features within an elementary tree that are c-commanded by a head H to percolate to the top feature structure of H's $X'$ projection. The infinitival elementary tree involved in the derivation of (101) will thus be as in (102).

(102)

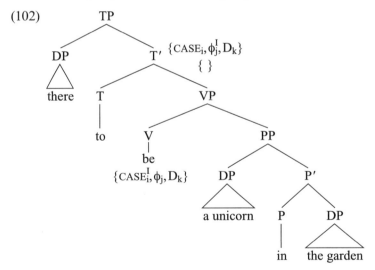

Since the uninterpretable Case and φ-features are configured just as in (93), this elementary tree will participate in raising derivations in an exactly parallel manner. This sort of derivation will permit a higher T head to enter into a long-distance agreement relation with the in-situ DP, since the DP's $\phi$-features, in the top feature set of T', will remain accessible to the finite T of an arbitrarily complex derived raising auxiliary. A similar pattern holds with the unraised nominative DPs in Icelandic, both with transitive expletive constructions, as in (69), and with quirky subject infinitivals, as in (67), suggesting that the Case and $\phi$-features of these nominative DPs percolate in a fashion similar to those of English post-verbal nominative DPs.[63]

# Chapter 5

# A Case Study:
# *Wh*-Dependencies

In the previous chapters, I explored raising-to-subject constructions within the context of the TAG-based theory I am developing. One significant property of the analysis I proposed for raising is the distinction it makes among cases of dislocation that had previously been treated uniformly in terms of transformational movement. Under the TAG analysis, some are produced by means of Adjoining, others by transformational movement within an elementary tree. In this chapter, I turn to another sort of dependency that has been tied to transformational movement: *wh*-movement. As in the case of raising, we will see that the TAG-based theory forces us to a view in which some dislocations of *wh*-elements are necessarily treated as the result of Adjoining, while others can be tied to elementary-tree-internal movement.

I begin this chapter by presenting the essentials of a TAG-based analysis of *wh*-dependencies deriving from work by Kroch (1987, 1989b) and myself (1992). I then show how the structural assumptions underlying the elementary trees involved in this analysis can be seen to derive from properties of the system of feature checking developed in chapter 4. In this context, I discuss how the phenomenon of superiority can be understood as yet another reflection of the Maximal Checking Principle proposed in chapter 4. I then demonstrate how the TAG analysis of *wh*-movement derives without additional stipulation the restrictions on movement embodied in Subjacency and the Adjunct Condition. While doing this, I take a detour to look closely at languages that systematically violate *wh*-islands, and I propose that such liberty in movement can be understood in terms of crosslinguistic differences in the structure of the elementary trees different languages allow. Finally, I turn to cases of grammatical extraction from weak islands, so-called long movement, and pursue a possible means for dealing with them in the context of TAG.

## 5.1   Movement and Adjoining in *Wh*-Dependencies

*Wh*-questions involve a dependency between a fronted *wh*-element and the position in which such an element is canonically interpreted.[1]

(1)  Which book$_i$ did Alice read $t_i$?

In the TAG context, there is no way to assimilate the dislocation of the *wh*-element from its base position to its fronted position to a case of Adjoining. As noted in chapter 3, Adjoining can only "move" an element from a position of one type to a position of identical type. The dependency between the *wh*-element and its trace, however, is "hybrid" in the sense that the character of the position occupied by the gap, a verbal complement, is distinct from the nonargument surface position of the *wh*-element, which I assume to be the specifier of CP. Thus, the dependency between the gap and the *wh*-phrase in (1) is one that I will assume is established via movement within an elementary tree.

As is well known, *wh*-questions have the interesting property that the distance over which the dependency between the *wh*-element and its base-generated position may hold is unbounded.

(2)  Which book has Leona said that Fred thought (that Leslie had heard that Bill had hoped . . .) that Alice would read *t*?

It should be clear by this point that the TAG framework does not permit us to treat these cases through a single application of transformational movement: in the TAG context, movement must remain within the bounded domain of a single elementary tree/extended projection. This result is in fact a welcome one. For reasons we will turn to shortly, it has been assumed at least since Chomsky 1973 that such apparently unbounded dependencies are not formed through a single unbounded application of movement, but are instead created by iterated applications of (local) movement (or equivalently the combination of local dependencies). Leaving aside the empirical motivations for such an assumption, it has never been clear conceptually why a transformational movement operation ought to be restricted in this way. In contrast, the mechanism by which dependencies are formed in the TAG framework provides a potential resolution to this conceptual quandary: since they must be established within an elementary tree, dependencies are necessarily local.

Translating an analysis involving iterated local movements into a TAG analysis involving elementary-tree-local dependencies is not, however, straightforward. Some of the local movements posited in a transformational analysis of a sentence like (2) cross extended projection boundaries and thus cannot be recast as elementary-tree-internal movements. It is interesting to note in this context that in almost all contemporary movement-based analyses of *wh*-movement, all steps but the first in the derivation involve homogeneous, as opposed to hybrid, dependencies, moving successively from the specifier of CP of one clause to the specifier of CP of the next higher clause.[2] As just noted, such homogeneous dependencies are precisely what Adjoining is capable of creating. Capitalizing on this observation, Kroch (1987) proposes that the "comp-to-comp" portion of successive-cyclic *wh*-movement is the result of Adjoining.[3] He suggests that in order to produce a long-distance *wh*-dependency, we need first of all an elementary tree involving local *wh*-movement, as in (3).[4]

(3)

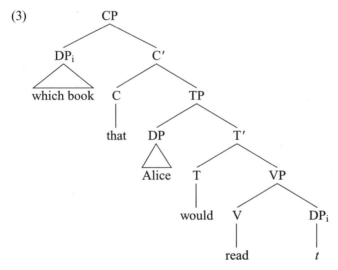

To accomplish the dislocation of the fronted *wh*-phrase to the specifier of CP position of a higher clause, we stretch the preexisting filler-gap relation in (3) using Adjoining to interpose lexical material. Specifically, if we adjoin an elementary tree like that in (4) to the C′ node of the tree in (3), the derived structure in (5) results, an apparent instance of successive-cyclic extraction.

(4)
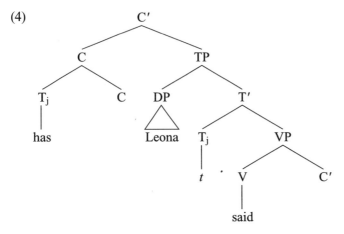

(5)
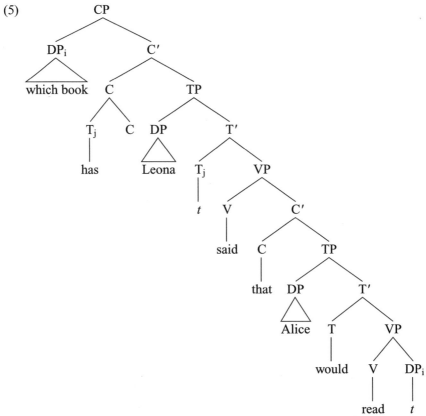

To extend even further the distance across which a *wh*-dependency stretches, we would instead begin the derivation by adjoining the C′ auxiliary tree in (4) to the root of another C′ auxiliary tree, like that in (6a), resulting in the complex C′ auxiliary tree in (6b).

(6) a.

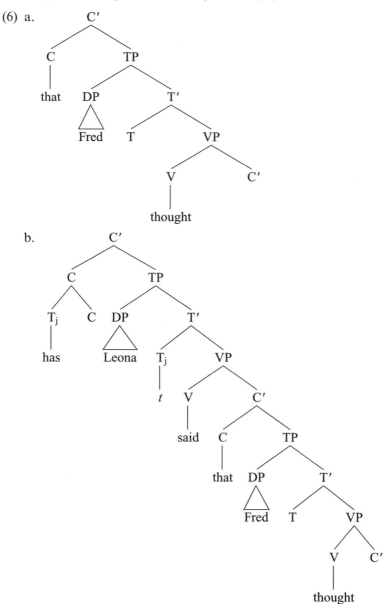

If we now adjoin this complex auxiliary tree to the C' node of the elementary tree in (3) containing the *wh*-dependency, we stretch the dependency across two clausal boundaries. By iterating the process of adjoining C' auxiliary trees to one another to create an even larger derived C' auxiliary tree, we can indefinitely extend the domain over which *wh*-dependencies can hold.

This derivation of *wh*-dependencies clearly parallels the derivation of raising constructions from earlier chapters. Indeed, the TAG derivations involved in *wh*-movement and raising constructions are virtually identical, the sole difference being whether Adjoining takes place in the C domain, as in *wh*-movement, or in the T domain, as in raising.[5] This parallelism in derivation highlights the fact that both types of constructions involve an initial heterogeneous movement, from an argument position to the specifier of CP in the *wh*-movement case and from VP-internal position to the specifier of TP in the raising case, with all subsequent movements creating only homogeneous dependencies.

The auxiliary trees in (4) and (6a), which are crucially involved in the derivation of long-distance *wh*-dependencies, are noteworthy in at least two respects. First, the root of these auxiliaries is the nonmaximal projection C'.[6] Second, the frontier nonterminal that is the complement to the verb heading each auxiliary tree is similarly a nonmaximal C'. These structural assumptions are necessary if we are to use Adjoining to separate a *wh*-element fronted to the specifier of CP from the rest of its elementary tree. If the tree is to be inserted below the *wh*-element, the auxiliary tree cannot project higher than C', and if the structure is to meet the formal characterization of an auxiliary tree as a recursive structure, there must be a foot node that is identically labeled. Nonetheless, it would be helpful to better understand what allows the root and foot nodes of these auxiliary trees to exhibit these exceptional structural properties. In the next two sections, I take up these issues in turn.

## 5.2   Bridge Verbs and Nonmaximal Complements

Consider first the presence of nonmaximal C' complements in auxiliary trees like (4). Just as I proposed in chapter 3 that only a limited class of verbs selecting for a projection of T permit a T' complement, thereby permitting raising, so we might expect to find a similar division among verbs selecting for a projection of C. Under the derivation I have just sketched, only verbs permitting C′ complements could head an auxiliary tree like (4), thereby licensing *wh*-movement. In contrast, a verb requiring a fully projected CP complement would not permit *wh*-movement from its complement, as it could not head such an auxiliary tree. I would like to suggest that this ability to select for C′ complements is what characterizes the class of so-called bridge verbs (Erteschik-Shir 1973). Bridge verbs, like *say* and *think*, permit *wh*-extraction to take place quite freely out of their complements, while nonbridge verbs, like *doubt* and *forget*, do not.[7]

(7) a. Who do you think [that Claude gave a book to *t*]?
    b. Why did she say [that she had left *t*]?

(8) a. ??Who do you doubt [that Claude gave a book to *t*]?
    b. *Why did you forget [that she had left *t*]?

Under the assumption that nonbridge verbs cannot take C′ complements, the TAG approach to *wh*-movement I have laid out derives the intolerance of such verbs to extraction from their complements.

Why should bridge and nonbridge predicates differ in this way? One potential line of explanation relates the selectional difference to the distinctive semantic properties of the nonbridge class. One subclass of nonbridge verbs, the factive verbs (including *know*, *forget*, and *regret*), is characterized by the presupposed truth of the proposition expressed by their complement. Melvold (1986) has proposed that this factive interpretation derives from the presence of an empty factive operator in the specifier of CP of the complements to these verbs. Progovac (1988) makes a similar proposal for another subclass of nonbridge verbs, the inherently negative verbs, such as *doubt* and *deny*. She suggests that the specifier of the CP complements to such verbs is also filled by an empty operator, this time one with negative force. In order for factive or inherently negative verbs to satisfy their semantic selectional requirements, then, their complements must include the relevant sort of empty operator in their specifier, thereby implicating a fully projected CP complement. There are, however, other predicates (including *whisper*, *emphasize*, and *be certain*) that are neither factive nor inherently negative yet belong to the nonbridge class in not permitting free extraction from their complements. Hegarty (1992) suggests that this last class is characterized as taking sentential complements assumed to be familiar to the listener in the context of use. If we assume that the semantic force of familiarity is conveyed structurally by an empty operator in the specifier of CP, we can derive the necessity of CP complementation in this case as well.[8]

## 5.3   Nonmaximal Projections, *Wh*-Features, and Superiority

Let us turn now to the issue of the nonmaximally projected C$'$ root in auxiliary trees like those in (4) and (6a). What permits the C head to project only to the C$'$ level in these cases? We can approach this problem by asking what it is that licenses the presence of a *wh*-phrase in a specifier of CP position, assuming this is necessary to project to the CP level. Fukui and Speas (1986) suggest that the licensing of such a *wh*-specifier is determined by C's lexical makeup: C licenses the projection of a specifier only when its lexical specification includes what they call a WH feature. Fukui and Speas take WH features to be present on just the C heads of interrogative clauses. Rizzi (1996) advocates a similar idea: he proposes a *Wh*-Criterion according to which any C head specified as [+wh] must contain a *wh*-operator in its specifier. Let us adopt this basic idea, as recast by Chomsky (1995, 2000) into his feature-checking framework. Following Chomsky, I will suppose that there is an uninterpretable selectional feature on C analogous to T's EPP feature, which I will call wh-*EPP*. Such a *wh*-EPP feature may be checked only by the merger of a *wh*-element into the specifier of CP.[9]

Now let us return to the C$'$-rooted auxiliary trees in (4) and (6a). For the latter auxiliary tree, it is plausible to assume that the C head *that* is lexically specified as lacking a *wh*-EPP feature. Consequently, there is nothing to license the merger of a *wh*-element into the specifier of CP, leaving us with a C$'$-rooted elementary tree. In the case of (4), the fronting of the auxiliary verb in this auxiliary tree would seem to indicate the presence of an interrogative complementizer, and hence *wh*-EPP features. Why doesn't this force the insertion of a *wh*-phrase into the specifier of CP? The answer here is the same one we discovered in the context of raising auxiliary trees in chapter 4: since there is no element in the elementary tree capable of checking the *wh*-EPP feature (i.e., there is no DP with *wh*-features), the MCP permits this feature to remain unchecked within the auxiliary tree, meaning that we are again left with a nonmaximal C$'$ root.[10]

Consider now what would happen if we were to alter (4) slightly so that it now includes a wh-phrase, as in (9).

(9)

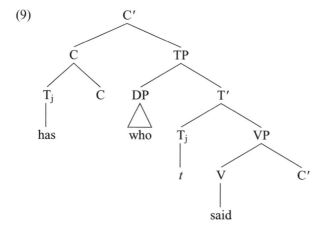

Were this a well-formed auxiliary tree, we would be able to derive the ungrammatical (10), by adjoining it to the C′ node of the elementary tree in (3), in the process stretching the *wh*-dependency in the latter tree.

(10) *Which book has who said that Alice would read?

Such examples have traditionally been treated in terms of the following constraint on movement (Chomsky 1973, 246):

(11) a. *Superiority*
         No rule can involve X, Y in the structure
         $\ldots$ X $\ldots$ [$_\alpha$ $\ldots$ Z $\ldots$ – WYV $\ldots$] $\ldots$
         where the rule applies ambiguously to Z and Y and Z is superior to Y
     b. $\ldots$ the category A is superior to the category B in the phrase marker if every major category dominating A dominates B as well but not conversely.

The Superiority Condition, a forerunner of Shortest Move, blocks (10): no transformation can move *which book* to the matrix C, since that same transformation could also move *who* to the matrix C, and *who* is superior to *which book*. As was the case with many violations of Shortest Move discussed in chapter 4, the MCP provides the means to rule out Superiority violations like (9). Since the *wh*-phrase in this tree is capable of locally checking C's *wh*-EPP feature, the MCP requires that it do so, as the resulting elementary tree will contain one fewer uninterpretable feature. Thus, (9) is ruled out in favor of the elementary tree in (12).[11]

(12)

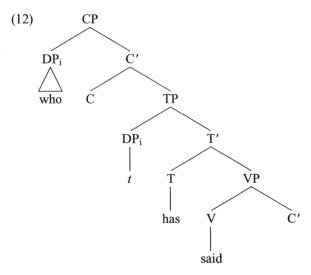

To form a multiple *wh*-question from the lexical material underlying (10), we would instead substitute a C′-rooted elementary tree like (13) into the C′ complement of *thought*, producing (14).

(13)

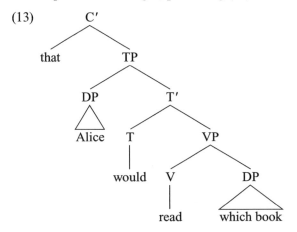

(14) Who has said that Alice would read which book?

Note that it is crucial that *that* in (13) lack *wh*-EPP features, lest raising of which book to the specifier of the embedded CP be forced by the MCP.

Under the conception of elementary trees I have proposed, modifiers to a verbal predicate are not present in the verb's elementary tree. If the MCP-based analysis of superiority just sketched is correct, it leads us to expect that unlike examples like (10) involving *wh*-arguments to a higher verb, examples involving *wh*-modifiers to such verbs should not induce superiority effects: the MCP cannot force such modifiers to raise to the verb's specifier of CP, as they are not generated within the verb's elementary tree.[12] The following examples, slightly modified from Tanaka 1999, suggest that this is correct:[13]

(15) a. What charge did the DA prove [that the defendant was guilty of *t*] during what trial?
   b. During what trial did the DA prove [that the defendant was guilty of what charge] *t*?

Let us turn next to the following example:

(16) *Which book has Leona said that who thought that Alice would read?

This case, another instance of a Superiority violation, can be derived in the manner discussed earlier for example (2): we first adjoin the auxiliary tree in (4) to the root of the auxiliary tree in (17) and then adjoin the resulting derived auxiliary tree to the C′ node in (3).

(17)

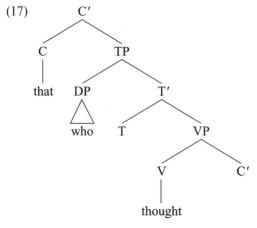

Since the only difference between this derivation and that of the well-formed example (2) lies in the use of the auxiliary tree in (17) rather than the one in (6a), it is natural to assume that a difference between these two trees is responsible for the contrast in well-formedness. Yet, given the assumption we made earlier that *that*-headed C projections lack *wh*-EPP features, the MCP-based explanation does not extend to this case: the absence of *wh*-EPP features on C in (17) means that *who* is not obliged to raise to the specifier of CP, just as in the elementary tree in (13).

Given the discussion in chapter 4, however, we already have reason to doubt our earlier claim that there are no *wh*-EPP features in auxiliary trees like (6a) and (17). Recall that the principle of Greed requires that all instances of Adjoining be associated with the elimination of uninterpretable features in the elementary tree that it targets. Under our current assumptions, then, the first step in the derivation of a long-distance *wh*-movement example like (2), in which the C′ auxiliary tree in (4) is adjoined into another C′ auxiliary tree, in (6a), should be blocked as there would be no features to be deleted (or identified) in either of these trees.

Suppose, then, that noninterrogative C heads may optionally be generated with *wh*-EPP features, continuing to assume that interrogative C heads must bear *wh*-EPP features.[14] Now, if the C head of (6a) is introduced into the derivation with a *wh*-EPP feature, the first step of the TAG derivation underlying (2) will be licensed by Greed, as the *wh*-EPP features projected by the C heads in (6a) and (4) will undergo feature identification, so that the top feature set on the root of the resulting C′ structure includes only one *wh*-EPP feature.[15] Returning now to the Superiority violation in (16), if C in (17) is generated with *wh*-EPP features, the MCP will force the *wh*-phrase in subject position to raise to the specifier of CP, as it is a potential local checker.[16] As just discussed, failure to generate *wh*-EPP features on the C head of the auxiliary tree will result in the TAG derivation's being blocked by Greed. For an elementary tree like (13), *that* may safely be generated without *wh*-EPP features, since this structure is inserted into the matrix clause via Substitution, an operation that is not subject to Greed, I am assuming.

The phenomenon of Irish complementizer agreement offers morphological evidence in favor of such widespread presence of *wh*-EPP features. McCloskey (1979) points out that whenever a complementizer intervenes along the path of *wh*-movement, the usual indicative complementizer *go* is obligatorily replaced by a leniting form *aL*.

(18) an rud   aL  shil    me aL  duirt tu   aL  dheanfa
     the thing that thought I    that said  you that you would do
     'the thing that I thought that you said that you would do'

McCloskey (see also Chung and McCloskey 1987; Rizzi 1990) interprets this alternation as a reflex of the presence of an intermediate trace in the intervening COMP positions, something that is not available in the TAG context, given the absence of intermediate traces. However, it would appear that this phenomenon can be equally well described by saying that unlike English, Irish does not allow optional generation of *wh*-EPP features on a single indicative complementizer, but instead has two distinct forms: *aL*, which has a *wh*-EPP feature, and *go*, which does not. Note also that a number of phenomena that have long been taken to provide evidence for the presence of intermediate traces in the specifier of CP position, including stylistic inversion in French (Kayne and Pollock 1978), complementizer deletion and subject-verb inversion in Spanish (Torrego 1983, 1984), and auxiliary inversion in Belfast English (Henry 1995), can be treated similarly to the Irish complementizer case, implicating instead the presence of *wh*-EPP features in an elementary tree.[17]

The MCP-based derivation of superiority effects exactly parallels the explanation of the impossibility of raising past a dative experiencer in Icelandic, as in (19a).

(19) a. *Margir menn virðast   mér    vera í herberginu.
         many men   seem.3PL me.DAT to be in the room
     b.  Mér    virðast    margir menn vera í herberginu.
         me.DAT seem.3PL many   men   to be in the room

As discussed at some length in chapter 4, although the MCP blocks the possibility of a feature F being checked by an element in a lower clause if there is a possible checker in the same clause as F, the MCP's consequences for the locality of movement are distinct from those of proposals based on a Shortest Move–like (or Superiority-like) condition. The MCP distinguishes only between cases in which the two potential checkers of some feature come from distinct elementary trees. When there are two (or more) potential checkers within a single elementary tree, the MCP requires only that one of them do so, but does not choose between them. As a result, the MCP-based explanation of the ill-formedness of Superiority violations like (10) does not extend to clause-local cases of superiority.

(20) *What has who read?

There is good reason to believe that the distinction between local Superiority violations like (20) and long-distance Superiority violations like (10) is an important one. The most straightforward evidence comes from German ((21)–(22)) and Spanish ((23)–(24)), both of which exhibit long-distance superiority effects, though not local superiority effects (Jaeggli 1982; Haider 1983; Büring and Hartmann 1994; Bošković 1997; Heck and Müller 2000).[18]

(21) a. Wer hat wen    getroffen?
       who has whom met
       'Who met whom?'
    b. Wen   hat wer getroffen?
       whom has who met

(22) a.   Wer hat gesagt, dass Maria wen   liebt?
          who has said    that Maria whom loves
          'Who said that Maria loves whom?'
    b. *Wen   hat wer gesagt, dass Maria liebt?
          whom has who said    that Maria loves

(23) a. Quién dijo qué?
       who   said what
       'Who said what?'
    b. Qué  dijo quién?
       what said who

(24) a.   Quién dijo que Juan compra qué?
          who   said that Juan bought  what
          'Who said that Juan bought what?'
    b. ?*Qué  dijo quién que Juan compra?
          what said who  that Juan bought

This is precisely the pattern the MCP leads us to expect, and it therefore provides strong support for my proposed analysis.[19]

But what should we make of English-type languages, which exhibit both local and long-distance superiority effects? Note first of all that it is not the case that English shows a uniform preference for moving the "higher" *wh*-phrase, as shown by the following examples from Chomsky 1973, 246, and Kayne 1984, 176:[20]

(25) a. John knows what books to give to whom.
    b. John knows to whom to give what books.

(26) a. ?I'd like to know where who hit what.
    b. ?I'd like to know what who hit where.

Even to the degree that English does exhibit a local superiority effect, however, it is important to note that this does not necessarily falsify the

MCP account of (10); instead, it suggests that something other than the MCP is involved in ruling out cases such as (20).[21] Of course, if the factors responsible for blocking local superiority cases also account for the impossibility of long-distance superiority, this line of retreat loses its appeal, as it would eliminate need for a principle like the MCP that explains only one of the cases. Fortunately, even within English, there is evidence that cases of local and long-distance superiority need to be distinguished. First of all, it has been pointed out by Bolinger (1978) and Pesetsky (1987) that English sentences violating Superiority can be rendered acceptable if the *wh*-elements involved are given what Pesetsky calls a D(iscourse)-linked interpretation: that is, the range of possible answers to the *wh*-element must be drawn from some contextually salient set of entities. D-linking is often, though not necessarily, encoded syntactically through the use of a *which*-headed *wh*-expression. Thus, the following example is much better than (20):

(27)  Which book did which student read?

Though judgments are delicate on these sorts of cases, as Pesetsky notes, it seems to me that D-linking yields improvement only in cases of local superiority, but not in cases of long-distance superiority.[22]

(28)  *Which book does which teacher think that we should read?

This suggests that some additional violation is involved in cases of long-distance superiority, which D-linking cannot overcome.

Another context in which Superiority violations are obviated in English, noted by Lasnik and Saito (1992, 118), involves indirect questions embedded within matrix *wh*-questions.

(29)  Who knows where who lives?

In the embedded indirect question, the *wh*-element *where* has raised past the higher *wh*-element *who*. In a simple monoclausal sentence, such movement would result in ill-formedness.

(30)  *Where does who live?

As Lasnik and Saito observe, this avoidance of superiority comes at a price: the embedded *who* in (29) cannot be interpreted as part of an indirect multiple *wh*-question, but must instead have matrix scope. This interpretive effect is demonstrated by the fact that (29) requires an answer to both the matrix and embedded occurrences of *who*, as in (31a), and does not permit an answer of the form in (31b).

(31) a. Gabriel knows where Adam lives, and Daniel knows where Elsa lives.

b. Gabriel does. (i.e., knows where who lives)

This contrasts with examples like (32), where the indirect multiple *wh*-question interpretation, requiring answer (31b), is the more accessible, though not only, interpretation.

(32) Who knows who lives where?

Long-distance superiority effects apparently cannot be avoided in a similar fashion, though judgments are once again delicate.[23] Thus, the following example seems to me unacceptable, even with matrix interpretation of the embedded *wh*-phrase *who*:

(33) *Who asked where who thought that Daniel lived?

I will refrain from offering an analysis of the difference between (29) and (30), or an explanation of why D-linking is necessary to avoid local Superiority violations in English. Nonetheless, the residual ill-formedness of (28) and (33) demonstrates that there is some additional grammatical factor at issue in cases of long-distance superiority that is not present in cases of local superiority. I propose that this factor is the MCP.

## 5.4   What Drives *Wh*-Movement?

Let us now examine elementary trees of the form depicted in (3), repeated here, in the context of the feature-checking system we are developing.

(3)

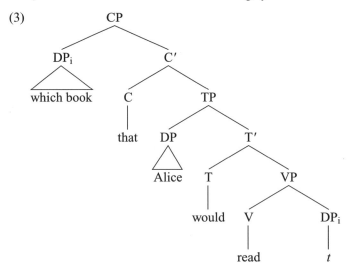

During the derivation of this tree, a [+wh] DP moves from the object position into which it was originally merged to the specifier of CP. What forces this movement to take place? Given the discussion of the previous section, one straightforward possibility is that the complementizer *that* comes into the derivation with a *wh*-EPP feature. By raising the *wh*-object to the specifier of CP, this feature is checked, as required by the MCP. Note, however, that the resulting elementary tree does not include an unchecked *wh*-EPP feature, this having been checked by movement of *which book* to the specifier of CP. Greed will therefore block subsequent Adjoining at the C′ node of this tree, unless there is some other uninterpretable feature in the elementary tree that could be checked during Adjoining. The impossibility of such Adjoining would be an unwelcome result indeed, as *wh*-phrases in English must not surface in the specifier positions of indicative (*that*-headed) CPs. It is therefore necessary to assume the presence of some other uninterpretable feature in (3) in order to ensure that an auxiliary tree projected by an interrogative C adjoins to the C′ node of (3).

What is the nature and locus of this mysterious additional uninterpretable feature? By the ANCR, we know that this residual feature cannot be part of C, as one of C's features, *wh*-EPP, has already been checked within the elementary tree. One natural possibility is that the residual unchecked feature comes from the *wh*-phrase, or more precisely the DP frontier nonterminal into which the *wh*-phrase will substitute. If this is correct, such a feature would play a role in the derivation of *wh*-movement almost identical to that played by Case features in raising derivations. Recall that in an infinitival elementary tree, a nominative DP raises to the specifier of TP to check T's EPP feature, but its own Case feature remains unchecked. This Case feature then forces the adjoining of a finite raising auxiliary to the T′ below this subject. In the case of *wh*-movement, an analogous feature on the *wh*-phrase could be used to force the adjoining of an interrogative auxiliary tree to C′ below the *wh*-phrase. Following this analogy, I will use the term wh-*Case* to refer to this uninterpretable feature on the *wh*-phrase. As with the usual sort of Case features on DPs, I assume that *wh*-Case features are not checked by (*wh*-)EPP features; instead, being uninterpretable features, they must be checked by an interpretable feature. Here, I will assume that *wh*-Case is checked by the specification of interrogative force on C, which I will label [+$Q$] following Baker (1970). In the system I am proposing, then, there is a pair of features, one interpretable and one uninterpretable, on

both C and the *wh*-phrase, which check one another and which regu-
late the movement of *wh*-expressions.[24] To summarize briefly, my current assumptions concerning the features underlying *wh*-movement are as
follows:

(34) a. *Wh*-EPP features on C are checked by interpretable *wh*-features
        from DP.
     b. *Wh*-Case features on DP are checked by [+Q] features.
     c. [+Q] C must contain *wh*-EPP features, while [−Q] C may
        optionally contain *wh*-EPP features.
     d. DPs with *wh*-features contain *wh*-Case.

Let us return to the derivation underlying the elementary tree in (3).
The C here is [−Q], as *that* is lexically marked as an indicative complementizer. Consequently, *wh*-movement to the local specifier of CP, driven
by a *wh*-EPP feature (optionally) generated on C, cannot check the moved
*wh*-phrase's *wh*-Case feature.[25] Just as with a Case feature of the usual
sort, I assume that *wh*-Case features present in a specifier position percolate to the top feature set of their sister X′ node.

(35)

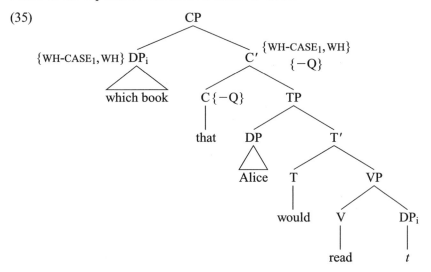

Since these *wh*-Case features are uninterpretable, a well-formed derivation involving this elementary tree must involve the adjoining at C′ of an
auxiliary tree with [+Q] features at its C′ root.

(36)

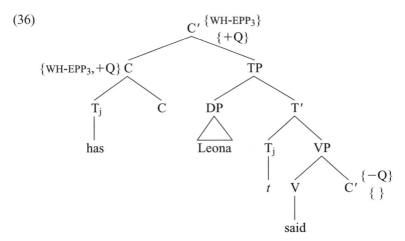

As was the case with T's EPP features, I assume that (*wh*-)EPP features on C percolate to the top feature set of C′, while other features on C (e.g., [+Q]), percolate to the bottom feature set. Now, when (36) is adjoined to the C′ of (35), the *wh*-EPP feature projected from the C head of (36) ends up in the same feature set as the *wh*-features projected by the *wh*-phrase in (35), thereby licensing checking and deletion of the *wh*-EPP features. Additionally, the *wh*-Case feature of the *wh*-phrase, projected to the top feature set of C′, ends up together with the [+Q] feature projected by the interrogative complementizer, allowing *wh*-Case to delete. The resulting structure is shown in (37).

(37)

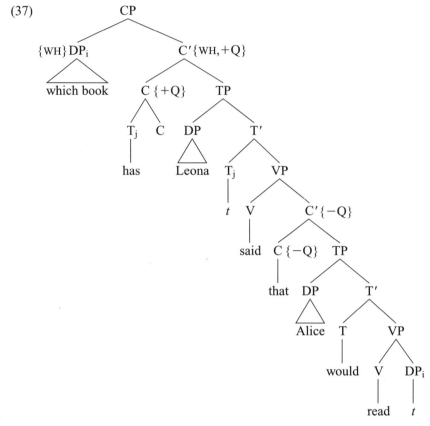

This structure has no unchecked uninterpretable features, meaning that it is convergent.

Contrast this derivation with a similar one, differing only in having a [+Q] complementizer in the elementary tree containing the *wh*-phrase. As noted above, such a complementizer will include a *wh*-EPP feature, forcing raising of a local *wh*-element. In this case, however, the [+Q] C will check *wh*-Case on the moved *wh*-element, leaving no unchecked features in the elementary tree. Thus, Adjoining should be generally impossible at the C′ node of such an elementary tree, as it would not serve to check any features, in violation of Greed. This allows us to explain the impossibility of examples like the following:

(38) *What do you wonder [John saw *t*]?

To generate this example, we would need to adjoin a C′ auxiliary tree headed by *wonder* between *what* and the [+Q] complementizer of the lower clause, selected by the matrix verb *wonder*.

(39)

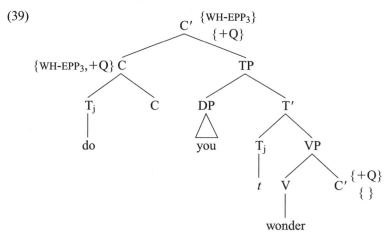

However, since *what*'s *wh*-Case feature, as well as C's *wh*-EPP feature, has already been checked in the lower clause's elementary tree, Greed blocks Adjoining. There is, however, an important caveat on this prohibition: if there were some other uninterpretable feature on the moved *wh*-phrase, then Greed would permit Adjoining to take place so long as it permitted this feature to be checked. The German *wh*-imperative construction studied by Reis and Rosengren (1992) is apparently just such a case.

(40) Wen sag mir, dass du  liebst!
     who tell me  that you love
     'Tell me who you love!'

Here, the *wh*-phrase *wen* 'who' raises out of its own interrogative clause, with the [+Q] complementizer selected by the verb *sagen* 'tell'.[26] To account for this possibility, we can assume, following Reis and Rosengren, that the elementary tree representing the subordinate clause in this example differs from the one in (35) in the presence of (uninterpretable) topic features on the *wh*-phrase.[27]

(41)

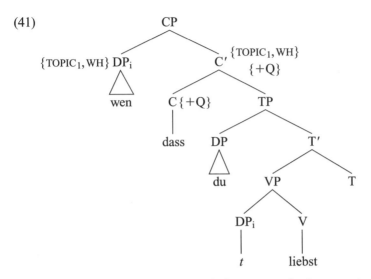

We will of course need to permit instances of *wh*-expressions that do not move to a specifier of CP within their elementary tree, not only to account for in-situ *wh*-questions in languages like Chinese, Japanese, and Malay, but also to analyze English multiple *wh*-questions. What should we conclude about the presence of *wh*-Case on such *wh*-elements? One possibility is that in-situ *wh*-elements include *wh*-Case features, but these features need not move to the specifier of CP in order to be checked. Following the assumptions made in chapter 4 concerning checking of Case and other nonselectional features, we should in fact expect that *wh*-Case can be checked under c-command by [+Q] within its elementary tree, or during Adjoining, when *wh*-Case features are projected to the top feature set of C′ within their elementary tree, following the discussion in section 4.6. Focusing on English multiple *wh*-questions, it is clear that this mechanism is inadequate, as it would permit only cases of multiple *wh*-questions in which all *wh*-expressions are clausemate arguments. The structural distance permitted between multiple *wh*-expressions appears to be unbounded, and indeed it is not subject to the usual sorts of locality restrictions constraining movement dependencies (Huang 1982, chap. 6).[28]

(42) a. Who remembers [why we bought what]?
　　 b. Who got jealous [because I talked to who]?
　　 c. Who thinks that [pictures of who] would please John?
　　 d. Who likes books [that criticize whom]?

Recall that in chapter 4, we achieved a slight extension in the domain in which nominative Case (and φ-) features could be checked (in Icelandic and Portuguese) by permitting the exceptional percolation of the features of a DP in the specifier of a deficient TP to the TP itself. Further, we saw that this characterizes precisely the domain over which nominative Case assignment and subject-verb agreement can obtain. However, an analogous extension would be inadequate to handle the cases given in (42). Yet, if we were instead to introduce additional machinery to handle the *wh*-in-situ cases, we would need to explain why such machinery does not apply in Case assignment and subject-verb agreement. This suggests, then, that we should try another path.

I will assume instead that in-situ *wh*-expressions lack *wh*-Case features and that neither they nor their features need to undergo any sort of movement or percolation during the derivation (Reinhart 1994; Cole and Hermon 1998). I assume, following Reinhart (1994, 1995), that such in-situ *wh*-expressions are interpreted via unselective binding of a choice function variable by an existential [+Q] operator, which I take to be expressed by an interrogative complementizer. This means that an in-situ *wh*-expression may form part of a coherently interpretable linguistic expression only if there is some [+Q] operator that takes scope over it. As [+Q] complementizers will, on my assumptions, necessarily include *wh*-EPP features, this means that there will also necessarily be some other *wh*-element in a higher specifier of CP, perhaps another *wh*-expression as in English multiple *wh*-questions, a *wh*-scope marker as in German partial movement constructions (McDaniel 1989), or an empty operator associated with the in-situ *wh*-phrase (Watanabe 1992; Aoun and Li 1993).

This proposal allows examples like (42) to be derived without difficulty, as the in-situ *wh*-elements need not include any uninterpretable features that require checking during the TAG portion of the derivation. For this solution to work, however, one problem remains to be resolved: at the point in the derivation at which the feature content of a *wh*-expression is determined, we will not know whether that expression will undergo movement or will remain in situ. To deal with this, I would like to suggest that it is sufficient to assume that *wh*-phrases (or more precisely the DP frontier nonterminals into which they substitute) may optionally be assigned *wh*-Case features. Thus, I revise (34d) in the following manner:

(43) DPs with *wh*-features may optionally contain *wh*-Case, while DPs without *wh*-features do not contain *wh*-Case.

To constrain the possibilities for overgeneration introduced here, I will also assume, following Chomsky (2000), that some uninterpretable feature, such as *wh*-Case, must be present on a *wh*-element in order for it to be visible to the Attract operation responsible for the checking of *wh*-EPP features.

Suppose now that, unlike the optional generation of *wh*-EPP features on [−Q] complementizers, the options of generating or not generating *wh*-Case features on a *wh*-element compete with one another in determining elementary tree well-formedness as determined by the MCP. This will imply that a *wh*-element generated in an elementary tree containing a [+Q] complementizer will always be generated with *wh*-Case features: this will allow the complementizer's *wh*-EPP features to be checked during the elementary tree derivation, along with the *wh*-element's *wh*-Case features.[29] Failure to generate *wh*-Case on the *wh*-element, in contrast, would yield an elementary tree with the *wh*-element in situ and the complementizer's *wh*-EPP feature unchecked, a structure with one more unchecked uninterpretable feature, and thus a structure dispreferred by the MCP.

In contrast, for *wh*-elements generated in elementary trees containing [−Q] complementizers, the latter lacking *wh*-EPP features, as in structures like (13), the MCP will always favor the absence of *wh*-Case. The *wh*-Case features would play no role in allowing *wh*-EPP features to be checked, as there are none present by hypothesis, and *wh*-Case would itself remain unchecked because of the absence of [+Q] features.[30]

The final case of a *wh*-element in an elementary tree with a [−Q] complementizer with *wh*-EPP features is somewhat more complex. *Wh*-Case features generated on such a *wh*-element would render this element visible to check C's *wh*-EPP feature. Yet, because C is [−Q], the *wh*-Case feature could not itself be checked. If *wh*-Case were not generated on this *wh*-element, however, C's *wh*-EPP feature would remain unchecked. In either case, a single uninterpretable feature would remain unchecked in the elementary tree, and therefore the MCP as it stands does not choose among these options. Given the discussion of example (16), we can see that this is not a satisfactory result. Failure to generate *wh*-Case on the *wh*-element would lead to the *wh*-element's not raising. This would produce an elementary tree like (17), giving rise to the generation of

Superiority-violating examples like (16). There are a number of ways around this difficulty, the most straightforward of which would make *wh*-EPP features more costly than *wh*-Case features for the purposes of the MCP. Let us tentatively assume this to be the case.

The analogy I have drawn between the T and C feature systems raises the question of whether there is an expletive element in the *wh*-domain that plays a role similar to that played by *it* or *there*. Such an expletive would check C's *wh*-EPP feature, thereby allowing a contentful *wh*-element to remain in situ. In fact, it has been been widely suggested that such *wh*-expletives do occur in a number of languages and constructions. Scope-marking elements like German *was* in partial *wh*-movement structures, as discussed in McDaniel 1989 and many subsequent works, can be taken to be the *wh*-expletive analogue to *it*, and the empty operator that Watanabe (1992) and Aoun and Li (1993) propose for Chinese and Japanese *wh*-in-situ structures can be viewed as the *wh*-expletive analogue to *there*. I leave the development of this analogy to future work, as it will require pursuing one of several possible refinements to the feature system underlying *wh*-movement that I have proposed.

## 5.5  Deriving Island Effects

As we have seen, *wh*-dependencies may span unbounded distances, and the TAG analysis I have proposed provides a way to produce such unbounded dependencies using iterated applications of Adjoining. There are nonetheless sharp restrictions on the sorts of structural boundaries that may intervene between a *wh*-element and its base position, syntactic domains that Ross (1967) famously refers to as islands. For example, *wh*-extraction may not proceed out of indirect questions (*wh*-islands), relative clauses, or "complex" NPs, each forming an island off of which syntactic movement may not venture.

(44)  a.  ?*What book did Mark ask [whom you had given *t*]?
      b.  ?*What book did you hear [the claim that Sofia wrote *t*]?
      c.   *What book did Karen meet the guy [who had written *t*]?

Beginning with the work of Chomsky (1964) and Ross (1967), various accounts have been proposed to explain why *wh*-movement is restricted precisely as it is. Virtually all of these accounts incorporate some sort of explicitly stipulated restrictions on the mechanism responsible for forming *wh*-dependencies. Since Ross's early suggestions, in which the various islands were accounted for with separate construction-specific constraints, subsequent theoretical developments have increased the abstractness and empirical coverage of the stipulated restriction(s) on movement. Chomsky (1977), for instance, shows how the ill-formedness of the examples in (44) follows from the principle of Subjacency.

(45) *Subjacency*

No rule can move an item from the position Y to the position X in the structure

X ... [$_\alpha$ ... [$_\beta$ ... Y ...] ...]

if $\alpha$ and $\beta$ are bounding nodes (TP and DP for English).

Subjacency blocks extraction from the *wh*-island in (44a) since the movement from the base position to the front of the clause crosses two bounding nodes: the TP boundaries of both the main and subordinate clauses.

(46) What book did [$_{TP}$ Mark ask whom [$_{TP}$ you had given *t*]]?

Extraction from the "complex NP" in (44b) is blocked since it crosses the DP and TP boundaries within the DP object, as well as the TP boundary of the matrix clause.

(47) What book did [$_{TP}$ you hear [$_{DP}$ the claim that [$_{TP}$ Sofia wrote *t*]]]?

Similarly, extraction from a relative clause in (44c) is ruled out since it crosses three bounding nodes: the TP boundary of the relative clause, the boundary of the DP inside which the relative is attached, and the TP boundary of the matrix clause.

(48) What book did [$_{TP}$ Karen meet [$_{DP}$ the guy who [$_{TP}$ had written *t*]]]?

On the face of it, Subjacency would also seem to rule out grammatical cases of long-distance extraction such as the one in (2), as the path from trace to *wh*-element crosses one TP node for each level of sentential embedding.

(49) Which book has [$_{TP}$ Leona said that [$_{TP}$ Alice would read *t*]]]?

To avoid this problem, Chomsky suggests that such examples are derived via a number of small movements, to the next higher COMP position (the specifier of CP in our terms).

(50)  Which book has [TP Leona said [CP *t* that [TP Alice would read *t*]]]?

As each of these successive-cyclic movements satisfies Subjacency, the apparent long-distance dependency is well formed. However, this sort of derivation is blocked in the cases in (44): in the *wh*-island and relative clause cases, the intervening specifier of CP position is filled by the other *wh*-element that has been fronted in the indirect question and relative clause, respectively. Furthermore, in both complex NP and relative clause islands, the unavailability of an intermediate specifier of CP landing site between the DP and the TP above it means that there is no way to avoid crossing these two bounding nodes during the derivation.[31]

The TAG analysis of *wh*-dependencies sketched in the previous sections does not permit anything analogous to successive-cyclic movement, since all instances of syntactic movement must take place within a single elementary tree. Consequently, there is no way to directly incorporate a locality principle like Subjacency into this framework. It is fortunate, therefore, that the TAG account of *wh*-movement has no need for any locality condition on movement at all, apart from the requirement that it take place within the elementary tree. Instead, as Kroch (1987, 1989b) demonstrates, the locality properties of *wh*-movement are derivable from the nature of the TAG combinatory operations coupled with independently motivated assumptions concerning the nature of elementary trees. In the remainder of this section, I review and extend Kroch's demonstration.

### 5.5.1  *Wh*-Islands
Let us turn first to the case of *wh*-island violations, as illustrated in (44a), repeated here.

(44)  a.  ?*What book did Mark ask [whom you had given *t*]?

Since both *wh*-expressions, *what book* and *whom*, are arguments of the verb *given*, the θ-Criterion requires that they both be generated in the same *given*-headed elementary tree. Given that all movement must be local to an elementary tree, this also means that both *wh*-elements must move to positions within this elementary tree. This means either that this CP must admit multiple specifiers, as in (51a), or that the CETM must tolerate recursive CP projections within a single elementary tree, each filled by a *wh*-element, as in (51b).[32]

(51) a.

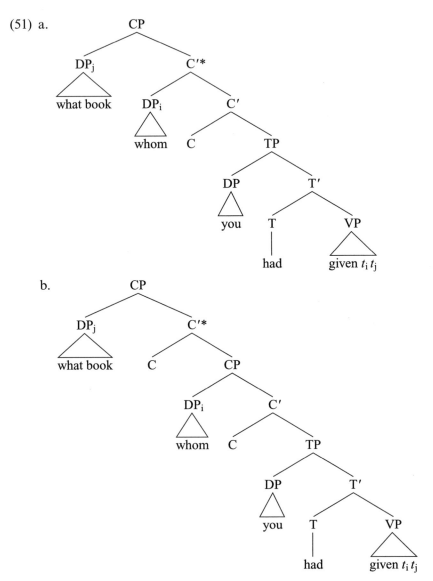

Given either of these trees, the TAG analysis of *wh*-movement can derive the *wh*-island-violating example by adjoining the auxiliary tree in (52) to the C′ node separating the two *wh*-elements, marked with a "*" in the elementary trees in (51).

(52)

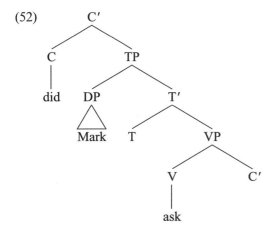

From the perspective of the TAG machinery, there is nothing wrong with this derivation. Consequently, the ill-formedness of the result must derive from some property of one of the elementary trees that we have exploited. Since a CP-recursive version of the auxiliary tree in (52) is needed to derive yes-no questions like (53), the problem must reside in whichever tree is chosen from those in (51).

(53) Did Mark ask whom you had given the book?

Kroch suggests that such elementary trees are ruled out because they contain two preposed *wh*-elements. This configuration is not permitted in monoclausal English questions, as seen in (54), and, Kroch argues, is not permitted in English elementary trees.

(54) a. *I wonder what book whom Mark gave.
     b. *I wonder whom what book Mark gave.

Kroch (1989b) observes that if this line of argument is correct, it predicts that languages that allow multiple *wh*-fronting in a single clause should license the presence of elementary trees like those in (51).[33] As a result, such languages should allow extraction out of *wh*-islands. Kroch notes that this prediction is confirmed by data from Romanian reported by Comorovski (1986). Comorovski points out that not only does Romanian allow multiple *wh*-elements to be fronted within a single clause, as shown in (55a), it also permits *wh*-extraction out of *wh*-islands, as shown in (55b).

(55) a. Cine$_i$ cui$_j$     ce$_k$   ziceai   că   $t_i$ i$_j$-a          promis   $t_k$ $t_j$?
        who  to whom what you say that    him.DAT-has promised
        'Who did you say promised what to whom?'

  b. Pentru care clauză$_i$    vrei        să afli    cine$_j$ $t_j$ nu a
     for     which paragraph you want to learn who     not has
     decis   încă ce$_k$   va    vota $t_k$ $t_i$?
     decided yet  what will vote
     'For which paragraph do you want to learn who has not decided
     yet what he will vote?'

Rudin (1988) argues that Bulgarian behaves similarly, allowing both
multiple *wh*-fronting and extraction from *wh*-islands.

(56) a.  Koj kogo  e vidjal?
         who whom is seen
         'Who saw whom?'
     b.  ?Koja ot tezi knigi$_i$ se    čudiš      koj znae  koj
         which of these books REFL wonder.2SG who knows who
         prodava $t_i$?
         sells
         'Which of these books you wonder who knows who sells?'

Guglielmo Cinque (personal communication) points out that this
analysis makes an even stronger prediction: a *wh*-phrase X should be
extractable out of an indirect question with *wh*-phrase Y in its CP specifier only if X may precede Y in a (monoclausal) multiple *wh*-question.
This follows for the simple reason that one of the elementary trees necessary for deriving the extraction of X from a *wh*-island with Y fronted,
will, like those in (51), include both of these *wh*-phrases at its front in
the order X Y. Following Kroch's hypothesis that the impossibility of a
particular multiple *wh*-configuration in a simple clause implies the impossibility of an elementary tree with that configuration, the conclusion
follows.[34] For this prediction to have interesting consequences, it is of
course necessary that there be restrictions on the ordering of multiple
*wh*-elements. As the Romanian examples in (57) and the Bulgarian
examples in (58) show, there are indeed such restrictions, at least in these
languages: subject *wh*-phrases must precede object *wh*-phrases.[35]

(57) a.  Cine despre ce    ți-a      vorbit?
         who about  what you-has told
         'Who told me about what?'
     b.  *Despre ce    cine ți-a      vorbit?
         about   what who you-has told

(58) a. Koj kakvo e    napisal?
who what   AUX wrote
'Who wrote what?'

b. *Kakvo koj e    napisal?
what   who AUX wrote

Given these patterns, we predict that Romanian should allow the extraction of *cine* 'who' out of an indirect question with *despre ce* 'about what' at its left periphery, but not vice versa. Similarly, Bulgarian should permit the extraction of *koj* 'who' out of an indirect question with *kakvo* 'what' at its periphery, but not vice versa. The following examples confirm these predictions:[36]

(59) a. Cine$_i$ ştii        [despre ce$_i$    $t_j$ i-a           povestit $t_i$]?
who  you know  about what   him.DAT-has told
'Who do you know what (he) has told him about?' (Carmen Dobrovie-Sorin, personal communication)

b. *Despre ce$_i$    ştii        [cine$_j$ $t_j$ i-a           povestit $t_i$]?
about   what you know  who    him.DAT-has told
'What do you know who told him about?'

(60) a. Koj$_i$ se    opitvat   da razberat [kogo$_j$ $t_i$ e    ubil    $t_j$]?
who REFL tried.3PL to find out  whom    AUX killed
'Who did they try to find out who (they) killed?'

b. *Kogo$_i$ se    opitvat  da razberat [koj$_j$ $t_j$ e    ubil    $t_i$]?
whom REFL tried.3PL to find out   who    AUX killed
'Whom did they try to find out who killed (them)?'

It turns out that in both Romanian and Bulgarian, the unacceptable orderings of *wh*-elements given in (57) and (58) can be rendered acceptable if the object *wh*-element has a D-linked interpretation. Thus, when the object is a *which* phrase, it may precede a *wh*-subject.

(61) a. Cine despre care    ţi-a      vorbit?
who about which you-has told
'Who told you about which one/what?' (Carmen Dobrovie-Sorin, personal communication)

b. Despre care   cine ţi-a      vorbit?
about   which who you-has told

(62) a. Koj   aftor   koja  kniga e    napisal?
which author which book AUX wrote
'Which author wrote which book?'

b. ?Koja kniga koj    aftor  e    napisal?
   which book  which author AUX wrote

Strikingly, in just such cases, the previously impossible extraction of the
object *wh*-phrase out of an indirect question is now well formed, just as
the TAG-based analysis predicts.[37]

(63) a.  Despre care$_i$ ştii        [cine$_j$ $t_j$ i-a         povestit $t_i$]?
         about  which you know who    him.DAT-has told
         'Which one do you know who told him about?'

   b.  ?Cine$_j$ ştii         [despre care$_i$  $t_j$ i-a        povestit $t_i$]?
       who  you know about which  him.DAT-has told
       'Who do you know which has told him about?' (Carmen
       Dobrovie-Sorin, personal communication)

(64) a.  Koj    kontinent$_i$ te  popita učitelja [koj$_j$ $t_j$ e    otkril      $t_i$]?
         which continent you asked teacher who   AUX discovered
         'Which continent did you ask the teacher who had discovered
         (it)?'

   b.  Koj    otkrivatel$_i$ te  popita učitelja [kakvo$_j$ $t_i$ e
       which explorer   you asked teacher what    AUX
       otkril      $t_j$]?
       discovered
       'Which explorer did you ask the teacher what (he) had
       discovered?'

Kroch (1989b) analyzes a pattern in English that bears a certain simi-
larity to the one we have just reviewed in Bulgarian and Romanian. As
Baltin (1986) notes, English permits topicalized, though not *wh*-moved,
PPs to extract freely from *wh*-islands.

(65) a.  After the party, I wonder [who will stay *e*].
   b.  *When do you wonder [who will stay *e*]?

(66) a.  ?On that shelf, I wonder how many books you can fit.
   b.  *On which shelf/Where do you wonder how many books you
       can fit?

Under the view of *wh*-movement we are pursuing, the derivation of the
well-formed cases will require an elementary tree of the following form,
in which both the PP and the *wh*-phrase have been fronted.[38]

(67)

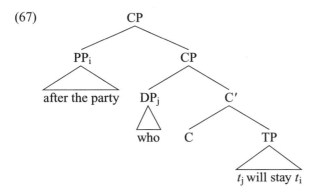

This elementary tree is virtually identical to the multiple *wh*-fronting structure in (51a), which, following Kroch, I suggested is impossible for English, but possible for Romanian and Bulgarian. Following the same line of reasoning as before, a structure like (67) must be licensed in the grammar of English, if we are to generate monoclausal sentences like the following, where a PP may be topicalized to a position immediately preceding a *wh*-element:

(68) a.   After the party, who will stay?
     b.   ?On that shelf, how many books can you fit?

Furthermore, the structure in (67) leads us to the correct prediction that both the PP and the *wh*-phrase could simultaneously be fronted, by adjoining a bridge-verb-headed auxiliary tree like (4) to the C′ node, producing examples like the following:[39]

(69) a.   After the party, who do you think will stay?
     b.   On that shelf, how many books do you think you can fit?

### 5.5.2  Complex NPs

Consider next the case of extraction from a complex NP, as in (44b), repeated here.

(44) b.   ?*What book did you hear [the claim that Sofia wrote *t*]?

Under the TAG conception of derivations I am assuming, instances of syntactic movement, including the one that creates a dependency between the base position of a *wh*-element and its surface position in the specifier of CP, must take place during the process of elementary tree formation, hence within a single elementary tree. Since the base position of the *wh*-

phrase in (44b) is the object of the verb *wrote*, the *wh*-dependency will be represented in the *wrote*-headed elementary tree shown in (70).

(70)

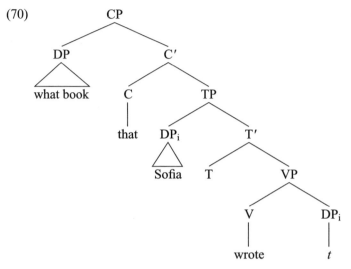

To derive (44b), we must adjoin a C′ auxiliary tree of the form in (71) at C′.

(71)

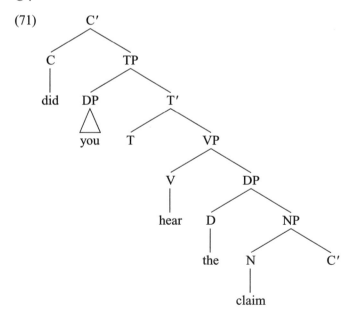

As this auxiliary tree includes both an extended projection of the verb *hear* and an extended projection of the noun *claim*, it must itself be derived from two separate elementary trees: a *hear*-headed C′ elementary tree with a DP complement nonterminal, and a *claim*-headed DP elementary tree with a C′ complement nonterminal.[40] Since neither of these is itself a C′ auxiliary tree, the derived structure cannot function as a C′ auxiliary tree: recall that TAG derivations must meet a local well-formedness condition, such that the possibility of combining two structures must be determined on the basis of the properties of the elementary trees underlying those structures.[41] Once again, we conclude that the TAG machinery, coupled with our constraints on elementary trees, makes it impossible to derive the anomalous example.

### 5.5.3 Relative Clauses

Let us turn next to the ill-formedness of extraction from relative clauses, illustrated in (44c), repeated here.

(44) c. *What book did Karen meet the guy [who had written *t*]?

As the base position of the moved *wh*-element is the object of *written*, movement must proceed to a specifier of CP position within *written*'s extended projection. There is a problem, however, since this position is already filled by the *wh*-element *who* moved from the subject position of this clause. Suppose for the moment that movement to an outer specifier of CP was possible, as shown in (72):

(72)

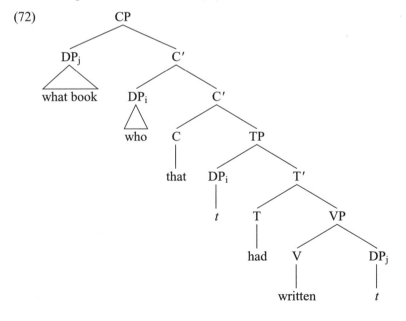

Now, to accomplish the fronting of *what book*, we must adjoin a structure like the one in (73) at the C′ node of this elementary tree.

(73)

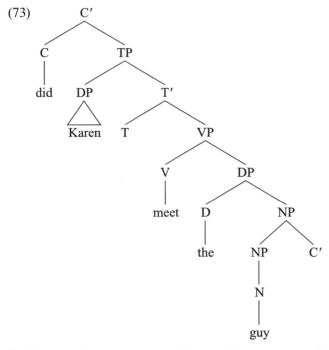

In this case, there are two problems with such an auxiliary tree. First, as
in the complex NP case, this auxiliary structure consists of two extended
projections and hence must itself be derived. Once again, neither of the
separate elementary structures would be a C′ auxiliary tree: the *meet*-
headed elementary tree is rooted in C′ but has a DP frontier nonterminal
node, and the *guy*-headed elementary tree is rooted in DP but has a
C′ frontier nonterminal node. Consequently, their combination could not
function as a C′ auxiliary. A second problem concerns the C′ frontier
nonterminal node in (73) representing the relative clause modifier. This
node, as a modifier, violates the θ-Criterion, as it is not assigned a θ-role
within this elementary tree.[42] Thus, once again, there is simply no TAG
derivation for the locality-violating example involving only well-formed
elementary trees.

### 5.5.4  Adverbial Modifiers
It is interesting to note that the TAG analysis, unlike the Subjacency
Condition, captures the islandhood of adverbial modifiers.

(74) *What did you fall asleep [because you were reading *t*]?

Subjacency does not rule out cases like (74), under standard assumptions, since *wh*-movement could move first through a specifier of CP position within the adjoined clause, crossing only one bounding node, and from there to the matrix specifier of CP, again crossing only one bounding node.

(75) What did [TP you fall asleep [CP *t* because [TP you were reading *t*]]]?

Under the TAG analysis, the base position of the *wh*-phrase is the object of *reading*, and hence *wh*-movement must take place within the extended projection of this verb. Supposing that *because* is a complementizer within *reading*'s extended projection, we are left with the elementary tree in (76).

(76)

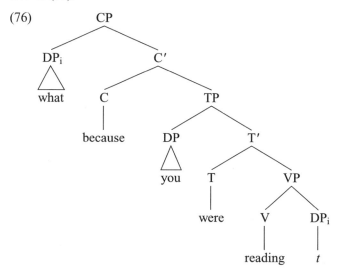

To form the example in (74), we must interpose a C' recursive structure like that in (77) containing the lexical material *did you fall asleep* between the *wh*-phrase and the remainder of its clause.

(77)

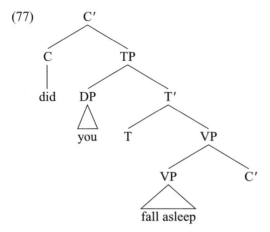

As in the case of extraction from relative clauses, this elementary tree violates the θ-Criterion, since it includes a C′ frontier nonterminal that is not assigned a θ-role (see note 42). Thus, under these structural assumptions, there is no TAG derivation for (74) involving only well-formed elementary trees.

Even if we analyze *because* not as the complementizer of the extended projection of *reading*, but as a distinct head—say, a preposition—that takes a CP complement, the derivation of (74) is still blocked, though for somewhat different reasons. Here, the *reading*-headed elementary tree would be as shown in (78).

(78)

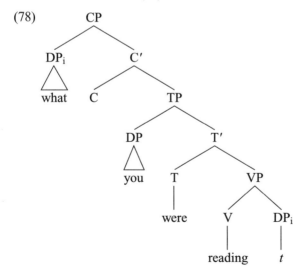

Now, to separate *what* from its clause, we would need to adjoin the auxiliary tree in (79).

(79)

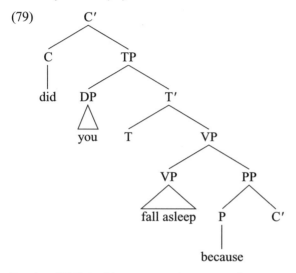

By the CETM, this structure is not an elementary tree, as it contains two extended projections, one verbal and one prepositional. Consequently, it must have been formed by some combinatory operation. Since the adverbial modifier is not assigned a θ-role by the verb *fall asleep*, there can be no frontier nonterminal within its tree into which the adverbial substitutes. Instead, the adverbial must head an auxiliary tree like that in (80a), which adjoins at the VP node of a C'-rooted elementary tree headed by *fall asleep*, shown in (80b).

(80) a.

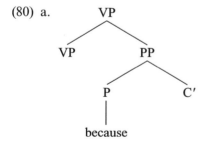

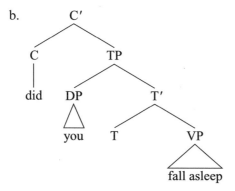

Now, although these two trees can combine to produce the structure in (79), this derived structure cannot function as a C′ auxiliary tree during the TAG derivation. Since neither of the trees in (80) is itself a C′ elementary tree, adjoining (79) into (78) violates the Markovian requirement on TAG derivations.

### 5.5.5 Subject Islands: A Case Apart

As is well known, extraction in English may not take place out of a sentential or DP subject.

(81) a. *I wonder which book [for me to read $t$] would upset Esther.
    b. *I wonder which book [a review of $t$] will be published in the next issue of *The New Republic*.

As with the case of adverbial modifiers discussed in the previous section, the ill-formedness of examples like (81a) does not follow from Subjacency.[43] For one could derive this example by first moving *which book* to the local specifier of CP, and then to the surface position, each movement crossing only one bounding node.

(82) *I wonder which book [$_{TP}$[$t$ for [$_{TP}$ me to read $t$]] would upset Esther].

To account for this other class of islands, Huang (1982) proposes his Condition on Extraction Domain (CED), according to which extraction may proceed only out of properly governed constituents. Since subjects are not properly governed, the CED blocks extraction out of these domains. Similarly, the CED blocks extraction from adverbial modifiers and from relative clauses, both of which, as adjuncts, are not properly governed. The CED does not entirely subsume Subjacency, however, as it provides no account for the islandhood of indirect questions or complex NPs: both are complements and therefore governed by the embedding head.

The TAG analysis proposed here cuts the cake a bit differently. As we have seen, it provides an account of the traditional subjacency cases (i.e., *wh*-islands, complex NPs, and relative clauses), adding to these the CED-violating extractions from adverbial modifiers. The TAG analysis does not fully subsume the CED, though, as it provides no explanation for the islandhood of subjects. To derive the embedded indirect question in (81a), we need only adjoin the auxiliary tree in (83a), with a C′ foot node in the specifier of TP, to the C′ node of the elementary tree in (83b).

(83) a.

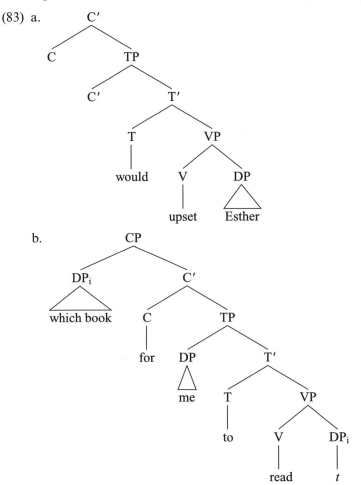

b.

Neither of these elementary trees violates any of the principles governing elementary trees that I have thus far proposed. In fact, the elementary tree in (83b) is identical to ones that are necessary for deriving grammatical extractions from sentential complements. Thus, if we are to rule out extraction from sentential subjects, it will be necessary to add some condition that rules out (83a) as a well-formed elementary tree.

Before turning to the content of such a condition, I want to point out that there is empirical support for the distinction that the TAG-based analysis makes between the island status of subjects and the island status of adverbial adjuncts, cases that are collapsed under the CED.[44] As noted perhaps first by Cinque (1978), and subsequently by many others, there exist languages (e.g., Japanese, Armenian, Hindi, and Turkish) in which *wh*-elements may be extracted from subjects. Even in these languages, however, extraction from adjuncts remains impossible. I take this asymmetry to suggest that separate factors must be involved in preventing extraction from subjects and adjuncts in a language like English. Moreover, the lack of variability in adjunct islandhood provides support for the TAG analysis, in which such extractions are blocked by fundamental properties of the TAG operations and elementary trees.

How, then, should we explain the impossibility of extraction from subjects? Kroch (1989b) proposes to rule out trees like (83a) by expanding the domain of application of the Empty Category Principle (ECP) to include not just traces of movement and base-generated empty categories like pro, but also foot nodes of auxiliary trees. According to the formulation given in Frank 1992, all empty nodes in Kroch's extended sense must be head governed.[45] If we assume that the specifier of TP is not a head-governed position, the C′ frontier nonterminal in that position in (83a) cannot function as a foot node. As a result, extraction from sentential subjects is blocked.

This idea is very similar to the Kayne's (1984, chap. 8) proposal to unify the ECP and the CED. As Kayne notes, this line of analysis provides a way of understanding the differences between languages that do or do not exhibit the Subject Condition. The Subject Condition obtains when the subject and object lie on opposite sides of the verb, as in SVO languages. When arguments lie either all to the left or all to the right of the verb, as in SOV and VOS languages, subjects behave like objects in permitting extraction.[46] Kayne suggests that this correlation derives from the fact that head government within a given language is restricted to one canonical direction, the subject being head governed only when it lies on the same side of its governor as the object.

By viewing the ECP as a condition on empty nodes in elementary trees, we also have a straightforward analysis of comp-trace effects.

(84) a. *Which book did Lenny say that *t* had just been published?
  b. *Who would Lenny have preferred for *t* to have married his daughter?

Under our assumptions concerning elementary trees, the derivation of an example like (84a) will involve an elementary tree of the form shown in (85).

(85)

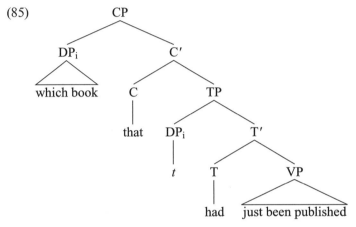

Given the presence of the comp-trace configuration within a single elementary tree, the ill-formedness of examples like (84a) and (84b) can be straightforwardly derived from the usual assumption that traces in subject positions are not head governed by *that*.[47] This account can be extended in a straightforward fashion to the *que/qui* alternation with French complementizers, with *qui* appearing just when it is required to govern a trace in the specifier of TP position of its own elementary tree.

Recent work has moved away from the idea that government and the ECP play a central role in the grammar, leading us to question the ECP-based account of sentential subjects I just outlined. One particularly appealing alternative explanation of the Subject Condition in the TAG context, suggested by Kulick (2000), makes crucial use of the idea that subjects are first merged into a VP-internal position and then moved to the specifier of TP. As noted earlier, an auxiliary tree that permits extraction from a sentential argument must have C′ foot and root nodes.

Kulick proposes that C's, as nonmaximal projections, understood here in an inherent sense, are invisible to the movement operation. Consequently, such a C', while capable of being merged into a thematic VP-internal position, cannot be moved to the specifier of TP, leading to the impossibility of the elementary tree in (83a) and the underivability of (82). In cases like (86), we are led to conclude that the sentential argument has not been extraposed from subject position, as suggested by Rosenbaum (1967), but is instead left in situ, the subject being filled by an *it* expletive.

(86) I wonder which book it would upset Esther for me to read.

To capture crosslinguistic differences in the presence or absence of the Subject Condition, we might follow Takahashi (1994) in assuming that the subjects of SOV and VOS languages need not leave their base positions (but see Stepanov 2000). As a result, auxiliary trees in such languages with apparent C' sentential subject frontier nonterminals would actually be like the auxiliary trees responsible for the derivation of (86) with C' within VP. Unlike the ECP proposal, this analysis does not extend to comp-trace effects. It is worth noting, however, that just about any account of the comp-trace effect and the Subject Condition that has been proposed outside the TAG context can be straightforwardly incorporated into a TAG context, often with considerable simplification, since they almost always come down to locally enforced constraints on well-formedness.

### 5.6 Long Movement

The discussion of island effects in the last section demonstrated how certain locality principles on movement, such as Subjacency, follow as a corollary from the TAG formalism's constrained mechanisms of structural composition coupled with independently motivated constraints on the form of elementary trees. There is, however, a significant problem with this derivation of locality, as pointed out by Kroch (1989b)—namely, that it works too well. As with proposals based on conditions like Subjacency and Shortest Move, the TAG analysis I have sketched fails to allow for a set of cases, commonly known as "long movement," in which movement takes place grammatically out of an island. One such example involves the extraction from a *wh*-island of a (D-linked) *wh*-phrase in verbal complement position.

(87)  Which car does Sally wonder how to fix?

Under our current assumptions, both *which car* and *how* will be generated in the lower clause's elementary tree (see note 12). Since movement, as we have conceived it, must take place within an elementary tree,
*which car* must therefore be fronted to the *fix*-headed elementary tree. As
noted earlier, English, unlike Romanian and Bulgarian, prohibits the
presence of multiple *wh*-elements (here, *which car* and *how*) within the CP
projection of a single elementary tree. Thus, there is no way to derive
(87).

   In order to generate examples like (87), then, we must relax some current assumption. One possibility, proposed by Cinque (1990), is that the
dependency involved in (87) is not derived from movement, but rather
involves the binding of a null pronominal variable by a *wh*-operator that
is base-generated in the specifier of CP of the main clause. Adapting
this idea into the TAG context, this means that we would no longer be
obliged to generate the fronted *wh*-element within the lower clause's elementary tree, as the internal argument role of *fix* is assigned to a DP
frontier nonterminal node (into which a null pronominal will substitute),
giving rise to the structure in (88).

(88)

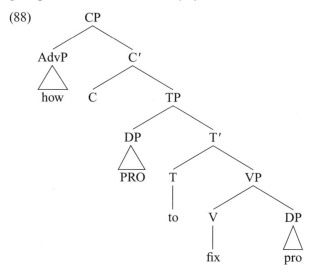

Instead, the *wh*-element appearing on the surface at the left periphery of
the matrix clause (or more precisely, a DP nonterminal node into which
a *wh*-element substitutes) is merged directly into the matrix specifier of

CP position during the derivation of the *wonder*-headed elementary tree shown in (89).

(89)

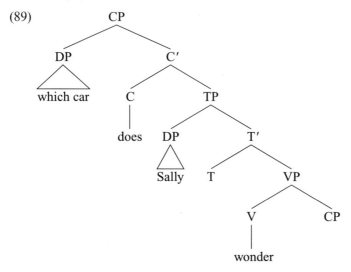

One might worry that the presence of such a DP in the specifier of CP position violates the θ-Criterion, as the DP is not assigned a θ-role. Recall, however, that we have reduced this half of the θ-Criterion to the requirement that Merge be associated with the satisfaction of some selectional requirement. Since the *wh*-expression checks the (selectional) *wh*-EPP features on the interrogative C in (89), this element is licensed within the elementary tree in a manner similar to that suggested above for *wh*-expletives and adjunct *wh*-phrases (see note 12). Using these two trees, the "long movement" example in (87) can now be generated by adjoining the CP-recursive tree in (89) to the root node of (88).

A serious problem remains, however, as this derivation fails to establish any linkage between the fronted *wh*-element and the in-situ pro. While this might be taken to be in the spirit of Cinque's proposal, such a linkage being established postsyntactically in the interpretive component, it leaves unexplained the sensitivity of this dependency to other islands. As Cinque notes, even *wh*-elements that are capable of undergoing grammatical long movement out of "weak" islands, such as indirect questions, nonetheless cannot extract out of "strong" islands, such as relative clauses or adjuncts.

(90) *Which car did Sally know a mechanic who could fix?

Under the assumption that island sensitivity reflects the operation of some syntactic process, the ungrammaticality of this example suggests that the syntactic derivation must play some role in establishing the *wh*-pro relation.

The analyses of *wh*-movement first proposed in Kroch 1987, 1989a, and further developed in Frank 1992 provide a possible means of establishing such a relation and in turn explaining the (limited) island sensitivity of long movement. These analyses make use of an extension to the TAG system, called *multicomponent TAG* (MC-TAG).[48] In MC-TAG, the basic objects of the derivation are not individual elementary trees, but (possibly singleton) sets of such trees, so-called multicomponent tree sets. At each step in an MC-TAG derivation, all of the trees in a multicomponent set must adjoin or substitute simultaneously into a single, as yet unaltered, elementary tree. Restricted in this way, MC-TAG can be shown to be identical to basic TAG in both weak and strong generative power (Weir 1988).[49]

The move to MC-TAG brings with it the expectation that the grammar should recognize two distinct types of locality domains for grammatical processes: the elementary tree and the multicomponent tree set. Let us continue to assume that movement is restricted to applying within a single elementary tree. We might imagine, however, that a syntactic process of establishing variable binding might apply over the broader domain of the tree set.[50] Of course, if the domain of a multicomponent tree set is to be restrictive, we will need to impose conditions on what kinds of elementary trees may be contained within a single tree set. I will adopt the idea, first explored by Bleam (2000), that the tree set as a whole is subject to the CETM, so that all of the components of a tree set must together form part of a single extended projection.

Returning to the *wh*-movement case, we can now represent the embedded clause as a tree set consisting of the pair of elementary trees shown in (91).

(91) DP$_i$

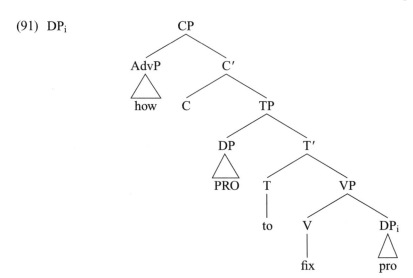

The first component of this tree set consists of a "degenerate" DP auxiliary tree, whose root and foot are the same node, while the second component is essentially identical to the elementary tree given in (88). This tree set satisfies the CETM since the degenerate auxiliary tree is not projected from a lexical head and therefore does not count as a distinct extended projection for the purposes of the CETM. For our purposes, the crucial property of this tree set is the dependency that holds across its two components, between the DP of the degenerate auxiliary tree and the in-situ pro, which I have represented via coindexing. I will take this dependency across members of a multicomponent tree set to be the structural representation of variable binding. In deriving (87), then, we can simultaneously insert these two components into the elementary tree in (89): the degenerate auxiliary tree adjoins to the DP node in the specifier of CP, while the CP-rooted elementary tree substitutes into the CP complement of *wonder*, to produce (92).[51]

(92)

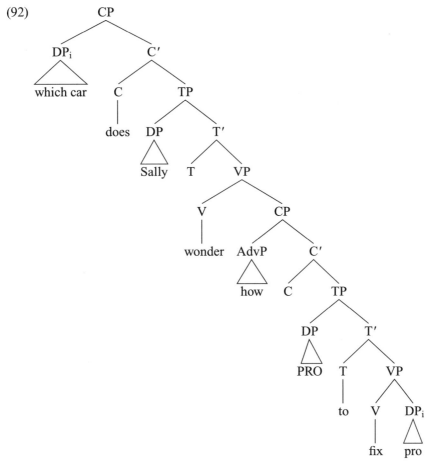

Although the adjoining of the degenerate auxiliary tree does not alter the structure of the embedded clause, it does establish a *wh*-pro dependency, as the DP node targeted by Adjoining inherits the index on the degenerate auxiliary tree. Since the establishment of binding relations requires c-command, we will need to ensure that the two structural composition operations take place in such a way as to yield the appropriate configuration. We can do this by imposing a c-command "link" between the degenerate auxiliary tree and pro, which has the effect of imposing the additional condition on the insertion of this tree set that the degenerate auxiliary tree must adjoin to a node that c-commands the node into which the CP tree in the tree set substitutes. It can be shown that such links add no formal power to the MC-TAG system.[52]

Of course, showing that the MC-TAG derivation can establish the *wh*-pro dependency is not enough. We must also demonstrate that it blocks the generation of illicit cases of long movement out of strong islands, as in (90).[53] On analogy with the derivation just sketched, we might imagine that such a sentence would be generated by adjoining the tree set in (93) into the main clause in (94) at the DP specifier and to the DP complement, respectively.[54]

(93) $DP_i$

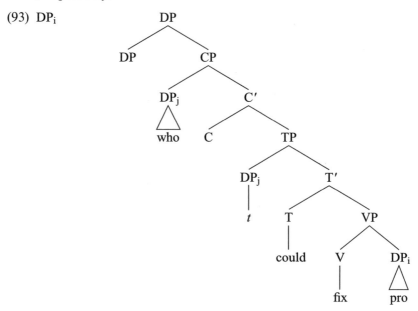

(94)

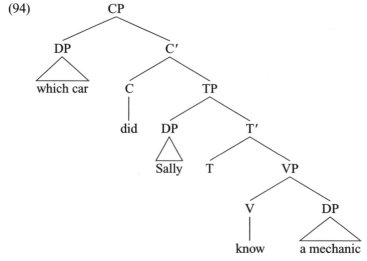

To block this derivation, I have elsewhere proposed a condition on the path connecting the coindexed elements in tree sets like (93) to the effect that it can pass through at most one extended projection (Frank 1992). Since the path in (93) passes both through the *fix*-headed verbal extended projection and through the DP extended projection at the root of this auxiliary tree, this tree set is ill formed, and hence (90) is correctly ruled out.[55]

A property of long movement that has received considerable attention is the distinction it draws between arguments and adjuncts. In contrast to the possibility of argument extraction, extraction of *wh*-adjuncts from even weak islands is impossible.

(95) *How$_i$ do you know [who fixed the car $t_i$]?

There is in fact a derivation very similar to the one I sketched for (87) that permits us to derive (95): namely, by simultaneously inserting the two components of the tree set in (96) into the elementary tree in (97) at CP and AdvP.

(96) AdvP$_i$

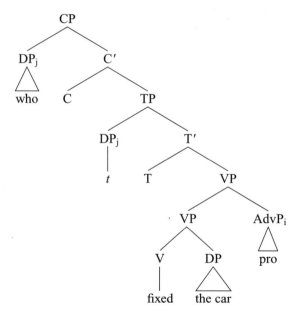

(97)

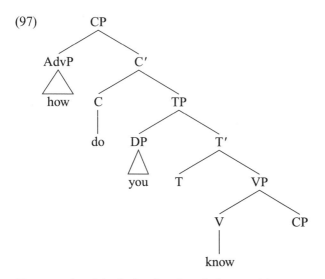

Fortunately, this derivation is ruled out without any additional assumptions, since one of the elementary trees in the set in (96) is ill formed. Specifically, the AdvP frontier nonterminal node (into which pro substitutes) in the second component of this tree set violates the θ-Criterion or its Merge-based equivalent, as it does not receive a θ-role or satisfy some selectional requirement.[56] Yet, if we fail to generate the adjunct pro within the embedded clause's elementary tree, there will be no way to adjoin both components of the tree set in (96) into a single elementary tree. Thus, there is no way for adjunct extraction to proceed using a multicomponent derivation, yielding the impossibility of extraction from weak islands.

It is interesting to observe that the analysis sketched here would seem to permit extraction not only from a single *wh*-island, but also from iterated *wh*-islands, as in (98).

(98) Which car$_i$ does Sally wonder who to ask how to fix $t_i$?

As noted by Cinque (1990), this is a welcome result, as the addition of *wh*-islands between the *wh*-element and its base position does not appear to degrade extraction, this example apparently being on a par with (87).[57] To derive this example, we would first adjoin a tree like that in (99) to the root node of the CP elementary tree in (91), and then insert the now derived multicomponent tree set into the main clause's elementary tree in (89).

(99)

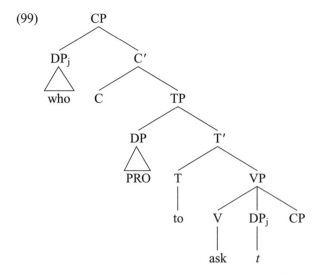

One potential hitch concerns the role of Greed in such a derivation, as it is not completely clear what feature is checked in the CP elementary tree in (91) when (99) is adjoined to its root node, or what element would be responsible for such checking. I put this issue aside for future investigation.

## 5.7  Long Movement from Nominals

As was discussed in the context of raising in section 3.5, the Adjoining-based approach to long-distance dependencies depends critically on the existence of recursion in the structural domain across which the dependency obtains. In cases of extraction from NP, however, such recursion is missing.

(100)  Which politician did you take a picture of?

Here, the base position of the *wh*-element is within a nominally headed DP extended projection, while the landing site is in the specifier of a verbally headed CP extended projection. Since these are extended projections of different types, there is no way to derive sentences like (100) with a simple application of Adjoining, as the structure that would need to be interposed could not have identical root and foot nodes. If we are to derive (100), then, we will need to make use of a different sort of derivation.

Kroch (1989b) and I (Frank 1992) have proposed that such examples be treated using the same MC-TAG machinery exploited in the long movement cases discussed in the last section. To derive (100), then, we will insert the multicomponent tree set in (101) into the elementary tree in (102), adjoining the degenerate DP auxiliary to the DP nonterminal in the specifier of CP and substituting the *picture*-headed DP into *take*'s complement position.[58]

(101) DP$_i$

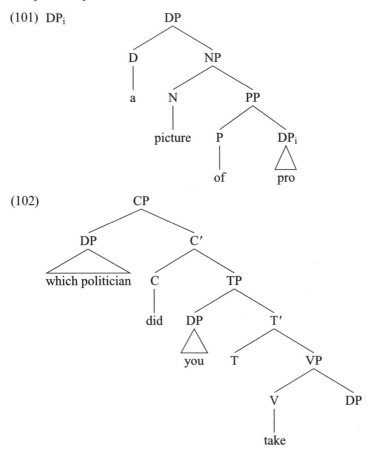

(102)

This treatment of extraction from NP as long movement contrasts with the proposal made by Stowell (1989), according to which such extractions are essentially an instance of successive-cyclic movement. Stowell suggests that the specifier of DP functions as an escape hatch for *wh*-movement in the same way that the specifier of CP does. As already noted, Stowell's suggestion cannot be transported into the TAG context, owing to the absence of recursive structure that can be adjoined. It is interesting to ask, then, whether there is any evidence bearing on the question of whether extraction from NP involves long or short movement. Frank and Kroch (1994) suggest that data concerning scopal interpretation provide just this sort of evidence and that this evidence argues in favor of the TAG long movement view of extraction from NP. In the remainder of this section, I review this evidence.

Cinque (1990) points out that in sentences like (103), the *wh*-amount quantifier (AQ) *how many* can have at least two interpretations in cases of successive-cyclic extraction.

(103)  How many books did they decide [to publish *t* this fall]?

Under the predominant reading, only a number is at issue, and no preexisting set of books is presupposed by the questioner. An appropriate answer for this interpretation might be "At most three, but they haven't chosen them yet." Another possible interpretation involves a set of books whose existence is presupposed by the questioner, who is asking which among these they have decided to publish. In this case, an appropriate answer could be of the form "Three: they are *Anna Karenina*, *The Unbearable Lightness of Being*, and *Call It Sleep*." Cinque labels these readings, respectively, the *quantificational* and *referential* interpretations of the AQ. In cases of extraction from weak islands, the range of interpretive possibilities for the AQ shrinks.

(104)  How many books did they decide [whether to publish *t* this fall]?

Here, the only available interpretation is the referential one, with a presupposed preexisting set of books.

Following Longobardi (1990), Cinque suggests that the interpretive difference between (103) and (104) derives from the presence of an intermediate trace position in one case and its absence in the other. For Cinque, the intermediate trace is necessary for establishing the chain of antecedent government relations between the AQ and its base position that is required for quantificational interpretation. Under the referential reading, on the other hand, no such sequence of antecedent government relations is needed, as the pro in the base position, a referential element, may be identified via binding, an option that is unavailable in the case of a nonreferential trace.[59] Though Cinque's proposal cannot be translated directly into the TAG context, owing to the absence of intermediate traces, it is nonetheless possible to maintain his intuition that the presence of pro is linked to the referential interpretation, while the presence of a *wh*-trace is linked to quantificational interpretation. Specifically, we can take derivations involving pro-variable-binding MC-TAG tree sets to be associated with referential interpretations of the AQ, while simple cases of elementary-tree-internal *wh*-dependencies, which are separated via simple Adjoining, will lead to the quantificational interpretation.[60]

As Frank and Kroch (1994) note, we can apply this interpretive diagnostic to the case of extraction from NP. They observe that when contrasted with the corresponding bridge verb cases like those in (105), extractions from nominal complements like those in (106) exhibit the same limited range of interpretations seen in extraction from *wh*-islands; that is, they allow only the referential interpretation.

(105) a. How many cities did they plan [to attack *t*]?
      b. How many rebels did the dictator insist on [capturing *t*]?

(106) a. How many cities did they make [a plan to attack *t*]?
      b. How many rebels did the dictator insist on [the capture of *t*]?

On this basis, we can conclude that extraction from NP involves long movement.

Cinque (1990, 12) cites Longobardi (1990) as identifying a similar interpretive contrast between long and short movement. For the Italian example in (107), where extraction takes place from the complement to a bridge verb, the fronted AQ may take scope either inside or outside the universal quantifier in embedded subject position.

(107) Quanti      pazienti pensi        che ognuno dei    medici
      How many patients do you think that each     of the doctors
      riesca     a  visitare in un'ora?
      manages to visit     in one hour?

Under the interpretation in which the AQ *quanti pazienti* 'how many patients' takes scope inside the universal quantifier, (107) is interpreted as a "family of questions" requiring an answer of the form "Dr. Spock is able to visit four patients, Dr. Kildare three patients, and Dr. Zhivago twenty-two patients." When the AQ takes wide scope, in contrast, an answer would need to specify the set of patients who are such that each of the doctors could visit them in one hour. As before, when long movement takes place, only the wide scope interpretation is possible.

(108) a. Quanti      pazienti ti chiedevi        come ognuno dei
         How many patients did you wonder how   each    of the
         medici  riuscisse a  visitare in un'ora?
         doctors managed to visit     in one hour?

  b. Quanti      pazienti ti lamenti      che ognuno dei    medici
     How many patients do you regret that each    of the doctors
     sia riuscito a  visitare in un'ora?
     managed   to visit    in one hour?

The family-of-questions reading is completely absent in these cases, and
the answer must instead be of the form "Three patients: Alice, Tom, and
Sue." Interestingly for the current discussion, Longobardi (1990, 90) also
notes that extraction from NP patterns with the cases of long movement
in (108) in its interpretive properties. Thus, in the following Italian and
English pairs, extraction from the nominal complement position permits
only the wide scope interpretation for the AQ, while extraction from the
verbal complement permits either scope (Raffaella Zanuttini, personal
communication).

(109) a. Di quanti      studenti consigli           la   presentazione
         Of how many students do you recommend the introduction
         ad ogni nuovo professore?
         to each new    professor?
      b. Quanti      studenti consigli           di presentare ad ogni
         How many students do you recommend to introduce  to each
         nuovo professore?
         new    professor?

(110) a. How many patients did they hear every doctor's description of?
      b. How many patients did they hear every doctor describe?

Once again, we find evidence supporting the implication of the TAG
analysis that the lack of recursion in extraction from NP implicates a
long movement derivation.

# Chapter 6

# Looking Onward

In this book, I have explored certain consequences that result from incorporating the TAG operations for structural composition into the architecture of syntactic derivations. My aim has been to give a sense of the explanatory possibilities that the TAG system offers. Inevitably, I have had to limit the scope of the discussion. Considerable work remains, of course, to explore in the TAG context the myriad syntactic phenomena not touched on here, but I must leave such explorations for another time. Similarly, my discussion of elementary tree derivations has also been limited in another respect, namely, that it has adhered largely to the mechanisms and vocabulary of Chomsky's Minimalist Program. There is no doubt that it would be useful and productive to carry out a similar study under a different conception of grammatical structure and derivation, such as those developed in LFG or Relational Grammar. Again regrettably, I must leave such an undertaking for another day.

In the remaining pages, I would like to raise two open issues, more in the interest of calling attention to them as areas for future work than in the hope of resolving them. The first issue is empirical and concerns a class of phenomena exhibiting dependency structures that cannot be expressed with the TAG mechanisms. The second issue is more conceptual and relates to the question of interfaces in the derivational architecture we have been exploring.

## 6.1 Difficult Dependencies

In the previous chapters, I have explored the consequences of using the TAG Adjoining operation for producing two types of dependencies that are traditionally derived via a movement operation: raising and *wh*-movement. As I noted in chapter 2, there are some traditionally movement-derived dependencies (e.g., those formed via the movement of a head) that have a more local character. I suggested that these dependencies are indeed derived via a movement operation, albeit one that can be safely confined to the domain of a single elementary tree. From this, I concluded that such local dependencies should not interact in any interesting way with the Adjoining operation. It turns out, however, that such interactions cannot be avoided when one considers the interaction between such local movements and other nonlocal dependencies.

Consider for example the sentence in (1), which exhibits both verb movement to C, a process I have taken to be elementary tree bounded, and subject raising, the derivation of which I have taken to crucially involve Adjoining.

(1) Does Gabriel seem to like gnocchi?

Under the analysis proposed in chapter 3, the raising predicate *seem* heads a T' auxiliary tree, which adjoins between the subject of the lower clause, *Gabriel*, and the lower inflectional element *to*. If we assume that the auxiliary verb *does*, which is raised to C, is part of the same elementary tree headed by *seem*, Adjoining no longer provides a way of "raising" the subject into the matrix clause in this case. That is, while adjoining at T' can separate *Gabriel* from *to like*, it cannot introduce the kind of interleaving necessary to derive (1). As Harley and Kulick (1998) point out, this problem is not simply a peculiarity of English subject-aux inversion but arises in all cases of subject-to-subject raising in a VSO language like Irish.

In Frank 1992, I suggested a possible solution to the problem just sketched, exploiting the multicomponent extension to TAG discussed in chapter 5. I proposed that the extended projection headed by the raising verb be spread out over the components of a multicomponent tree set, as in (2), so that the auxiliary verb attached to a C head is in a distinct elementary tree from the one projected by the raising predicate, which projects only as high as T'.

(2)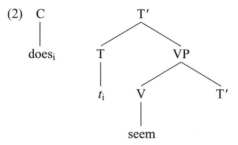

Example (1) can now be generated by inserting the two halves of this tree set into an infinitival elementary tree as in (3) projecting as high as C′, substituting the auxiliary verb into C and adjoining the raising predicate at T′.

(3)

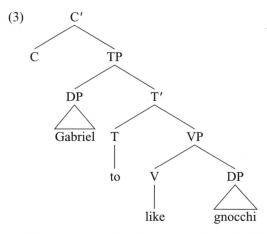

This analysis suffers from a number of difficulties, however. First of all, it relaxes the locality requirement on head movement, allowing it to take place across elementary trees of the same multicomponent set. This runs counter to the suggestion I made in chapter 5 that movement dependencies, though not variable binding, are subject to strict elementary tree locality. Even putting this issue aside, Kulick (2000) points out a more serious shortcoming of this multicomponent analysis: it is unable to generate the full range of cases so long as we respect the tree locality requirement on multicomponent combination, which requires all members of a multicomponent tree set to adjoin or substitute into the same underived elementary tree. This shortcoming arises with examples like (4), in which a PP experiencer argument to an intermediate raising verb has been fronted.

(4) To whom$_i$ was the CIA likely to have appeared $t_i$ to have been involved?

As before, the extended projection of the matrix raising predicate must be split across two elementary trees of a multicomponent tree set, along the lines of (2). Note as well that the extended projection of the intermediate raising predicate *appeared* must be spread across two elementary trees in a multicomponent tree set, this time to allow for the separation of the *wh*-moved dative PP from the lower raising predicate.

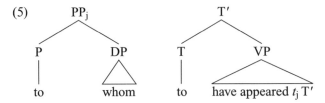

(5)

Given these trees, there are two ways we might go about generating (4). We might first try to combine the tree set in (5) with the one from the matrix clause, essentially like the one in (2). Observe, however, that neither of these multicomponent tree sets may be completely embedded into any single elementary tree contained in the other. Instead, the only possible combination is to adjoin one of the T′ auxiliary trees—say, that from the matrix clause's tree set—into the T′ auxiliary tree from the other set, producing a derived multicomponent tree set with three components, as shown in (6).

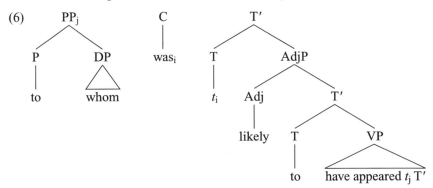

(6)

Example (4) can now be produced by combining this multicomponent tree set with an elementary tree headed by the most embedded predicate *involved*, substituting into PP and C and adjoining at T′.

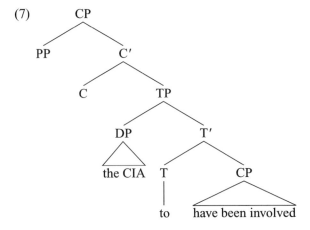

(7)

This derivation violates the tree locality requirement on multicomponent combinations, however. Pieces of the matrix clause's multicomponent tree set are combined into distinct elementary trees: the T′ auxiliary is adjoined into the T′ auxiliary tree from the middle clause's tree set, while the C-rooted tree that houses the auxiliary verb is substituted into the elementary tree headed by the embedded clause. Consequently, this derivation is ruled out. As an alternative, we might try to insert each of the multicomponent tree sets separately into the embedded clause's elementary tree in (7). Although each of these tree sets may embed completely into this elementary tree, this derivation will nonetheless violate the tree locality requirement, since only the first such combination will insert a multicomponent set into an underived elementary tree. Thus, the MC-TAG analysis cannot account for the possibility of cases like (4).

A similar problem arises in the phenomenon of Romance clitic climbing, exemplified in the following Italian sentence:

(8) Gabriele li     vuole mangiare.
    Gabriel  them wants to eat
    'Gabriel wants to eat them.'

If we assume that the pronominal object clitic *li* (or a node into which it substitutes) is generated as part of the same elementary tree as the verb *mangiare* 'eat', which assigns it a θ-role, Adjoining does not offer a means of combining the two clauses in this case, as it cannot achieve the necessary interleaving of elements from the matrix and embedded clauses. Bleam (2000) advocates a multicomponent analysis of clitic climbing, in which the clitic head is in a different component of a multicomponent tree set from its thematically licensing verb.

(9)

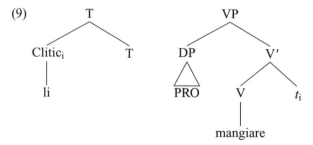

To derive (8), these two components adjoin and substitute into the matrix clause's elementary tree, at T and VP, respectively.

(10)

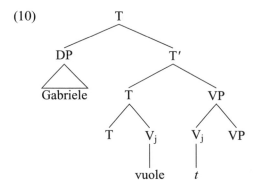

Just as in the raising case, however, a broader range of cases reveals a conflict with the elementary tree locality requirement of multicomponent tree combination. Thus, as Bleam (2000) argues, there is no way to generalize this analysis to generate cases like the following Spanish example, in which clitics raise from both the intermediate and embedded clauses:

(11)  Mari te lo    quiere permitir   ver.
      Mari you-it wants  to permit to see
      'Mari wants to let you see it.'

This is impossible for the same reason as the raising case: neither of the multicomponent tree sets representing the two embedded complement clauses can combine into a single elementary tree in the other multicomponent tree set.

   Finally, the same analytic difficulty arises in the context of scrambling, attested in languages such as German and Japanese. Once again, although an MC-TAG analysis can handle a considerable range of cases, the tree locality restriction we are assuming blocks the generation of certain more complex example types, which are nonetheless grammatical, as Rambow (1994) argues extensively. I will not go into these examples here; for details, see Rambow's discussion.

   The question we must address, then, is how to remedy the apparent insufficiency of the TAG model so that it can generate the types of dependencies seen in the examples above. Both Bleam (2000) and Rambow (1994) suggest a move to derivational systems whose formal power is considerably greater than that of TAG. Bleam advocates a version of MC-TAG that relaxes the tree locality requirement to one requiring only that all members of a multicomponent set combine with the members of some other set. Though this may be adequate to handle Bleam's clitic-climbing cases (though see Kulick 2000 for discussion), it fails to account for either the raising cases like (4) or the instances of scrambling discussed by Rambow (1994). Rambow advocates a variant of MC-TAG that is even less constrained than Bleam's set local version, arguing that such a system is necessary to generate the full range of scrambling cases.[1]

Such suggestions run against the spirit of the approach taken in this book, however; for at the same time that the power of the derivational architecture is increased, so too is the restrictiveness of the system decreased. This has the result that many of the empirical consequences of the TAG derivational architecture's restrictiveness are lost. In Rambow's proposed system, for instance, locality constraints are no longer derivable from properties of the elementary trees coupled with the nature of Adjoining; instead, they must be explicitly stipulated.

In seeking an extension or modification of TAG capable of capturing the phenomena just discussed, then, I take it to be crucial that the restrictiveness of TAG be maintained. Though I will not argue in favor of any particular alternative, I will mention two different revisions to TAG having this character. The approach suggested by Frank, Kulick, and Vijay-Shanker (2000) reconceptualizes TAG elementary trees as sets of c-command relations (see Frank and Vijay-Shanker 2001) and characterizes the formalism's combinatory operations in terms of monotonic combinations of such relations. As noted in Frank, Kulick, and Vijay-Shanker 2000 (see also Kulick, Frank, and Vijay-Shanker 2000), this system permits analyses for the phenomena discussed in this section, while retaining the ability to derive locality effects like that discussed here. A second possibility is proposed by Kulick (2000), who introduces a formalism called Segmented TAG, according to which Adjoining not only permits the insertion of one elementary tree inside another, but also allows the structure of one to collapse with that of another. Like the monotonic c-command proposal, Segmented TAG also retains an elegant explanation for locality phenomena like that discussed in previous chapters.

## 6.2  Interface Issues

In developing a TAG-based derivational architecture, I have drawn a great deal on ideas from work in the Minimalist Program, most notably the view that features are the driving force for movement, notions of derivational economy and full interpretation, and the like. Yet I have said very little about one of the central issues in the Minimalist Program, namely, the nature of the interfaces between the grammatical derivation and the systems for articulatory/perceptual and conceptual/intentional interpretation. In this final section, I would like to speculate on ways to address this issue.

In the framework I have developed, the phrase marker that results from a syntactic derivation corresponds to something like an S-Structure representation in Chomsky's (1981) Government and Binding framework. In Chomsky's (1993, 1995) minimalist framework, however, such a structure does not constitute a level of representation; instead, it is distinguished only by the fact that it is the input to the Spell-Out operation, which splits the representation in two, one piece being sent off for phonological interpretation, the other continuing on as the target of derivational operations. Since the construction of such a surface phrase marker marks the conclusion of the TAG derivation as I have conceived of it, one immediate implication of the current conception of derivations is that there is no place for the application of post-Spell-Out operations. We are led, therefore, to reject the idea of covert or LF movement.[2] This means that we must assume that the interpretive effects that have been assumed to derive from such movements result instead either from the mechanisms for semantic interpretation (as in, e.g., Cooper 1983) or from previously unobserved instances of overt (i.e., pre-Spell-Out) movement (as in, e.g., Groat and O'Neil 1996, Kayne 1998).

Even in the absence of such LF movement, this discussion leaves open the question of what constitutes the PF and LF interface levels. One natural possibility is that the phrase marker produced by the TAG derivation is the interface for both phonological and semantic interpretation, essentially following Groat and O'Neil (1996). That is, at the conclusion of the derivation, Spell-Out applies to provide interface representations for both the articulatory/perceptual and conceptual/intentional interfaces. There are a number of potential problems for such an approach, however. As noted in previous chapters (e.g., section 3.4.2), the absence of intermediate traces in the derived representations eliminates the possibility of recovering certain interpretive relations, such as scope and referential dependency, from the derived phrase markers. Though I will not be able to justify this claim here, I take it to be the case that the TAG derivation structure, which encodes the sequence of derivational steps taken to produce the derived structure, is sufficiently richly articulated to support the recovery of interpretations. Note that the idea that a derivational history serves as the interface to semantic interpretation is not a new one: it is the same proposal made by Chomsky (1955) with reference to the T-marker. The possibility I am suggesting here, then, is to return to that model not only in its use of kernel sentences (now elementary trees), but also in its assumptions concerning the interpretive interface.[3]

As noted in chapter 1, a single complex phrase marker will sometimes be derivable with multiple TAG derivations, meaning that there will be multiple derivation structures. If derivation structures are the locus of semantic interpretation, we might expect that there will be cases of multiple interpretations corresponding to ambiguity that is purely derivational and not structural.[4] One particularly compelling case of such ambiguity concerns examples like the following, which permits both idiomatic and nonidiomatic interpretations:

(12) Mark let the cat out of the bag.

A number of syntactic diagnostics suggest that both idiomatic and nonidiomatic interpretations are associated with the same phrase marker. However, following Abeillé and Schabes (1989), we can express the existence of this ambiguity in a straightforward fashion at the level of derivation structure. Specifically, we might assume the existence of both a standard elementary tree headed by *let* and an idiomatic elementary tree that includes all of the lexical material associated with the idiom.[5] The two derivations of this example would make use of different elementary trees and different derivational operations; the literal derivation would involve substitution of all arguments, while the idiomatic derivation would involve substitution of the subject alone.

Even if the structure of the TAG derivation is sufficient for determining a sentence's interpretation, it is interesting to note that certain aspects of interpretation can be fixed prior to the point at which an elementary tree enters into the TAG portion of the derivation. For instance, the scopal possibilities between elements within a single elementary tree are unaffected by the adjoining of additional structure. Thus, if an object quantifier may take scope over a subject in a simple clause, it may also do so if a raising auxiliary is adjoined between the two, as in (13). Likewise, as seen in (14), if a subject quantifier may take scope over a fronted *wh*-phrase, it may continue to do so even if a clause is adjoined between them.

(13) a. A translator was assigned to each visiting diplomat.
     b. A translator seems to have been assigned to each visiting
        diplomat.

(14) a. Which woman does every man love?
     b. Which woman do you think every man loves?

A similar point can be made concerning θ-role assignment: since elementary trees include positions for all of the arguments of a lexical head, the θ-roles assigned by that head can be determined at the level of the elementary tree. For aspects of interpretation such as these, then, it is natural to think of an interpretation process that applies cyclically during the derivation whenever an elementary tree is completed.

Of course, there remains a substantial part of semantic interpretation that requires reference to structure outside the bounds of a single elementary tree. Quite clearly, the scopal relation between elements in distinct elementary trees cannot be specified until after the TAG structural composition operations that link them have applied. And although a head can assign its θ-roles to the frontier nonterminals within its elementary tree, such θ-roles can be linked to the extended projections of other heads only after elementary trees have been combined. Further, the determination of referential dependencies must make crucial reference to aspects of syntactic structure that are not available within a single elementary tree domain.[6] Conceiving of semantic interpretation as a derivational process, these aspects of interpretation might be computed in parallel with the TAG derivation. As Kallmeyer and Joshi (1999, to appear) show, this can be done by associating with each syntactic operation during the TAG derivation a corresponding interpretive operation that composes the elementary tree interpretations in a well-defined fashion. Kallmeyer and Joshi explore the problems of computing predicate-argument and scopal relations; they also consider how the tight linkage between the syntactic and semantic computations might be exploited to rule out certain syntactic derivations that give rise to semantically incoherent results, as well as to block certain scopal interpretations, since they require a derivation violating the TAG-based restrictions on derivational locality. However, this work leaves open the problem of derivationally computing anaphoric dependencies.

Continuing along this line, let us consider finally the possibility that there is a PF analogue of the cyclic process of semantic interpretation. On such a view, (at least some aspects of) the phonological interpretation of elementary tree domains would take place as soon as an elementary tree is complete. On the empirical side, this would lead us to expect phonological/prosodic phenomena that are computed over elementary tree domains and that are insensitive to the insertion of additional structure via Adjoining or Substitution. In fact, Feng (1995, 1996) argues that this is precisely what is going on in the assignment of phrasal stress in classical and modern Chinese. Moreover, Feng (2000) shows how the assumption that prosodic structure is assigned to elementary trees provides an elegant account of the influence of prosodic constraints on syntax in the case of the Chinese *ba* construction. Note that in its most radical version, this proposal amounts to the assumption that Spell-Out applies to elementary trees. If this is on the right track, we might conclude that the objects manipulated by the TAG derivation are themselves PF representations, rather than pieces of syntax as I have assumed throughout. Since PF representations are characterized by different sorts of structural properties than traditional phrase markers, we will need to rethink the nature of the operations for structural composition that take place during the TAG part of the derivation. Moreover, it is not clear how to carry over the lines of argument I have pursued in this book in such a different representational context. Future work will reveal whether and how these lines of thought can be brought together.

# Notes

## Chapter 1

1. As has been pointed out, it is not completely clear whether the difference between representationally and derivationally oriented grammars is one of perspective or whether it is more substantial. It is often the case that the force of a set of well-formedness constraints on linguistic expressions can be instantiated in a derivational procedure, and vice versa.

2. If one views context-free rewriting as an operation that combines trees of depth one (i.e., the structural context specified by a single rewrite rule) via Substitution, it is perhaps more proper to take the basis to be the set of such depth one trees. Thus, for the set of rewrite rules in (i), we would have the basis in (ii).

(i) S → NP VP
    NP → Daniel
    NP → Gabriel
    VP → V NP
    V → admires

(ii)
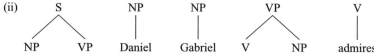

3. Since the phrase structure rules generating the kernel structures are nonrecursive, the set of possible kernel structures is guaranteed to be finite. Consequently, one could in principle take the set of kernel structures to constitute the basis of the grammar.

4. In this theory, even the derivation of simple sentences required the application of certain transformational operations, called the obligatory transformations. In the derivation of complex sentences, the application of these transformations was interleaved with the application of other singular and generalized transformations, as specified by some extrinsically imposed ordering on the transformations.

5. One might object that the application of Passive to the matrix after the insertion of the embedded clause in the derivation of (1) contradicts the assertion that Passive is in fact such an early transformation. In fact, this sort of complexity

raises problems for one of Chomsky's formal conditions on the derivational history or *T-marker*, his condition 5 (p. 394), since it does not allow Passive to apply at a unique place along a path through the T-marker. There is nonetheless a sense in which Passive is still applying to an unexpanded structure, as it must apply to a structure S prior to S's being embedded within some other structure T. This constraint is reformulated in the cyclic conception of derivations to which we turn shortly. As we will see, the use of the TAG Adjoining operation as a mechanism for structural composition allows us to avoid the interleaving of singular and generalized transformations entirely.

6. Fillmore's own response to these observations was to construct a derivational architecture in which this lack of such orderings follows from the nature of the derivations. See Fillmore 1963 for further details, and Bach 1977 for illuminating discussion.

7. Such locality conditions are also needed in the Chomsky 1955 model, since it allows singular transformations to apply to complex structures to form dependencies of arbitrary depth.

8. Even with this strengthened structural composition machinery, there remains a residue of transformational effects that are handled through the transformation of lexical specifications, as in LFG.

9. Though this statement is literally true, there is a sense in which such an intermediate-level structure does exist in LFG (as well as CCG), namely, the level of lexical representation. It is not clear what the difference between this representation's being lexical and its being syntactic amounts to beyond terminology. Indeed, the distinguished syntactic level I will propose in this book, the elementary tree, has been suggested to constitute the lexical representation of the lexical predicate that heads it. In LFG, however, the application of lexical rules to this structure accounts only for a certain range of dependencies (e.g., passivization and dative shift in English). Dependencies that apply over unbounded domains (e.g., raising and *wh*-movement), require the use of feature unification mechanisms, part of the formalism's structural composition mechanisms, to ensure that the dependents are compatible. Even restricting ourselves to local dependencies, substantive differences exist between the LFG proposals and the TAG analyses I discuss in this book, as a result of the functional material that I assume to be present in a lexical head's elementary tree structure (on which see chapter 2). Without such structure within the elementary tree, it is difficult to see how phenomena involving movement of the verbal head (e.g., French-style verb raising and auxiliary inversion (Emonds 1978; Pollock 1989)), can be handled locally. If they cannot, the combinatory machinery will need to be complicated accordingly.

10. This proposal also does not address very directly the near synonymy of the examples in (3). In the proposed derivation for (3b), a phonologically null object of *climb* undergoes *wh*-movement to the front of the infinitival clause, and it is left to some other process to establish the semantic linkage between this null element and the late-inserted subject.

11. Later in his paper, Uriagereka suggests an alternative characterization of DCs that attempts to address these sorts of issues. Specifically, he suggests that a DC is a minimal structure in which all grammatical properties are satisfied (i.e., allowing for a convergent derivation). In contrast to the linearization-driven proposal mentioned in the text, which allows arbitrarily large structures so long as they are strictly right branching, Uriagereka intends the latter proposal to break up structures at clausal (i.e., CP) boundaries. This proposal raises a number of questions, however. First, it leaves unclear precisely what it means for grammatical properties to be satisfied in a piece of structure: are the grammatical properties of a subordinate clause satisfied in a nonembedded context, for example? Additionally, as I discuss in the text in the context of Chomsky's proposal, the empirically observed "bleeding" that occurs across phase boundaries, as seen in successive-cyclic movement of *wh*-phrases for instance, leads to considerable complication of these proposals.

12. Chomsky takes *v* to be the head in whose specifier external arguments of lexical predicates are merged. Though the mechanics of Chomsky's system necessitate a distinction between predicates that take external arguments and those that do not, it is not clear conceptually why the projection of an unaccusative predicate, which does not include a *v* head, does not constitute a saturated lexical predicate, and hence a phase boundary. See Legate 1998 for arguments that the notion of phase should be extended to include all VPs, a proposal that Chomsky (2001) adopts in part in terms of the stipulative distinction between strong and weak phases.

13. Interestingly, not all instances of unbounded movement are forced into a successive-cyclic derivation by phase boundaries. Raising, the topic of chapter 3, is one such case. Since raising verbs like *seem* do not assign an external θ-role and since they select for TP complements, clauses containing raising predicates include neither a phase-inducing *v*P nor a phase-inducing CP projection.

(i) [TP Elizabeth [VP seems [TP *t* to [VP be likely [TP *t* to win]]]]].

In such cases, phases can grow to be unboundedly large structures. Chomsky assumes that the successive-cyclic movement that takes place in constructions like (i) is forced instead by the need to check the EPP features of all intermediate T heads.

It seems plausible that there ought to be a single driving grammatical force behind all cases of successive-cyclic movement wherever it exists—say, the presence of phase boundaries. This leads to one of two possibilities: (a) the TPs in successive-cyclic raising constructions do constitute phase boundaries, or (b) there is no movement to intermediate positions in raising constructions. I am not aware that anyone has pursued the former possibility, perhaps because of the complexities it would introduce for nonraising constructions. Castillo, Drury, and Grohmann (1999) pursue the latter possibility, eliminating EPP features in the T heads of raising complements.

14. Chomsky (2001) takes a somewhat different perspective on the apparent "bleeding" that occurs across phase boundaries, suggesting that a phase P is sent off for PF and LF interpretation, and hence frozen, only once the next higher

phase Q above P is completed. This means that elements can be moved out of P, even if they are not at its left edge, so long as Q has not yet been completed. This proposal integrates the notion of phase more tightly into the derivational mechanics of the system, so that the immutability of phases is not stipulated in the same way as before. However, Chomsky retains his Phase Impenetrability Condition as well, so that P's left edge remains accessible even after Q is complete. Needless to say, this weakens the tight linkage between the process of PF/LF interpretation and syntactic immutability.

15. In these trees and throughout this book, I adopt the phrase structural assumptions of Stowell (1981), Chomsky (1986), and Abney (1987). Specifically, I take clauses to be projections of functional heads (tense (T) and complementizer (C), respectively, for the traditional labels S and S'), and nominal phrases to be the projections of determiner (D) heads.

16. This operation, then, can be seen as violating the formulation of cyclicity in Chomsky's (1993) Extension Condition as it adds structure to an internal node. Indeed, virtually all applications of the TAG operations will have this property. This means that the effects of cyclicity will need to be enforced through some other means in the TAG context. I return to this topic in chapter 3.

17. Observe that the recursive character of auxiliary trees guarantees that any instances of (direct) dominance and c-command relations that hold within an elementary tree will continue to hold even after additional structure is adjoined. If the inserted auxiliary tree structure did not have identically labeled root and foot nodes, then either the mother of the adjoining site would come to dominate a node of a different label, or the nodes that are attached below the foot node of the auxiliary tree would come to have a mother node of a different label. This gives rise to an alternative characterization of Adjoining as a dominance-/c-command-preserving expansion of a tree structure, pursued in Rambow, Vijay-Shanker, and Weir 2001 and Frank, Kulick, and Vijay-Shanker 2000.

18. This is not to say that transformations are not involved in the creation of the elementary trees themselves. However, the limited domain of the elementary trees will mean that the transformational component will be considerably weaker than usually assumed, and will consequently need fewer (if any) externally imposed restrictions. I return to this issue below.

19. See XTAG Research Group 1992 for an English grammar constructed at least in part in this way, with impressive coverage.

20. Though not formulated in a TAG context, Grimshaw's (1997) conception of optimality-theoretic syntax also seems to advocate such a local conception of grammatical well-formedness, in which optimality is determined for individual extended projections. Given the conception of elementary trees as extended projections that I advocate in chapter 2, it is a natural next step to try to combine these lines of work. I leave this for the future.

21. It is worth noting that this perspective diverges somewhat from other conceptions of TAG in which elementary trees are thought to be on a par with lexical entries and subject to considerable idiosyncrasy.

22. I assume here that certain verbs may take "nonmaximal" C's as their complements. I discuss the issue of $X'$ complementation in the context of raising and *wh*-movement at considerable length in chapters 3, 4, and 5.

23. Empirical considerations aside, there remains the conceptual issue of why the grammar should reify the notion of elementary tree in the way that it does. That is, why should grammatical derivations make use of two different mechanisms for structural composition, one for creating elementary trees and another for combining them, when one ought to be enough to produce recursive structure? Though I cannot offer anything decisive, one might look for an answer in the nature of the systems with which the grammar interacts. It may be that the mechanisms by which elementary-tree-internal relations are interpreted in order to establish phonological and semantic representations are qualitatively different from those by which these local phonological and semantic representations are combined. If this is so, it would suggest that the grammar ought to proceed by first constructing the local units constituting elementary trees, which can be sent off for interpretation. Subsequent combinations of these elementary trees would be accompanied by distinct types of information being sent to the articulatory and interpretive systems. Though I return briefly to such speculations in chapter 6, making this idea precise will require considerable further work.

24. Note that divergences in derivation structure will not necessarily correspond to divergences in the derived phrase marker, that is, structural ambiguity as usually understood. As noted above, the structure in (13c) can be derived either by substitution of the embedded clause into the matrix clause or by adjoining of the matrix clause into the embedded clause. One might take such spurious ambiguity to be an unfortunate property of an interpretive interface. There is certain evidence, however, that this sort of ambiguity in derivation structure is not spurious at all. Frank and Kroch (1994) suggest that various interpretive distinctions between gerunds and nominalizations follow from the availability of both Substitution and Adjoining derivations only in the case of gerunds, nominalizations requiring Substitution. Abeillé and Schabes (1989) argue that idioms constitute another case in which multiple TAG derivations must exist for a single derived phrase marker, the multiple derivations of a sentence like *The farmer kicked the bucket* corresponding to the literal and nonliteral interpretations of the idiom.

25. I put off until chapter 4 the general question of the factors governing the placement of features in elementary trees.

26. As we will see in subsequent discussion, local derivational constraints of the sorts we will consider can be viewed as properties of elementary trees themselves.

27. A number of cases have been cited in the literature as lying even beyond the generative power of TAG (Miller 1991; Radzinski 1991; Becker, Rambow, and Niv 1992; Rambow 1994). However, each of these cases is problematic in some way, defusing the argument that the grammatical systems of natural language are more formally expressive than TAG. Miller's argument depends crucially on the existence of certain anaphoric relationships between fronted *wh*-elements and resumptive pronouns in Swedish question forms, relationships that are plausibly

semantic rather than syntactic (cf. Pullum 1985 for similar arguments in another context). Radzinski discusses the case of Chinese number names, whose patterns of well-formedness are in all likelihood determined by an extralinguistic cognitive faculty for mathematical thought, or via the interface between the linguistic and mathematical faculties. Consequently, results about the complexity of such structures tell us little about grammatical complexity on its own. Becker, Rambow, and Niv's argument, which is the most persuasive, concerns the Germanic scrambling phenomenon. As is often the case for such proofs of the formal complexity of natural language, it requires that we assume that the unacceptability of certain sentences derives from some kind of processing limitation and not from the grammar, as Miller and Chomsky (1963) argued for the case of center-embedded sentences in English. As Joshi, Becker, and Rambow (2000) note, however, the plausibility of such an assumption depends on the presence of a concrete processing model that explains the contrasts in acceptability, and the absence of a simple grammatical explanation of the same contrasts. In the scrambling case, Joshi, Becker, and Rambow note that there is such a grammatical explanation, leaving open the conclusion that linguistic descriptions of the scrambling phenomenon require mechanisms beyond the power of TAG.

28. See Kroch and Santorini 1991 for arguments in favor of this sort of grammar, in which, contrary to many analyses of Germanic verb raising, the sequence of verbs at the end of the sentence does not form a syntactic cluster. Kroch and Santorini show how the crosslinguistically observed word order variation in the Germanic verb cluster can be elegantly captured through simple changes in the derivational constraints that are assigned to the nodes of these elementary trees.

29. Joshi (1985) conjectures that natural languages are characterized by the formal property of constant growth, a notion related to the property of semilinearity (but see Michaelis and Kracht 1997). The intuition behind constant growth comes from the observation that natural languages do not leave larger and larger gaps between their well-formed strings. Rather, between any two strings there is in general a constant bound on the difference between their lengths. This notion of constant growth may be formally defined as follows (taken from Michaelis and Kracht 1997).

(i) A language $L$ has the constant growth property iff there is some constant $c_0 \in \mathbb{N}$ and some finite set of constants $C \subset \mathbb{N}$ such that for any $w \in L$ with $|w| \geq c_0$, there is some $w' \in L$ and some $c \in C$ for which $|w'| = |w| + c$ holds (where $|w|$ indicates the length of $w$).

Every TAL exhibits the constant growth property. To a first approximation, this can be seen by taking the $C$s to be the length of the strings at the frontiers of the elementary trees in the grammars, and $c_0$ to be the length of the shortest string that can be derived by the grammar. Such a string can then be extended by adjoining a single auxiliary tree, whose length is by hypothesis among the $C$s.

30. Another type of support for the role of TAG in grammatical competence comes from "external" evidence, specifically, the degree to which TAG supports the development of models of, for example, language comprehension, production,

and acquisition. For applications of TAG to comprehension, see Joshi 1990, Rambow 1992, Frank 1992, Rambow and Joshi 1994, and Kim, Srinivas, and Trueswell, to appear. For applications to production, see Badecker and Frank 1999, Ferreira 2000, and Frank and Badecker 2001. For applications to acquisition, see Joshi 1989 and Frank 1998, 2000.

**Chapter 2**

1. These proposals differ in the nature of the VP-internal position in which the external argument is generated. Koopman and Sportiche argue that the external argument is generated in a nonspecifier subject position of a small clause formed with the VP. In contrast, Fukui and Speas propose that the external argument is generated in a position adjoined to V'. A more recent variant, stemming from ideas of Larson (1988) and developed by Chomsky (1995), posits an additional verbal head $v$ that takes the VP containing the lexical verb and its internal argument as a complement and hosts the external argument in its specifier. For the sake of concreteness and simplicity, I will represent external arguments as being generated in the specifier of VP. I will note whenever variations in this assumption affect the discussion.

2. If we take external arguments to be assigned inside the projection of the lexical predicate, even lower functional heads like TP would not be included in a verbally headed elementary tree.

3. See Rambow 1993 for a related proposal using a somewhat different formal system.

4. In the structure in (4) and those that follow, I sidestep the issue of whether a predicate's elementary tree also includes the functional projections that embed the external argument. Such arguments are usually taken not to be selected, so this might lead one not to include such structure. As I abandon this view shortly, I will not aim to resolve this issue here.

5. It might be possible to resolve this problem by exploiting the alternative formulation of Adjoining as monotonic combination of c-command relations pursued in Kulick, Frank, and Vijay-Shanker 2000 and Frank, Kulick, and Vijay-Shanker 2000.

6. Abney's (1987) analysis of gerunds as projections of determiner heads that take VP complements is one prominent counterexample to this claim. I return to this issue in section 3.5.

7. It is not clear whether prepositions with more thematic content than *of* ought to head their own extended projections. Grimshaw notes that the evidence here cuts both ways, but ultimately assumes that they are uniformly functional heads that are part of other lexical heads' extended projections. For the moment, I leave the matter open. See Van Riemsdijk 1996 for relevant discussion.

8. Such small extended projections might be argued to arise in cases of small clause complements. I return to such structures in chapter 3.

9. Ouhalla (1991), Zanuttini (1997), and Bobaljik and Thráinsson (1998), among others, argue that languages may in fact differ in the ordering and presence or absence of certain functional projections, negation and agreement to take two examples. As noted earlier, languages do not appear to differ along the dimension of which functional heads are allowed to appear in the extended projection of a particular lexical head. See Cinque 1999 for arguments that whatever variation exists in this domain is extremely limited.

10. In these trees, I have for simplicity put aside the possibility that external θ-roles are assigned VP-internally, with subsequent movement of the subject. I return to this issue below.

11. Bill Badecker (personal communication) suggests that the plurality requirement imposed by *gather* is of a somewhat different sort than that imposed by *merge* or *combine*, the latter requiring syntactic plurality.

(i) They merged the *army/armies.

If this is correct, I have no explanation for why these cases of selection should differ in this way. However, I suspect that what is going on here is that the semantic requirement imposed on the object by *merge* or *combine* is rather more severe than that imposed by *gather*, requiring a plural entity whose members themselves are complex entities that can be combined.

12. It is important to note that this selectional restriction of *serve* does not constrain the embedded subject directly, as is sometimes assumed. Were this the case, we would expect judgments for the examples in (13b) to be identical, as they have the same embedded subject. The divergence in acceptability on these examples can be explained via reference to the θ-roles that the verbs *melt* and *chill* assign to their subjects, patient in the first case and instrument in the second. Consequently, Higgins's condition that a given DP be interpretable as an instrument must relate to θ-roles assigned by the embedded verb, and hence the selectional properties of *serve* must constrain the embedded verb itself.

This poses a puzzle for the "degree-0 and a little bit" learning theory proposed by Lightfoot (1991). Lightfoot argues that during syntactic acquisition, children have access to matrix clauses and embedded subject positions, but not to embedded verbs. He suggests that the problem of learning the selectional properties of *serve* poses no difficulties for this view, under the (apparently incorrect) assumption that the relevant property is a property of the embedded subject. Consequently, if something like Lightfoot's proposal is correct, we will need to extend to some degree the syntactic domains that constitute children's primary linguistic data.

13. Peter Sells (personal communication) points out a potential problem with viewing selectional properties of the type I have considered here as configurationally governed at all. The constraint I have posited on the complements to *decide*, for example, persists even when the complement does not seem to be in a position that is syntactically selected by *decide*, as in pseudoclefts.

(i) What Lester needed was to speak/know French.

(ii) What Lester decided was to speak/*know French.

The same effects obtain in the selection of indicative and subjunctive mood.

(iii) What Lester said was that his secretary types/*type all of his letters.

(iv) What Lester required was that his secretary types/type all of his letters.

From this, we might conclude one of two things. One possibility is that we should rethink the notion of configurationally governed selection, reformulating it instead in semantic terms. A second, perhaps less drastic, conclusion is that we need to reconsider the way in which selection is enforced in the particular case of pseudoclefts in such a way that they do involve configurationally governed selection at some level of representation. Tony Kroch (personal communication) mentions the following fact about anaphor binding which suggests that if binding is configurationally governed, then so is selection.

(v) What Lester$_i$ said about the exhibition was that pictures of himself$_i$ will be on display.

Here, the reflexive is bound by the matrix subject even though the reflexive is apparently not embedded within a complement of the verb *say*. Assuming that there is some level of representation in which the *that* clause is "reconstructed" to be the complement to the verb *say*, we could assume that binding and selection operate there. If this is on the right track, then a fact about the selection properties of the verb *insist* suggests that the appropriate level is quite abstract indeed. In (vi), we see a pseudocleft in which the verb has different subcategorizations in the *wh*-clause and in the *that* clause.

(vi) What Lester insisted on was that he be/*is allowed to shower.

In the *wh*-portion of the pseudocleft, the verb *insist* exhibits a subcategorization frame that is restricted to NP objects.

(vii) *Lester insisted on that he be allowed to shower.

The verb nonetheless enforces the restriction that the *that* clause following the copula be subjunctive. I leave the difficult question of resolving these issues open.

14. If P also forms part of the nominal extended projection, we would expect to see, say, gender agreement on prepositions. I do not know whether any such cases exist.

15. As noted earlier, this result requires that even semantically contentful prepositions like *under* be analyzed as functional heads so that they can form part of nominal extended projections. In the TAG context, this raises the question, which I leave open, of how this notion of extended projection can be reconciled with the conception of elementary trees as being centered around a single thematic head.

16. The impossibility of pied-piping beyond the extended projection boundary shown in example (22c) for indirect questions contrasts with what is seen in direct questions.

(i) Pictures of which college do you like?

(ii) Under the assumption that John went to which college would you hire him?

These examples, taken from Hegarty 1993a, indeed sound better than (22c), though they do seem to demand a particular context, perhaps a generalization of the "quizmaster" context. Note that both of these examples are impossible as indirect questions.

(iii) *I wonder pictures of which college you like.

(iv) *I wonder under the assumption that John went to which college you would hire him.

Hegarty does cite the following example of an indirect question with pied-piping beyond the extended projection.

(v) I was wondering under pictures of which college we would find the records.

This sentence does strike me as somewhat better than (iii) and (iv), though I am not certain that it is completely well formed. Leaving aside such murky cases, I continue to maintain the claim that pied-piping is restricted to extended projections, at least in embedded questions.

Note that the pattern in relative clauses is different still. As discussed in Kayne 1984, 184–186, *wh*-elements in (appositive) relative clauses may pied-pipe considerably more structure than a single preposition (example (vii) from Cinque 1982).

(vi) John, to speak to whom now would be a mistake, ...

(vii) I   suoi studenti, il   non aver    promosso i    quali, potrà essere
      the his  students the not having promoted the which may   be
      interpretato tendenziosamente, ...
      interpreted  tendentiously
      'His students, whose not having been promoted may be interpreted
      tendentiously, ...'

17. If the following cases of suppletion involving P and D combinations, drawn from German and Dutch, respectively, are taken to derive from head movement, they could constitute further evidence for the presence of the prepositional head within an extended projection ((ii) from Van Riemsdijk 1996):

(i) Der Mann geht in   das/ins     Haus.
    the man  goes into the/into-the house

(ii) Hij gaat *voor  het/er  voor   altijd  golfen.
     he  goes before it/there before always play-golf

18. This raises the question of whether there is any need for a locality condition beyond the requirement that movement remain within an extended projection, to which I return later.

19. An alternative representational view of elementary trees might allow for the coindexation of frontier nonterminals via an elementary-tree-internal process of chain formation, with traces inserted via Substitution.

20. For the sake of readability, I will often depict elementary trees with their DP arguments already filled in, when such insertion plays no crucial role in the derivation. Of course, since these DPs constitute separate extended projections, the CETM will imply that they are distinct elementary trees, inserted via Substitution.

21. In order for a derivation involving such an "ambiguous" auxiliary tree to be well defined, a particular application of Adjoining will need to choose which node

is serving as the foot node. If TAG derivations proceed in a bottom-up fashion, as determined by the derivation structure, the ambiguity will have been resolved at the point of Adjoining, since the other potential foot node will already have been filled by Substitution. Indeed, since the locus of substitution is marked in the derivation structure, one need not encode which frontier nonterminal is serving as the foot node in a derivation structure, as it can be recovered indirectly as the node into which substitution has not taken place.

22. I assume that the selectional requirements that are imposed upon each of the CP arguments, which for example guarantee the insertion of the *plutôt que* complement into the second argument slot, are enforced through some featural specification on the CP foot/substitution nodes.

23. Kroch (1989b) dubs such trees *athematic auxiliary trees*, as he assumes that the foot node is not thematically related to the lexical head of the elementary tree. Since I reject this assumption, taking a subject-predicate relation to hold between the adjoined element and the phrase to which it attaches, I adopt the more transparent alternative term *modifier auxiliary*.

24. Grimshaw's formulation of the GTC is slightly different from this, but amounts to the same thing. Specifically, Grimshaw states that phrases must be licensed either by being assigned a θ-role or by being part of an extended projection with a phrase that is assigned a θ-role. I see no empirical or conceptual reasons for maintaining the difference between θ-role-assigned or non-θ-role-assigned phrases, so I will maintain the simpler statement given in the text.

25. I have said nothing about how root extended projections are licensed. I will follow Grimshaw (1991) in assuming that this case is handled by special stipulation.

**Chapter 3**

1. Nontransformational frameworks, including LFG, HPSG, and Categorial Grammar, deal with the displacement of the subject using other mechanisms, feature unification for the first two and function composition for the third (Bresnan 1982a; Pollard and Sag 1994; Jacobson 1990). These approaches, most especially the latter, have certain similarities with the TAG Adjoining-based approach I propose in this chapter, though significant differences remain. I return to these briefly at the conclusion of section 3.8.

2. I ignore for the moment the complexities introduced by VP-internal subjects.

3. For the sake of readability, DP arguments are filled in these elementary trees. However, according to the CETM, they could not be present in the same elementary tree as a verbal head. I will assume that they are inserted using Substitution during the course of the derivation, prior to the relevant application of Adjoining.

4. Note that the elementary tree in (9) is not entirely unproblematic in that it violates the formulation of the EPP given in chapter 2. I put this issue aside for the moment, returning to it extensively in chapter 4.

5. Of course, if we assume that subjects are generated internal to the projection of the verb, there remains the possibility of movement internal to the elementary tree from the VP-internal base position to the specifier of TP position. If one were to decompose the elementary trees even further, one could derive even these cases of displacement using Adjoining. For one such proposal, see Hegarty 1993a. However, I will argue below that this more fine-grained view of elementary trees fails to capture certain differences between dependencies obtaining within and across extended projection boundaries.

6. Alternatively, we might adjoin the nonfinite auxiliary tree in (13) into the finite auxiliary tree in (9), this time at the foot node. It is sometimes suggested in linguistic work on TAG that adjoining at foot nodes ought to be prohibited since it introduces a systematic ambiguity into derivations, but see Kulick 1998 and note 16 of this chapter for considerations pointing in the other direction. However this issue is resolved, one derivation of these cases that is not permitted in the TAG system is one in which the two auxiliary trees are combined by means of Substitution (i.e., (13) into (9)). Conceptual, formal, and empirical reasons for this prohibition will be discussed in section 3.3.

7. The issues of successive cyclicity and the presence of intermediate traces are in principle separable. Under a derivational view of the grammar, one could enforce locality through a Shortest Move–like requirement, as is widely assumed, without obliging the movement operation to leave a trace in each position from which movement takes place. Such a separation is, of course, impossible under a representational view since one cannot talk of locality except in terms of conditions on chains, that is, the relation between a moved element and its trace.

8. This leaves open the question of why (i) is ill formed.

(i) It seems $t$ was certain Eleanor to know the answer.

In Chomsky 1995, it is assumed that a derivation producing this sentence would leave the Case features of the DP *Eleanor* unchecked. However, as noted by Chomsky (2000, 149), citing Eduardo Raposo (personal communication), this analysis does not explain why such Case features cannot be checked covertly by feature raising. To avoid this problem, Chomsky (2000) assumes that although *it* is the closest element that could check the matrix T's EPP features, it is in a sense "defective," as it cannot actually move because it lacks Case features, these having already been checked by the intermediate T. This leaves the derivation at an impasse, what Chomsky calls a defective intervention effect, with the result that after the point illustrated in (17), the derivation is blocked and cannot proceed.

9. While the Extension Condition is adequate for the case at hand, it brings with it a number of conceptual oddities. Crucially, Chomsky assumes that only overt movement abides by the Extension Condition and that adjunction does not. Chomsky attempts to reduce the former condition to the latter, assuming that covert movement involves adjunction of features exclusively. The formulation of the Extension Condition in Chomsky 1995 states that strong features (i.e., those that trigger overt movement) cannot be embedded. Chomsky is forced to complicate the characterization of embedding invoked here in order to permit one head

to adjoin to another with unchecked strong features. It would of course be desirable if we could eliminate such a stipulative constraint on derivations.

10. The question arises of what exactly licenses this expletive subject position in the elementary tree, given that this is not a position to which a θ-role is assigned and that it hence is not compelled by the TAG version of the θ-Criterion. For now, let us assume that nonthematic subject positions in an elementary tree may be licensed via some association (a chain, say) with the predicate's complement clause. This will require a slight reformulation of the θ-Criterion as given in chapter 2, so that it refers to chains rather than individual frontier nonterminals, along the following lines:

(i) *θ-Criterion (TAG version) (part 2)*
  If A is a frontier nonterminal node of elementary tree T, A must be a
  member of a chain that is assigned a θ-role in T.

An alternative to this analysis is suggested in Bennis 1986, where expletive *it* is generated within the complement domain of the raising predicate and is moved to the higher subject position. This idea could be adapted into the TAG framework by assuming the following structure for the raising predicate's complement clause:

(ii) [$_{TP}$ it [$_{T'}$ T [$_{CP}$ that ... ]]]

The derivation of an example like (iii) would then be identical to that for simple raising cases like (7), adjoining a T′ auxiliary tree headed by *seems* at the T′ node in (ii).

(iii) It seems that Eleanor knows the answer.

Note that this analysis will still block the generation of the superraising cases. However, it is not clear to what degree the structure in (ii) constitutes an extended projection, since TP appears above CP. If it does not, such a structure would violate the CETM. I therefore put aside this intriguing possibility.

11. Note that raising to object, whether understood in Postal's (1974) sense or the revised sense of Lasnik and Saito 1991 as movement to the specifier of a Case-assigning functional head, does not qualify as an instance of this type of movement, as the type of position is changed from one clause to the next. However, because this movement crosses an extended projection boundary, it is not possible to analyze it as an application of Move within an elementary tree. Since the GPSG analysis of such structures, where the verb takes NP and VP complements, is incompatible with my assumption that the lexical heads of elementary trees are saturated, I am led to adopt the exceptional-Case-marking (ECM) analysis of such structures, in which the embedded subject remains in the lower clause. Modifications to the TAG formalism allow incorporation of Lasnik and Saito's version of raising to object (Rambow and Santorini 1995; Frank, Kulick, and Vijay-Shanker 2000).

12. Since use of Adjoining allows us to eliminate the Extension Condition, we are free to eliminate the distinction between substitution and adjunction that Chomsky posited (see note 9). Thus, neither adjunction structures nor substitution structures, recast into their TAG guises, will be required to extend their targets.

13. Implementing this idea would require an augmentation to the TAG formalism that allows some properties of the site of adjoining to percolate above the interposed auxiliary tree—for example, the addition of top and bottom feature descriptions proposed by Vijay-Shanker and Joshi (1988). Pursuing this analysis would require an extensive tangent to the main discussion, but no issues of principle arise. In chapter 4, I return to the role of such a system of bifurcated node descriptions.

14. Lasnik (1999) suggests that scope reconstruction in cases of raising is in fact impossible. Instead, he argues that the only possible locus of interpretation is the surface position, giving rise to a wide scope interpretation. Apparent cases of reconstruction, instances of narrow scope interpretation, he takes instead to derive from certain interpretive properties of indefinites, unrelated to syntactic operations. Naturally, such a view is compatible with the Adjoining-based view of raising, as there is even less reason to suspect the existence of reconstruction given the absence of a trace in the embedded clause. Indeed, if Lasnik is correct that A-reconstruction is generally impossible, it perhaps suggests that subjects might be generated directly in their specifier of TP position, rather than being moved from a VP-internal position, as this would avoid the question of why reconstruction does not take place to even this base position. Note that since I take θ-roles to be assigned within elementary trees, prior to the application of Adjoining, the absence of this trace will not affect our ability to recover θ-role information even after raising has taken place.

15. It might be argued that the contrast between the examples in (25a) and (27a) is due not to the presence of raising, but to the contrast in finiteness in the clause that hosts *not*. However, in examples involving ECM verbs, where the subject plausibly remains in the subject position of the lower clause, the narrow scope interpretation of the quantifier with respect to the matrix predicate is possible.

(i) I expected many/several unicorns not to be in the garden.

Like those given in the text, these examples do not permit a narrow scope interpretation of the quantifier with respect to negation. In these cases, however, where the quantifier does not raise to matrix subject position, the quantifier takes scope within the matrix predicate, though judgments are admittedly delicate. If the ECM verb is passivized to produce a raising structure, the judgments are like those of the examples given in (27): the quantifier must take widest scope.

(ii) Many/Several unicorns are expected not to be in the garden.

16. Further questions arise with respect to examples involving multiple raising predicates.

(i) Many unicorns are likely to seem to be in the garden.

Under a reconstruction-based analysis, one would expect that the quantifier could take scope in at least the following three places: outside all of the predicates, between *likely* and *seem*, or below *seem*. Under the line of analysis I am pursuing in which there are no traces in intermediate subject positions, it is not immediately obvious how the middle scope reading could be generated. I am not certain whether these readings are all possible, since it is not clear to me how to clearly distinguish the latter two. Assuming, however, that all such readings are distinguishable and available, there is in fact a simple way to generate them that exploits the many-to-one mapping from derivation structures to derived trees. Note that the derivation for (i) can begin in one of two ways: either by adjoining the auxiliary tree for *are likely* into the auxiliary tree for *to seem* at the latter tree's root, or by adjoining the auxiliary tree for *to seem* into the auxiliary tree for *are likely* at the latter tree's foot. In either case, the resulting derived auxiliary tree adjoins into the elementary tree for *many unicorns to be in the garden*. This gives rise to the following pair of derivation structures:

(ii) a.  many unicorns to be in the garden

to seem

are likely

   b.  many unicorns to be in the garden

are likely

to seem

Suppose that when a raising predicate R is adjoined into an elementary tree, DPs that c-command R's locus of adjoining, like the subject, are optionally assigned scope immediately outside R. For the derivation in (iia), this will mean that *many unicorns* takes scope between the raising predicates, while for the derivation in (iib), the wide scope interpretation results. (Recall that narrow scope interpretation results from the quantifier's being interpreted in the position of its elementary-tree-local trace within the small clause, a position that in any case does not c-command the locus of adjoining.) Of course, many details remain to be worked out for this to constitute a full account of the interactions of scope and movement, and I leave such an account for future work.

17. This condition would be rendered more complex under proposals that take PRO to be assigned (null) Case (Chomsky and Lasnik 1993).

18. It has also been noted that intermediate traces of *wh*-movement do not block contraction (Jaeggli 1980).

(i) a.  Who do you want [*t* PRO to visit *t*]?
   b.  Who do you wanna visit?

Kroch and Joshi (1985) observe that since the TAG analysis of *wh*-movement does not posit such intermediate traces, as we shall see in chapter 5, their invisibility to contraction is unsurprising.

19. This says nothing about the locality required between *there* and the indefinite, often tied to requirements of assigning nominative Case to the associate, either

via the expletive or directly by the T head (Burzio 1986, 1994; Chomsky 1991, 2000). I consider how Case assignment to the indefinite DP associate might be handled in the TAG context below.

20. In chapter 4, I consider why this should be so. I show that the locality of the expletive-associate relation can be derived from more general principles of elementary-tree-local feature checking. Concerning the licensing of the position of *there* in such a tree, see note 10.

21. In so doing, we also avoid problems for the Merge-over-Move preference noted by Wilder and Gärtner (1997) arising from examples of the following form:

(i) There was a rumor [that a unicorn was in the garden] in the air.

Under the assumption that a complement C to a head H must be fully constructed before H is embedded within a larger structure, as required by the Extension Condition, it follows that the complement clause *that a unicorn was in the garden* will need to be constructed before *there* is inserted into the matrix specifier of TP. On Chomsky's (1995) analysis, the presence of the expletive in the sentence's numeration ought, via the Merge-over-Move preference, to block the DP *a unicorn* from raising out of the small clause in which it is generated, preventing this example from being generated. Chomsky (2000) resolves this problem by dividing the derivation into pieces, which he dubs *phases*, each of which is generated from independent lexical numerations. As CPs constitute distinct phases in this account, the presence of *there* in the matrix clause is irrelevant to the determination of derivational economy in the nominal complement.

Even though the analysis proposed here does not require the notion of phase to deal with cases such as those we are discussing, there is a natural affinity between the idea that economy is computed over separate derivational phases and the idea that well-formedness, perhaps sensitive to economy conditions, is computed over separate elementary trees. Clearly in the TAG context, the question of a Merge-over-Move preference, if there is one at all, would need to be resolved within a single elementary tree, just as Chomsky assumes it is resolved in a single phase. In chapter 4, I return to a comparison of phase-local and elementary-tree-local notions of economy.

22. In this structure, I show the infinitival verb *vera* not raising to T. Jonas (1996, 183) cites the following example, to demonstrate that raising of V to T is possible in the infinitival complement to a raising verb:

(i) Það    virðast ekki margir stúdentar vera  alltaf    hér.
    there seem    not   many    students  to be always  here

This follows on the assumption that the base position of *vera* 'to be' is below that of *alltaf* 'always'. As noted by Sigurðsson (1989) and others, movement of V to T is obligatory in control infinitivals, though Jonas (1996, 182n. 20) notes that the situation is more complex with the infinitival complements to raising and ECM predicates. However this is resolved, it does not affect the TAG analysis so far as I can tell.

Example (i) also provides evidence that the DP associate in these Icelandic partial raising cases can remain within the embedded clause, under the assumption that negation patterns with VP adverbials like *alveg* 'completely' in appearing in a position below that of the subject (Jonas 1992, 181).

(ii) a.  Það  hafa sennilega einhverjir stúdentar alveg         lokið
         there have probably some      students  completely finished
         verkefninu.
         the assignment

    b. *Það  hafa sennilega alveg      einhverjir stúdentar lokið
        there have probably completely some       students finished
        verkefninu.
        the assignment

23. It should be noted that the structure in (40) differs in one crucial respect from that of a canonical TEC, in not abiding by the verb-second constraint (compare with (42b)).

(i) *Það  einhver köttur hefur étið   mýsnar.
     there some    cat    has   eaten the mice

Since adjoining of a raising auxiliary tree can alter the relative position of elements with respect to the finite verb, we will need to assume that the verb-second constraint is enforced via constraints on Adjoining, perhaps reducible to economy as discussed in chapter 4 or perhaps related to phonological or morphological well-formedness conditions that filter the output of the syntactic derivation (Anderson 1993).

24. Such a derivation yields a derivation structure that diverges from the one suggested for examples involving multiple raising like (11). In those cases, one raising auxiliary adjoins to the other, with the complex auxiliary adjoining into the embedded clause's elementary tree. In the derivation for examples like (37b), however, the two raising predicates adjoin separately. Under our current assumptions, English examples like (i) will also implicate such independent instances of Adjoining.

(i) What do you think John was likely to buy?

Here, auxiliary trees corresponding to *do you think* and *was likely* will adjoin separately to an elementary tree corresponding to *what John to buy* at C′ and T′, respectively. I leave open the desirability of such derivations, returning briefly to the topic in chapter 6.

25. Possessor raising, as illustrated in the Chickasaw examples in (i) from Munro and Gordon 1982, is an apparent instance of movement out of DP into the clausal domain.

(i) a. John im-ofi'-at      illi-h.
       John III-dog-NOM die-TNS
       'John's dog died.'
    b. John-at   ofi'(-at)   im-illi-h.
       John-NOM dog(-NOM) III-die-TNS

For reasons similar to those discussed below for raising out of nominals, and in note 11 for raising to object, this dependency cannot be established via Adjoining.

I am therefore led to conclude that what is labeled possessor raising does not actually involve syntactic movement, but instead involves an anaphoric dependency.

26. See Alexiadou 1999 for a notable exception. Her analysis is discussed in further detail below.

27. It is unclear on Alexiadou's analysis, however, why the feature that is sufficient to drive movement of genitive DPs to prenominal position generally is insufficient to drive raising. In a footnote, she suggests that the surface position of prenominal genitives is in fact their base argument position. From this, we can conclude that the head of the projection hosting these genitives lacks the features to attract a lower DP.

28. As Guglielmo Cinque (personal communication) points out, this predicts that in a language in which tense morphology can be attached to nouns, as for example in Somali and varieties of Salish, raising should be possible with nominals. I do not as yet know what the facts are in Somali. However, this prediction cannot be tested in Salish, since the varieties in question lack raising constructions of the relevant sort quite generally (Henry Davis, personal communication). Though Japanese does not permit tense morphology to attach to nominals, the Japanese construction discussed by Sells (1991) shown in (i) might nonetheless be an instance of this kind of case, providing support for the prediction Cinque points out.

(i) Ame-ga [huru]    hazu          da.
    rain-NOM  fall-PRES expectation COP-PRES
    'Rain is expected to fall.'

Sells argues that in this example, the subject *ame-ga* 'rain' raises from the subject position of the clausal complement to the nominal *hazu* 'expectation' to the subject of the matrix. Crucially in the present context, the matrix clause expresses tense, on the copula. Thus, it is plausible to take the derived subject position to be the specifier of TP. The raising auxiliary tree necessary to derive this kind of example, then, could be of the form in (49b), where the nominal is embedded within a T projection.

29. Note also the following contrasts:

(i) a.  *I was astonished at headway's having been made on the problem.
    b.   I was astonished at headway having been made on the problem.

(ii) a.  *I was astonished at there's being a riot.
     b.   I was astonished at there being a riot.

These data suggest that independent of raising, there is some sort of prohibition against nonreferential genitive subjects of DP. If this is correct, the raising data are not decisive, as there are other reasons why such cases are not possible. Neither should they be viewed as evidence against the line taken here, however.

30. Since the CETM does not force elementary trees with verbal heads to include T projections, one might try to construct a raising auxiliary tree for *made* that was rooted in V', as shown in (i).

(i)
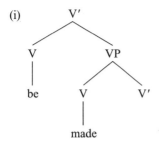

This tree could then be adjoined into the elementary tree in (63a) between the bare infinitive and its external argument. The resulting structure could then be substituted into the complement of another bare infinitive complement-taking verb, which could then assign accusative Case to the raised subject.

(ii)  *I saw her be made leave the party.

As seen in (ii), however, such sentences do not appear to be possible. Nothing in what I have said rules such cases out. However, (ii) violates an independently attested property of bare infinitive complements, namely, that they cannot include auxiliary verbs.

(iii)  *I saw her have left the party.

(iv)  *I made her be leaving the party.

If auxiliary verbs are generated in or obligatorily moved to functional heads above V, this restriction would follow directly from the selectional properties of the causative and perception verbs. On this line of reasoning, passive clauses would necessarily project beyond VP, in order to provide a structural locus for the passive morpheme *-en*, perhaps in T. This would mean that elementary trees of the sort in (i) would need to project beyond VP and would fail the recursivity requirement imposed on auxiliary trees.

31. I do not at present understand why these verbs tolerate T′ complements in their passive versions, but not TP complements in their active versions.

(i)  *I saw John to leave.

(ii)  *I made John to leave.

Paul Portner (personal communication) has pointed out to me that the cases in (66) probably should not be analyzed as the passive analogues of the examples in (62), since they tolerate a broader range of meanings. Focusing specifically on the perception verb cases, (62a) demands direct perception of the leaving event, while (66a) does not. We should be cautious of concluding much on the basis of this interpretive contrast, however, as the same active/passive interpretive contrast holds for the Italian examples (i) and (ii) in note 32, without any apparent change in the form of the infinitival verb.

32. This active/passive contrast with causative and perception verbs is altogether absent in Italian.

(i) Maria l'ha      visto partire.
    Maria him-has seen  leave
    'Maria saw him leave.'

(ii) Lui é stato visto partire.
     he  is been  seen  leave
     'He was seen to leave.'

The infinitival complements in these cases are not bare to the same degree as the English cases, however: they show the same infinitival morphology present in control constructions. This leads to the suggestion that the infinitival complement clauses in (i) and (ii) include the projection of a functional head beyond VP, a head I will assume to be T. The presence of this head's projections permits the instance of Adjoining implicated in raising to take place.

33. I am assuming that this head F is not required and indeed is not possible in verbally headed small clauses, that is, in the bare infinitive complements to causative and perception verbs discussed earlier. If it were possible in such cases, there would be nothing to block the analysis proposed for raising out of other cases of small clauses from applying in this case. This asymmetry between verbal and nonverbal small clauses may derive from the fact that only nonverbal predicates may appear in contexts in which they are locally unsaturated (e.g., in cases of secondary predication or modification), while verbal predicates may not. Alternatively, it may be the case that verbal predication is also mediated by an additional head, perhaps the $v$ head discussed by Chomsky (2000); but in this case, the head is categorially distinct from T.

34. Such inverse copular sentences are possible only with definite DP predicates.

(i) a.   Kevin is at home/happy with his job.
    b.  *At home/Happy with his job is Kevin.

(ii) a.   Kevin is a pain in the neck.
     b.  *A pain in the neck is Kevin.

The reason for the categorial restriction perhaps derives from the fact that the EPP requires a DP subject. I have no explanation to offer for the definiteness requirement.

35. Heycock (1995) notes the existence of examples that do allow "inverted" small clause complements.

(i) If Bill has an alibi for 6 p.m., that makes the murderer John!

(ii) If that's so, that would make the most likely cause of the problem the pictures of Stalin.

Heycock argues that the small clause complement of *make* is structurally richer than that of *consider* in containing the projection of a functional head, which she labels *Aspect*. Inverted small clause complements are possible in these cases, then, because the specifier of this aspectual projection provides a landing site for the inverted predicate.

36. Speakers who accept examples like (81a) provide a bit of evidence that bears on the analysis of *there*-insertion given by Moro (1990, 1997). Moro suggests that

*there* in examples like (i) functions as a predicate of a small clause that is raised to subject position, parallel to (74b).

(i) There$_i$ is [a serious problem $t_i$].

On my judgments, there is a close correspondence between situations that allow inverse copular constructions and those that allow *there*-insertion, supporting Moro's analysis. However, speakers who accept (81a) and reject the inverse version (81b) find the *there*-insertion cases with raising predicates nearly perfect.

(ii) There seems little point in us continuing this discussion.

(iii) ?There seems a major problem with this analysis.

This divergence in judgments suggests that any parallelism between inverse copular constructions and *there*-insertion is only apparent and that the two cases should not be assimilated, contra Moro's claims.

37. If a functional verb is simply one that assigns no θ-roles, one would expect passives of unergative verbs to qualify as well, as in the following Dutch example:

(i) Er wordt hier (door de jonge lui)     vell gedanst.
    it was   here (by   the young people) a lot danced
    'There was a lot of dancing here (by the young people).'

If this were the case, it would not be at all clear what could count as the lexical head of the verbal elementary tree needed to generate (i). One resolution to this dilemma denies the assumption that *wordt gedanst* 'was danced' fails to assign θ-roles in (i), perhaps building on the fact that there is a need to establish some sort of thematic linkage with the *by* phrase. This would leave *gedanst* as a lexical verb, capable of heading an elementary tree's extended projection. A compatible assumption might follow Hale and Keyser (1993) in their hypothesis that unergatives are underlyingly transitive. Consequently, passives of unergatives would continue to assign their internal θ-role. Evidence in favor of this assumption might come from the fact that unaccusatives, which on Hale and Keyser's account are monadic predicates, do not tolerate passivization.

(ii) *Er werd door de  bloemen binnen een paar dagen verflenst.
     it was by   the flowers in      a few days wilted
    'There was wilted in a few days by the flowers.'

If this suggestion is on the right track, we could derive the ill-formedness of such examples from the absence of a lexical verb to head a clausal elementary tree.

38. This raises the issue, which I leave open, of the sense of extended projection that could include *be*, the verbal functional projections that dominate it, and its small clause complement.

39. I use the label *CopP* so as to be neutral between my speculative functional verb idea and Moro's more conservative functional head proposal. I also ignore possible raising of the finite copula from Cop to T.

The functional element F heading the copula's small clause complement is the same functional head needed to generate examples like (68) and (69). Recall that I am following Baker and Stewart (1997) in assuming that this head is necessary to mediate the semantic relation between the subject and the predicate of a (non-verbal) small clause. Consequently, even though there is no TAG-internal reason to force us to posit such a projection, I take it to be present in postcopular small clauses as well in the interest of uniformity. Of course, it would be more satisfying if there were some evidence for the existence of this functional projection in this context. One strong sort of evidence for this projection would come from the possibility of adjoining a raising predicate here, as in (68) and (69). And indeed, given the discussion so far, there is nothing to prevent the adjoining of a *seems*-headed auxiliary tree like that in (9) to the F′ node in (84). This would produce a structure of the type shown in (i).

(i)

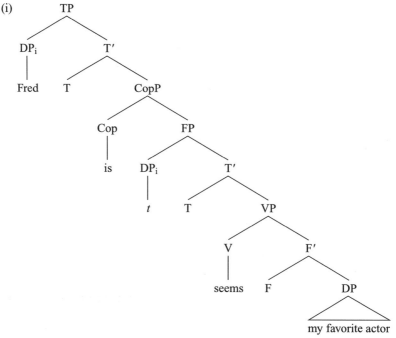

Unfortunately, such sentences are crashingly bad. One could take this fact as evidence against the presence of the F projection in such cases. I will assume instead that the ill-formedness of such sentences derives from the same principle that rules out examples like the following:

(ii) *Fred seems appears my favorite actor.

I return to the analysis of such examples in chapter 4.

40. I assume that the small clause subject does not pass through the specifier of the copula's projection. One reason for this assumption is the absence of examples in which this landing site is overtly occupied.

(i) *[TP There have [CopP[many different people]i been [FP ti my favorite actor]]].

If we assume that the copula is inserted to provide support for morphology generated in T, much like *do*-support, it might plausibly lack features that would drive movement to its specifier.

41. But see Cinque 1999, where it is argued on the basis of restructuring phenomena that such aspectual verbs are generated within a clause's functional structure.

42. Heycock exploits the presence of this aspectual projection in a somewhat different fashion. Heycock follows Den Dikken (1993) in assuming that movement of the small clause predicate past the specifier position occupied by the subject is in general impossible, unless the head of the small clause moves to a higher head position. By doing this, the head extends the domain of the lower specifier position (Chomsky 1993) and renders the higher specifier position equidistant from the base position of the predicate. Den Dikken suggests that in the case of the copula, the functional head of the small clause, which he assumes to be Agr, moves up and incorporates. Heycock extends this idea suggesting that for raising predicates like *remain* and *become*, it is the aspectual head that adjoins to the higher raising predicate. What is not clear on this account is why raising predicates of the *seem* variety should not tolerate such adjunction of the lower functional head. In the current context, the complexities of "domain-extending" head movement are unnecessary. Rather, the only constraint on movement is that it remain within a single elementary tree. Inversion in the absence of AspP is blocked by this requirement alone.

## Chapter 4

1. I have included the expletive element in the elementary tree in (2) and in all subsequent trees. If the internal structure of an expletive constitutes an independent extended projection, such an elementary tree would violate the CETM. In such a case, we could assume that these expletives are substituted into these positions. As we will see, this has certain consequences for the formulation of the second part of the θ-Criterion.

2. This suggests the possibility of an alternative conception of elementary trees that abandons the idea that θ-role assignment must take place within an elementary tree, but insists that Case assignment take place within such a domain. Such a view of elementary trees substantially changes the range of possible grammatical analyses. Since this possibility would take us far afield, I put it aside.

3. This nonlocality of Case assignment might appear to endanger the fundamental TAG hypothesis that grammatical dependencies are all expressed within a single elementary tree. In section 4.6, we will see how Case requirements can in fact be expressed locally through constraints on the application of the TAG derivational operations.

4. In Frank 1992, I state the following constraint on elementary trees, similar in spirit to the θ-Criterion in (7):

(i) If α is a non-terminal which appears along the frontier of an elementary tree τ, then α is part of a chain whose tail is selected in τ, either through theta role assignment or predication.

This differs in one crucial respect from the θ-Criterion given in (7), in allowing frontier nonterminals that are licensed through predication. The notion of predication referred to includes the relation between T′ and its specifier, thereby licensing the *it*-type expletive subjects in (6). However, there seems to be no principled reason for assuming that a similar predication relation does not hold between *there* and T′ in (2), so that this constraint does little to block the occurrence of that tree.

5. The presence of the P projection within this tree might be taken to violate the CETM, as it presumably forms part of the extended projection of the N head within the dative. On this view, then, the correct structure for this elementary tree would have a PP frontier nonterminal instead of the DP. One might now be tempted to say that the EPP goes unsatisfied within this tree since there is no DP within the elementary tree capable of moving to the specifier of TP, the dative DP now being invisible because it is not present within the elementary tree. Instances of locative inversion, however, apparently constitute cases in which PPs raise to subject position, satisfying the EPP requirements of a clause (Bresnan 1994). Thus, in any case, some additional stipulation will be needed to ensure that the dative PP is incapable of raising to subject position.

6. See Boeckx 1999 for possible extensions of this pattern to Romance.

7. Languages differ with respect to when they allow potential specifiers of TP to remain in situ, the specifier of TP being filled by an expletive. English speakers typically find *there*-insertion with unaccusatives fully acceptable, with passives somewhat less so, and with transitives virtually impossible.

(i) ?There was recently written a brilliant critique by someone from India.

(ii) *There has someone from India written a brilliant critique.

On the other hand, Icelandic allows expletives even with transitive verbs. Here, I will leave open the question of why such differences exist both among English verb types and crosslinguistically.

8. This line of argument runs into problems with predicates like *seem* and *appear* in which the subject must be filled by an expletive, even though their CP complements may not raise to the specifier of TP.

(i) It seems/appears [CP that Fred will be elected].

(ii) *[CP That Fred will be elected] seems/appears.

I return to such cases in section 4.4. It also remains to be explained why speakers use the expletive *it* rather than *there* in this case. One can simply assume that *there* is used with DP associates, while *it* is used with CP associates, but this is little more than a restatement of the problem. I return to this issue below.

9. This sort of generalization suggests an optimality-theoretic formalization of constraints on elementary trees. In particular, suppose the existence of two constraints representing the θ-Criterion and the EPP (with a simple formulation requiring that every projection of T have a specifier). By ranking the θ-Criterion above the EPP, we get the desired effect: violations of the EPP are preferred to the introduction of a frontier nonterminal that is not assigned a θ-role. I leave open the further development of what seems to me an attractive line of inquiry.

One central issue that remains to be resolved in this context concerns how the presence of constraint violations within an elementary tree affects the TAG derivation (cf. the discussion in section 4.6 in the context of the economy-based proposal I adopt) and whether the latter is itself constrained by optimization computations.

10. See Legate 1998, however, for arguments that Chomsky's restricted notion of phase is too limited to account for the sorts of phonological isolation effects that he uses in part to motivate the notion of phase itself.

11. The presence of nonprojected nonterminals in elementary tree numerations violates Chomsky's (2000) Inclusiveness Condition, which requires that phrase markers be composed only of combinations of lexical items. See Castillo and Uriagereka 2000 for discussion of this issue and a possible modification of the TAG derivational architecture that avoids it.

12. I ignore here the question of whether the verb phrase includes the projection of a light verb *v*. Adding such a projection would require no substantive changes to the proposal in the text, so far as I can tell.

13. On the other hand, the part of the θ-Criterion requiring that a lexical head assign all of its arguments within its elementary tree does not follow from the derivational machinery. Instead, I take this requirement to constitute an inter-pretability condition on elementary trees, under the assumption that unsaturated predicates are not coherently interpretable.

14. For the moment, I leave aside the reason why the subject raises, as opposed to the object.

15. I assume with Chomsky that the ability of some element to serve as a feature checker (the *goal* in Chomsky's terminology) depends on two properties of the element hosting the feature to be checked (the *probe* in Chomsky's terminology) and the structural relation between the probe and the goal. First, the probe must c-command the goal. Second, the goal must itself contain some uninterpretable feature prior to entering into the checking relation with the probe. For DPs checking the EPP, this is a structural Case feature. Chomsky ties the inability of dative experiencer DPs to check the EPP in English and their ability to do so in Icelandic to the absence or presence, respectively, of structural Case features on dative DPs in these languages.

16. It is worth noting, however, that with respect to the cases considered so far, we could also assume that the reference set of derivations includes all elementary tree numerations containing some particular lexical head under a particular choice of subcategorization. This restriction to identical subcategorizations is necessary if we are to permit both raising and nonraising forms of *seem*: elementary trees of the latter sort will include an *it* expletive subject, which checks T's EPP feature, while the former will include no subject and hence will have an unchecked EPP feature. If the MCP compared all derivations including *seem*, the nonraising variant would block the raising variant, as the former would allow T's EPP feature to be checked by expletive *it*.

17. As noted in chapter 3 (note 21), however, Chomsky's argument for a phase-based notion of derivational economy as it relates to preference for Merge over Move does not go through in the TAG context, as the Merge-over-Move effects are derived without reference to such an economy principle.

18. If we assume that all uninterpretable features must be checked by the conclusion of the (TAG) derivation, we must allow uninterpretable features to be checked across an elementary tree boundary, one example being the EPP features of the T in the extended projection of a raising predicate. The MCP allows such cases, so long as there is no possibility for elementary-tree-internal checking. I postpone discussing the mechanism for intertree feature checking during the TAG derivation, taking it up in section 4.6.

19. In fact, as Frank and Kroch (1995, 131–132) note, there has been little motivation for exploiting the complex aspects of Shortest Move outside of clausal domains. See also note 42 of chapter 3.

20. As Chomsky notes, this line of analysis needs to be extended to account for the insufficiency of $\phi$-features for nominative Case assignment in languages like Greek (Iatridou 1993).

21. I assume that the subject cannot be assigned accusative Case since it does not stand in the appropriate structural relation (c-command) to the relevant Case-assigning head.

22. To account for the British English/Swedish pattern, Ura (1996) exploits the idea that certain pairs of DPs can be rendered equidistant from a higher feature via movement of the lower object to a position close to the higher one. To capture the Georgian/Albanian pattern, McGinnis (1998) proposes that indirect object DPs in these languages can bear "inert" Case, rendering them invisible for feature checking.

23. This numeration differs from the one considered in (32) not only in the presence of *there*, but also in the particular nonprojected nonterminal that is present: TP here and T′ previously. I assume that nonprojected nonterminals may appear freely in a numeration, but that any such nonterminals must be merged (under selection) into the elementary tree that is derived. This requirement will limit significantly the range of possible nonprojected nonterminals in any lexical head's elementary tree numeration. I also assume generally that if a predicate can select for the X′ projection of some head X, it can also select for the XP projection of the same head. Consequently, raising predicates capable of selecting T′ will also select TP. It is tempting to assume that this is the result of the general nondistinctness of X′ and XP projections, in a system like that of Chomsky (1995) with no inherent notion of bar level. On this line of reasoning, differences between X′ and XP would result from the presence or absence of unchecked features, and their effects on Adjoining discussed in section 4.6. For the moment, I leave open the further development of this possibility, noting only that it brings with it a number of potential pitfalls concerning the impossibility of superraising, and the like.

24. Since the MCP compares derivations that begin from the same numeration, we are in the position of allowing both the raising auxiliary tree in (8) and the

problematic structure in (2). If instead we allow a more liberal notion of reference set, as hinted in note 16, where the MCP compares all elementary tree derivations including the same lexical head, we end up with the perhaps even more problematic result that the auxiliary in (2) is favored by the MCP over the one in (8), leaving only the former structure well formed.

25. Since the content of this DP will be filled in during the TAG derivation, these features cannot be seen as projected from some head; rather, they are assigned freely. Upon substitution, we will require that the features of the substituted DP match those of the DP frontier nonterminal into which it is substituted.

26. Perhaps on analogy with the invisibility of fine-grained syntactic details to phonological derivation.

27. We might imagine relating this prohibition in some way to Stowell's (1981) idea of Case resistance. We would need to tread carefully here, since CP, when raised to the specifier of TP, is apparently able to check T's $\phi$-features. We might try to tie this variability in CP's $\phi$-feature-checking potential to the fact that when CP moves to the specifier of TP, it does so for the purpose of checking the EPP features. T's $\phi$-features are checked as a sort of "free rider" in the sense of Chomsky 1995. We might then hypothesize that CP can check $\phi$-features only when they are checked as free riders. Alternatively, we can follow Koster (1978) in claiming that CP never moves to the specifier of TP, instead landing in some higher position. In this case, it is not CP, but some other element—say, an empty analogue of *it*—that checks both the EPP and $\phi$-features on T. This leaves open the nontrivial problem of constraining the distribution of this empty expletive.

28. The MCP and ANCR also permit the derivation of a tree headed by an argumentless predicate lacking a specifier of TP, deriving from a distinct numeration. Such trees, though generable by the first part of the derivation, turn out to be unusable by the TAG part of the derivation and hence harmless, for reasons that will become clear in the next section. In brief, I assume that at the conclusion of the TAG derivation, all uninterpretable features must be checked. Given the assumptions I will make in the next section about how uninterpretable features may be checked during applications of Adjoining, the geometry of such trees will prevent T's EPP features from being checked.

29. See also Taraldsen 1995.

30. On this line of reasoning, English differs from Icelandic in not permitting superimposed Cases.

31. Burzio's argument that these reflexives lack even (third) person features derives from a contrast in compatibility with impersonal antecedents: reflexives allow them, and true third person forms, such as the object pronouns *lui* 'him' and *loro* 'them', do not (Burzio 1991, 88).

(i) a.  Sarebbe  presuntuoso  [PRO$_i$ parlare sempre di sé]$_i$.
        would be presumptuous       to talk always of REFL
        'It would be presumptuous to always talk about oneself.'

   b. *É presuntuoso    [PRO$_i$ dire    che  Maria parla di lui$_i$/loro$_i$].
      is presumptuous         to say that Maria talks  of him/them
      'It is presumptuous to say that Maria talks about him/them.'

32. Burzio (1991) observes that there is crosslinguistic variation in the range of feature values that are compatible with PA. Icelandic and Italian both appear to restrict PA to third person forms.

33. The restriction of nondeletion to cases of PA blocks the possibility of clauses in Icelandic with multiple DPs all marked with nominative Case—a clause type that is indeed not observed.

34. A similar derivation is presumably involved in (53). I have not explained why the result shows singular rather than plural agreement in either case, as I take PA to induce only third person. This is presumably related to the relative markedness of singular and plural agreement. For discussion, see Burzio 1991, 1992.

35. The impossibility of default agreement in (57) contrasts with the behavior of certain other dative-nominative predicates (Sigurðsson 1996).

(i) a. Henni   leiddist/leiddust       strákarnir.
       her.DAT bored.3SG/bored.3PL  the boys.NOM
       'She found the boys boring.'
    b. Henni   líkaði/líkuðu         ekki þessar athugasemdir.
       her.DAT liked.3SG/liked.3PL  not  these  comments.NOM
       'She didn't like these comments.'

Sigurðsson (p. 28) suggests that this variability is due to an in-progress reanalysis of object nominative from structural to inherent Case. In support of this point, he notes that default agreement is impossible with nominative objects in the dative-nominative passives of ditransitive forms, an instance of object nominative Case that could not be inherent.

As discussed in note 36, for some speakers at least default agreement is marginally possible for monoclausal Italian impersonal constructions. In such cases, it might be suggested that the object does not bear structural nominative Case, but instead bears inherent partitive Case (Belletti 1988).

36. The third person restriction in Romance impersonals shows a similar local/long-distance contrast. Though some Italian speakers fully accept lack of agreement with objects, there is a uniform preference for agreement (example from Taraldsen 1995).

(i) Si   ammirano/(??)ammira    troppo  i   giocatori di calcio.
    REFL admire.3PL/admires.3SG too much the players   of soccer
    'Soccer players are admired too much.'

In long-distance impersonal constructions, however, even those speakers who disprefer nonagreement in (i) find it fully acceptable.

(ii) Si   vorrebbe/vorrebbero               invitare tutti i   senatori, ma non
     REFL would want.3SG/would want.3PL to invite all    the senators but not
     ci   sarà    posto.
     there will be room
     'One would want to invite all the senators, but there won't be room.'

And, just when agreement is absent, so too is the restriction to third person.

(iii) a. Si   *ammiriamo/(??)ammira troppo     tutti noi.
REFL   admire.1PL/admires.3SG too much all   us
'We are all admired too much.'

  b. Si   vorrebbe/*vorremmo                invitare tutti noi, ma non ci
REFL   would want.3SG/would want.1PL to invite all   us   but not there
sarà     posto.
will be room
'One would want to invite all of us, but there won't be room.'

Person restrictions in Icelandic monoclausal sentences work in a similar though perhaps nonidentical way. See Sigurðsson 1996, 35.

Luigi Burzio (personal communication) suggests that the optionality of agreement in (ii) derives from the optionality of restructuring in such examples. When restructuring fails to take place, the DP object of the embedded clause remains outside the domain in which the matrix T finds a controller for agreement. As noted by Bleam (2000), restructuring-based analyses are not tenable in a TAG context, as the restructuring operation, if part of the derivation of individual elementary trees, could create elementary trees unbounded in size. We must therefore pursue an alternative, though the locus of the nominative object in object position of the embedded clause prevents us from directly importing the Icelandic analysis I propose in the text. One possibility might turn on the elementary tree in which *si* is generated: if it is generated in the embedded clause and raised to the matrix via Adjoining (see Kulick 1999), agreement with the nominative results; if generated in the matrix clause, the result is nonagreement as required by the ANCR. I leave the details of such an analysis for future work.

37.  Taraldsen (1995) notes that the presence or absence of agreement also correlates with the possibility of coreference between an embedded nominative pronoun and the dative subject.

(i) Konunum_i     *fundust/fannst        þær_i     vera gáfaðar.
the women.DAT   seemed.3PL/seemed.3SG they.NOM to be gifted
'The women thought they were smart.'

This contrast suggests an analogy between ECM and the nominative Case assigned to the embedded subject under agreement. One might expect, therefore, to see differences between the agreeing and nonagreeing form on Thráinsson's (1979) *í barnaskap X-um* 'in X's foolishness' test, which he argues to provide an argument that ECM subjects undergo raising to a matrix object position. There is no contrast between the agreeing and nonagreeing forms in this case, however: both permit a matrix subject interpretation with the adverbial positioned after the embedded subject (Halldór Sigurðsson, personal communication).

(ii) Mér      virtist/virtust          þær í barnaskap mínum hafa    gert
me.DAT seemed.3SG/seemed.3PL they in foolishness my      to have done
þetta vel.
that   well
'They seemed to me in my foolishness to have done that well.'

If I am correct in assuming that lack of agreement between matrix T and the embedded subject implies that nominative Case is being assigned from within the embedded clause (and hence there is no need to raise the DP to some matrix nominative object position), the lack of contrast in (ii) casts doubt on this test, as Halldór Sigurðsson (personal communication) notes.

38. As noted by Raposo (1989, 291), the presence of agreement morphology on the embedded infinitive renders impossible the binding of a reflexive in the embedded subject position by the matrix subject, something that is possible in the absence of agreement morphology (Eduardo Raposo, personal communication).

(i) Os actores$_i$ viram-se [uns aos outros$_i$ *representarem/representar a
    the actors    saw          each other          represent.3PL/represents.3SG the
    cena].
    scene

Under the assumption that the presence of φ-features on the infinitival T is what blocks the possibility of agreement between a lower subject and matrix T (more on this below), this is analogous to the situation in the Icelandic cases mentioned in note 37. As Raposo (1989, 302n.13) observes, however, the situation with pronouns and Condition B effects is somewhat different.

39. One could of course propose that EPP features can fail to delete in some cases, just as we have been doing for φ-features. This would not help us in the case of examples like (58), however, if we assume that such EPP features must ultimately be checked in the course of the TAG derivation (see section 4.6). If feature checking during Adjoining requires a specifier-head relation, there can be no element that could check T's EPP features after Adjoining. Pursuing this line of thought, one might be tempted to posit a null expletive that does in fact raise out of the embedded clause to become an (invisible) outer subject of the raising predicate. This would lead us to predict the existence of a definiteness effect on the embedded nominative, a prediction that is falsified by the possibility of a nominative pronominal subject seen in (58).

40. As in the preceding discussion, I assume that nonfinite T may in some cases include uninterpretable φ-features, allowing assignment of nominative Case along the lines just discussed. See below for discussion of the interaction of such non-finite-TP-internal nominative assignment with the possibility of matrix agreement. Additionally, I leave open the questions of the presence and interpretability of φ-features on other verbal projections, for example, CP. McCloskey (1991) shows that conjunction of CPs in subject position that denote semantically incompatible propositions can lead to plural agreement (as in (i)), suggesting perhaps that CPs (or at least conjunctions of them) contain interpretable φ-features.

(i) a. [That the president will be elected and that he will be impeached] seem
       equally likely at this point.
    b. [That the march should go ahead and that it should be canceled] have
       been argued by the same people at different times.

If this is true, my analysis would lead us to predict that sentences of the form "*there* plural-raising-verb conjoined-CP" should be possible, apparently contrary to fact.

(ii) a. *There are likely [that the president will be elected and that he will be impeached].

b. *There seem [that the march should go ahead and that it should be canceled].

Unfortunately, the semantic incompatibility condition makes it impossible to construct sentences of the relevant form that have a coherent interpretation, so far as I can see.

41. The inability of *there* to check T's ϕ-features might be taken to follow from this restriction, given the uninterpretability of its ϕ-features. We would, however, need to assume that *it*-type expletives contain interpretable ϕ-features. Possibly the restriction that only interpretable features can check uninterpretable features also provides a partial explanation for (55), since plausibly the zero ϕ-features in the outer shell of the dative subject are uninterpretable. It remains to be explained why deletion is even possible in such cases.

42. Raising of the embedded subject is apparently also possible when the raising predicate fails to show agreement with the raised subject.

(i) As coisas parece    estarem  quentes em Belfast.
     the things seems.3SG to be.3PL hot      in Belfast

However, the absence of agreement in the matrix predicate almost certainly indicates that the "raised" DP has moved to a nonsubject position with an *it*-type empty expletive in the specifier of TP, as such movement is also possible out of finite CPs, a configuration incompatible with raising crosslinguistically.

(ii) As coisas parece    que estão   quentes em Belfast.
      the things seems.3SG that are.3PL hot      in Belfast

Raposo (1989, 297) cites a case of apparent raising with agreement in both clauses, in what he calls the prepositional infinitival construction.

(iii) Os meninos foram     vistos a comerem o   bolo.
       the children were.3PL seen   to eat.3PL  the cake

In this construction, however, the relation between the embedded infinitival and the embedded subject is rather different, since, as Raposo observes, with an active matrix predicate, the embedded subject cannot bear nominative Case (assigned by the inflected infinitive on my assumptions), but only accusative Case (assigned by the matrix verb). On the basis of this fact and others, Raposo suggests that these inflected infinitives take PRO subjects, with the overt DP subject controlling PRO from the specifier of the projection of the preposition *a*.

43. These cases differ from their Icelandic analogues in at least two respects, so we must perhaps be a bit tentative in our conclusion. First, note that the embedded infinitival verb precedes the embedded subject in (64), undergoing raising to C in Raposo's (1987) analysis. This means that percolation of the subject's interpretable ϕ-features, even if it is responsible for agreement with the matrix T, is likely taking place via a somewhat different mechanism. A second difference relates to the element that fills the matrix specifier of TP position: a zero-feature dative subject in Icelandic, and a covert expletive in Portuguese. In the Icelandic cases, I

suggested that agreement with the embedded subject depends on the (non)deletion of matrix T's ϕ-features under pseudo-agreement with the dative subject, in accordance with (55). In the Portuguese cases in (64), in contrast, the presence or absence of agreement plausibly derives from whether the expletive filling the matrix specifier of TP position is a covert analogue of *it* or of *there*. Even so, my proposed analysis still explains the perhaps otherwise mysterious incompatibility between matrix and embedded agreement seen in (65a), with insertion of covert *there* directly into matrix subject position.

44. Given what I have said, it is possible for the finite T to check its ϕ-features on both the matrix quirky subject and the embedded quirky subject, if the latter projects its features. At present, I see neither adverse consequences nor empirical benefits from this curious result.

45. I assume that *það* is generated in the matrix clause's elementary tree, a plausible assumption given the absence of a definiteness effect on the embedded nominative.

46. Those speakers who find (69) somewhat degraded find (70) similarly degraded, independent of the presence or absence of agreement. Note also that whatever gives rise to the mild deviance in such cases must be qualitatively different from the source of the ill-formedness in (66), as speakers judge the latter example to be considerably worse.

47. Compare the conclusion of section 4.3. Observe also that the existence of this definiteness effect suggests that Icelandic shares with English the property of disallowing elementary trees like (2).

48. On the basis of examples in which there is no DP that can check T's ϕ-features, it might be argued that *það* is sometimes able to check T's ϕ-features (examples from Maling 1990, 84; Andrews 1990, 184).

(i) a. Ég veit    að   það   er ekið    vinstra megin í   Ástralíu.
       I  know that there is driven left      side    in Australia
       'I know that people still drive on the left side in Australia.'
    b. Það   virðist að    hann sé veikur.
       there seems COMP he   is sick
       'It seems that he is sick.'

While this is no doubt a possibility, it is also imaginable that some other language-particular process allows T's ϕ-features to be checked by unmoved CP complements, in contrast to English. I leave the proper analysis of such cases open.

49. Similar facts obtain in Greek. For discussion, see Iatridou 1993, 185.

50. See also Motapanyane 1994 for further evidence that Romanian raising involves movement to an A-specifier of TP.

51. Grosu and Horvath note that there is significant idiolectal variation on the latter point, whereby some speakers tolerate such sentences without *ca*. I will take possible nonappearance of the complementizer in nonraising cases to implicate a nonovert complementizer. In contrast, Grosu and Horvath note that there is no variation in the unacceptability of the complementizer in raising contexts.

52. As argued by Motapanyane (1994, 733), one cannot take the incompatibility of the complementizer with raising to derive from a *that*-trace effect, as analogous *wh*-extractions are well formed.

53. Kayne (1984) suggests that the impossibility of (80) should be assimilated to a *that*-trace violation, derived from the ECP, a proposal that seems problematic in the face of the possibility of extraction from postverbal subject position, at least in cases of Ā-movement. On the TAG analysis I am proposing, these two are unrelated.

54. For a different view and possible counterarguments, see McCloskey 2000, 71n. 20.

55. Chomsky (2000) provides a different perspective on the same intuition, according to which feature checking of an element E is not necessary for E to move, but the possibility of moving E depends on E's including some uninterpretable features that will need to be checked for the derivation to converge. Under this conception, once the DP *Daniel* in (74) has its Case features checked by the embedded T, it is no longer visible for checking any of the features of the higher T.

56. It is not clear that Greed will apply in cases of Adjoining involving modifier auxiliaries, which plausibly do not induce any feature checking. There is reason to believe, however, that such cases of Adjoining are rather different from those involving complement auxiliaries. See Schabes and Shieber 1994 and Frank, Kulick, and Vijay-Shanker 2000 for some discussion.

57. Two notes are in order here.

First, if we adopt Chomsky's (2000) proposal that the presence of uninterpretable features on an element E is necessary for E to check features on some other element, this application of Adjoining will not be capable of checking the EPP features on T either. This might allow us to alter the previous formulation of Greed to require checking of features either in the adjoining auxiliary tree or in the elementary tree that is the target of Adjoining.

Second, one might wonder how Greed is compatible with raising from finite clauses in Romanian as discussed above. One technical solution would allow optionality in the checking of nominative Case when subjunctive T's $\phi$-features are checked. Romanian differs from the Icelandic and Portuguese cases discussed above, then, in that its optionality resides not in the presence or absence of agreement features on nonfinite T, but in the effect of these agreement features on Case assignment.

58. At least in cases of adjoining of complement auxiliary trees, like those involved in raising. See also note 56.

59. This is often (perhaps always) accompanied by feature checking within the auxiliary tree, though even this is on the highest head in the auxiliary, distinct from the selecting lexical head in all but cases involving auxiliary trees with no functional projections.

60. Steedman's (1987) use of the S combinator in his categorial framework accomplishes a similar effect, though in a different empirical domain.

61. Assuming that examples like (99) are permitted in Romanian and Greek, where raising proceeds from finite (subjunctive) clauses, this might suggest that the φ-features of T may (exceptionally) percolate to the top feature set of T′ in those languages, for reasons that are at present obscure to me. There is, however, an alternative to this difference in projection between the two language types. We could instead say that crosslinguistically, a head's uninterpretable features always percolate to the X′ projection's top feature set, but that the process of feature identification may be restricted in its application: in English, EPP features undergo feature identification, while φ-features do not, whereas in Romanian and Greek, both can undergo feature identification. Assuming that a single set of interpretable φ-features projected from a DP can check only a single instance of φ-features, Adjoining of the derived auxiliary tree (in English) would leave one of the two sets of unidentified φ-features unchecked. A related alternative would prohibit feature identification of φ-features generally, but would permit φ-features projected from Romanian and Greek DPs to check multiple instances of φ-features, as suggested earlier. At present, I do not see a basis for choosing among these different analytical options.

62. If Case and φ-feature checking are to work out in cases of successive-cyclic raising, this line of analysis will require the opposite derivation from the one I have been assuming, namely, adjoining of the nonfinite auxiliary tree to the foot of the finite auxiliary tree. Otherwise, these features, projected from finite T, will not be local to the features of the postcopular DP in the T′ node's bottom feature set. Recall, however, that this derivation violates Greed, as currently formulated. Thus, this principle and its consequences would need to be rethought. Additionally, the derivation we are forced to, whose result is depicted in (97b), yields EPP features that are "stranded" in a position in which they cannot be checked. Consequently, we might want to consider the possibility that nonfinite T, at least in raising complements, lacks EPP features, as suggested by Castillo, Drury, and Grohmann (1999). If this is correct, it raises the question of why the subject ever moves in infinitival elementary trees like (93). A number of possibilities are open, including a view according to which movement within an elementary tree is cost free. Pursuing this matter would take us far afield, so I leave it for future work.

63. As noted earlier, the presence of a dative subject prevents the nominative object's φ-features from percolating further to TP, as the dative blocks the possibility of higher agreement (see (66)). I do not know whether expletives similarly block the percolation of a VP-internal nominative's φ-features to TP; that is, I do not know the status of examples like (i).

(i) Mér      virðast    það   vera margir menn      í  herberginu.
    me.DAT seem.3PL there to be many   men.NOM in the room
    'It seems to me that many men are in the room.'

Even if (i) is ill formed, it is not clear whether this ill-formedness arises from problems with agreement or with the occurrence of *það* in TP complements, asserted to be possible by Andrews (1990, 173) (see (ii)) and impossible by Jonas (1996, 185) (see (iii)).

(ii) a. Ég tel      það hafa     verið dansað á  skipunu.
   I   believe there to have been  danced on the ship
   'I believe there to have been dancing on the ship.'
   b. Ég tel       það kveða    að honum.
   I   believe there imports at  him
   'I believe him to be important.'
   c. Ég tel       það hafa     verið beðið  eftir honum.
   I   believe there to have been  waited for   him
   'I believe him to have been waited for.'

(iii) *Ég tel       það vera marga stúdenta í  þessum bekk.
   I   believe there to be many  students in this      class

Andrews's examples differ from Jonas's in all being impersonal constructions with no associate for the expletive. Exploring why this difference should affect the possibility of *það* would take us far afield, and I therefore put the matter aside.

## Chapter 5

1. Alternatively, this dependency can be taken to hold between the *wh*-element and the lexical predicate that assigns it a θ-role, as in LFG, HPSG, and Categorial Grammar. This sort of view renders the formulation of configurational requirements on θ-role assignment more complicated, but avoids the postulation of an abstract gap.

2. I put aside the proposal made in Chomsky 1986, and its recent instantiations in Fox 1999 and Nissenbaum 1998, in which *wh*-movement proceeds from the specifier of CP to a VP-adjoined position back to the specifier of CP.

3. Kroch assumes that *wh*-movement takes place to a position adjoined to CP (S' in his terms). As noted in the text, I assume instead that *wh*-movement proceeds to a specifier position, as in Chomsky 1986 and much subsequent work. This divergence produces some rather significant differences in analysis, particularly with regard to the bridge/nonbridge verb distinction, as we shall see.

4. As noted in chapter 2, the presence of the trace of *wh*-movement within this elementary tree can be argued to be compatible with the CETM, as it lacks phonological and (plausibly) semantic content, the latter being filled in upon substitution into the DP frontier nonterminal at the head of the chain. The function of movement within the elementary tree, then, is simply to establish a chain among a number of distinct positions, with only the highest requiring filling in the course of the derivation. Alternatively, we might require that substitution take place into all positions along the chain, with features on the different members of the chain determining whether an empty category or contentful phrase must be substituted.

5. This naturally leads to the question of whether there is a third type of derivation involving adjoining of a V' auxiliary tree. If Adjoining is constrained by Greed as I suggested in chapter 4, it is possible that such instances of Adjoining would be blocked, if lexical categories like V may not contain uninterpretable features. In the context of a somewhat different derivational system, Kulick,

Frank, and Vijay-Shanker (2000) propose an analysis of restructuring predicates involving V′ auxiliary trees.

6. I use the term *nonmaximal* projection here in an absolute sense, that is, not projected to a second bar level. If the notion of maximal projection is instead understood relationally, as in Chomsky's (1995) bare phrase structure proposal, even these C′s would be seen as maximal within the elementary tree, since they are not further projected. (Note that this is not true under Muysken's (1982) related suggestion whereby a C′ projection could be characterized as [+projected, −maximal].) Observe, however, that even under Chomsky's proposal, what we call maximal CP and nonmaximal C′ projections must nonetheless remain distinct, at least for languages like English. Assuming that projections of C may merge with at most one specifier, some property, perhaps the presence of *wh*-EPP features on C discussed below, will serve to distinguish C′ from CP so that only the former tolerates the attachment of an element as a specifier. It should therefore be straightforward to reconstruct the current discussion of nonmaximal projections within a bare phrase structure view.

Note incidentally that in the case of the C′ in (4), the TAG derivation will embed this C′ within the matrix projection, so that it now becomes nonmaximal, even in a relational sense, while the relationally nonmaximal C′ in the elementary tree in (3) becomes relationally maximal (meaning that Chomsky's (1995) requirement that structure remain uniform in phrase structure status cannot apply during the TAG derivation).

7. I put aside for the moment the contrast between the marginal status of argument extraction from nonbridge complements and the sharp ungrammaticality of adjunct extraction. I return to this issue in section 5.6, where I suggest that argument extraction from the complements to nonbridge verbs makes use of a rather different derivation.

8. Hegarty (1992) proposes a different unification of these cases, arguing that the complements to factive, inherently negative, and familiar complement predicates share the property of having a complementizer with semantic content. For negative predicates, he follows Laka (1990) in taking the negative force to be conveyed by a negative complementizer. For familiar and factive predicates, he assumes that the complementizer binds an event variable of the lower predicate, producing a sort of definite description of an event. He then provides an analysis under which the presence of semantic content in the complementizer blocks the possibility of antecedent government and hence of free extraction. Though it is possible to translate Hegarty's analysis into the TAG context, it is less straightforward to derive locality effects under such an analysis than under the one I adopt, in which complements to nonbridge verbs uniformly include an empty operator in the specifier of CP.

9. Unlike T's EPP feature, which is present on all instances of T, Chomsky assumes that some C heads lack *wh*-EPP features. Chomsky's proposal diverges, however, from those of Fukui and Speas and Rizzi in that *wh*-EPP features appear not only on complementizers heading interrogative clauses, but also on all

C heads whose specifiers serve as intermediate landing sites for *wh*-movement. As will become clear, we will need to adopt Chomsky's view into the TAG context for theoretical and empirical reasons.

10. To satisfy the ANCR as well, we must assume that C does not have any other uninterpretable features that are checked within this elementary tree. This implies, then, that the movement of the auxiliary from T to C cannot have been driven by the presence of an uninterpretable feature on C. Otherwise, the C head in (4) would have had some but not all of its uninterpretable features checked within its elementary tree, triggering an ANCR violation. Note, incidentally, that the same argument holds for V-to-T movement in raising auxiliary trees in French-type languages, as these T heads will have unchecked EPP and, in the case of finite T, $\phi$-features. One potential resolution for this conflict could take the EPP/*wh*-EPP feature to be assigned to the $T'/C'$ itself during the derivation, rather than projected from the T/C head. In the case of C, checking of a T-attracting uninterpretable feature would leave it with no remaining unchecked features, in accordance with the ANCR. In the case of T, however, this proposal would not resolve the problem of the unchecked $\phi$-features, which are less plausibly a property of the $T'$ projection. I will assume, therefore, that the factors governing head movement are distinct from those involved in XP-movement.

11. I put aside the difficult issue of why moving the subject *wh*-element *who* to the specifier of CP obviates the need to raise the auxiliary to C. Note, though, that it should be straightforward to incorporate any proposal about this issue into the TAG-based derivational architecture, as a constraint on elementary tree derivations.

12. This raises the question of how *wh*-modifiers can ever appear in specifier of CP position, if they are not present in the verbally headed elementary tree and therefore cannot move to such a specifier position during the elementary tree derivation. One possibility is that they are substituted into a *wh*-DP frontier nonterminal that has been merged directly into the specifier of CP position to check *wh*-EPP features, just as with the proposal below for *wh*-expletives. This means that adjunct *wh*-elements are not interpreted via an operator-variable relation, but are instead interpreted directly in the specifier of CP position (Williams 1994). If this is correct, it provides a potential explanation for the strict locality of adjunct extraction, as adjunct *wh*-elements, unlike argument *wh*-elements (see section 5.6), must always be construed in the clause into which they are substituted.

13. Tanaka's original examples use the D-linked *wh*-phrase *which trial* (on D-linking, see Pesetsky 1987). As discussed below, in-situ D-linked *wh*-phrases do not give rise to superiority effects. Nonetheless, the general pattern that Tanaka observes appears to hold independent of issues of D-linking.

14. See note 9. We must assume that the two variants of C do not compete during evaluation by the MCP, lest examples like (2) be ruled out entirely.

15. Assuming that *wh*-EPP features, like EPP features, project to the top feature set of the head's $X'$ projection.

16. Giving rise to a comp-trace effect here, but not necessarily in general.

17. See Kroch and Joshi 1985, 81–84, for an analysis of French stylistic inversion in the TAG context, essentially along these lines. See also Frank and Kroch 1995, where it is demonstrated that arguments for intermediate traces on the basis of connectivity effects like that illustrated in (i) can be given an alternative TAG treatment.

(i) Which picture of himself$_i$ does Carl$_i$ think that Mary prefers $t$?

18. It is possible that Serbo-Croatian may pattern in this way as well, as it fails to show local superiority effects (examples from Richards 1997, 32).

(i) a. Ko   je   koga   vidjeo?
       who AUX whom seen
       'Who saw whom?'
   b. Koga je   ko   vidjeo?
       whom AUX who seen

In cases of long-distance superiority, the pattern of relative acceptability appears to be in the expected direction, though unfortunately, a number of interfering factors conspire to produce an overall low degree of acceptability (Željko Bošković, personal communication).

(ii) a. ???Kome      koga      rece    da je   Ivan sreo?
         whom.DAT who.ACC told.2SG that AUX Ivan met
         'Whom did you tell that Ivan had met whom?'
    b. ?*Koga      kome      rece    da je   Ivan sreo?
         who.ACC whom.DAT told.2SG that AUX Ivan met

19. A number of proposals have tried to relate the lack of local superiority effects in German and Spanish to the relatively free word order in these languages, with apparent superiority effects deriving from alternative word orders. See Grewendorf 2001, 110n. 37, for arguments against this line of analysis. My proposal here has little to say about such a correlation, if one exists.

   It is also worth noting that the German contrast I reported between local and long-distance superiority is not observed by some speakers, who permit both orders in (22). I have little to say at present about why some speakers permit such examples, or why others admit examples like the following, taken from Fanselow 1997, in which a lower *wh*-phrase is able to move past a *wh*-phrase generated in a "higher" elementary tree:

(i) a. Über wen   hat wer [ein Buch t] kritisiert?
       about whom has who a   book   criticized
       'Who criticized a book about what?'
   b. Wem  hat wer versucht [t dabei     zu helfen]?
       whom has who tried       there with to help
       'Who tried to help whom in this respect?'

For further discussion, see Büring and Hartmann 1994 and Haider 2000.

20. Lasnik and Saito (1992, 120) note a related pair, with divergent judgments.

(i) a.   What did you give to who?
    b. *Who did you give what to?

A possible explanation for the divergence in judgment between (ib) and (25b) could derive from the assumption that the indirect object in the elementary tree headed by *give* is represented by a PP frontier nonterminal into which a *to*-headed PP must substitute. In such an elementary structure, a [+wh] DP object of *to* would not be accessible to an elementary-tree-local movement operation (in contrast to a [+wh] PP) and hence could not check a *wh*-EPP feature on C when another *wh*-element is present in *give*'s elementary tree. Under such an analysis, extraction of *to*'s object would necessitate recourse to multicomponent Adjoining, as discussed in section 5.6.

21. A problematic case would be a language that showed either no superiority effects at all, or only local superiority effects. At present, I am not aware of languages that exhibit either of these patterns.

22. Pesetsky (1987, 106) cites the following case of long-distance superiority as being well formed:

(i) Which book did you persuade which man to read?

I agree that this sentence is considerably better than (28), and perhaps even on a par with (27). It seems to me to degrade considerably, however, if we make the clausal complement finite.

(ii) ?*Which book did you persuade which man that we all should read?

This contrast might be taken to suggest that examples like (i) admit an ECM structure, alongside their usual object control structure, in which the *wh*-phrase *which man* is in embedded subject position. Under such a structure, the well-formedness of (i) is compatible with the MCP. Such an alternative structure is clearly not possible in (ii). The distribution of emphatic reflexives, as discussed by Baltin (1985, 874), provides evidence in favor of this view. Baltin notes that object control verbs like *persuade* differ from ECM verbs like *believe* in whether or not they permit subject-bound emphatic reflexives after the DP to which they assign accusative Case.

(iii) a.   John persuaded Sally himself to visit Marsha.
     b.  *John believed Sally himself to visit Marsha.

Unsurprisingly, this contrast is generally unaffected by *wh*-extraction across the verb.

(iv) a.   Who did John persuade Sally himself to visit?
     b.  *Who did John believe Sally himself to visit?

In examples with the structure of (i), however, I find the placement of an emphatic reflexive after the in-situ *wh*-phrase degraded, just as with ECM verbs.

(v) a.  ?*Which director did John persuade which actress himself to visit?
     b.  *Which director did John believe which actress himself to visit?

If this pattern is robust, it suggests that examples like (i) do not involve *wh*-elements from separate clauses.

23. Lasnik and Saito (1992, 121) cite an example that constitutes an apparent counterexample to this claim.

(i) Who wonders what you told who [PRO to read *t*]?

In this example, *what* moves from the most deeply embedded clause past *who* in the *told* clause. Lasnik and Saito mark this example as acceptable under the reading in which the embedded *who* takes matrix scope. I am not sure that I share their judgment concerning this example. Nonetheless, taking their judgment to represent one grammatical option, it is possible that in such grammars, *told* admits an ECM structure, alongside the usual control structure. See note 22.

24. See Shima 1999 for a similar proposal, in which C and *wh*-phrases contain two features each, one interpretable and one uninterpretable.

25. Note that the checking of Case features on a DP whose *wh*-Case features are unchecked does not violate the ANCR, as formulated, since this DP is not a lexical item. It is plausible, in fact, to assume that *wh*-Case features are not part of any lexical item, but are generated only on DP nonterminals in an elementary tree numeration, into which the *wh*-phrase's content is later substituted.

26. As Reis and Rosengren note, this would seem to imply that the incompatibility of *dass* with a *wh*-element in its local specifier cannot be due to *dass*'s being marked [−Q]; instead, it must arise from something like the Doubly Filled Comp Filter.

27. Note that the ANCR implies that the unchecked feature in this elementary tree cannot be on C, since C's *wh*-EPP feature has already been checked. Therefore, the uninterpretable feature, which I take to be [topic], must be on the *wh*-expression. Of course, if there were more levels of projection within the C domain, as suggested by Rizzi (1997), the uninterpretable feature might instead be on some head within the C complex.

28. But see Büring and Hartmann 1994 for a different opinion. Also, as Huang (1982) notes, in-situ *wh*-adjuncts do exhibit apparent island effects.

(i) a. *Who knows [if they left why]?
    b. ?*Who likes the man [who fixed the car how]?
    c. *Who drove away [after I laughed why]?

It seems clear, however, that the impossibility of such cases is due not to the presence of islands, but to the oft-noted impossibility of in-situ *wh*-adjuncts more generally.

(ii) a. *Who left why?
     b. ?*Who fixed the car how?

Reinhart (1994, 1995) suggests that the ill-formedness of such cases can be derived from the assumption that adverbial, unlike argument, *wh*-phrases do not denote first-order choice function variables.

29. In the case of multiple *wh*-elements in such an elementary tree, it would be sufficient for any one of the *wh*-elements to be generated with *wh*-Case. Note, though, that if *wh*-Case can be checked under c-command by [+Q] within an elementary tree, further instances of *wh*-Case on nonfronted *wh*-elements would still be checked during the elementary tree derivation.

30. This means that a *wh*-element generated as part of a sentence containing a [−Q] complementizer without *wh*-EPP features would be generated without a *wh*-Case feature and would consequently not give rise to any unchecked uninterpretable feature. Such a structure should therefore be well formed. Yet, there is something undeniably odd about such sentences.

(i) #Esther thinks that Cullen said what.

This sentence lacks a normal question interpretation, unsurprising given our earlier assumption that [+Q] is the locus of interrogative force. I suggest that the ill-formedness of (i) is semantic: the absence of a [+Q] operator means that the in-situ *wh*-expression cannot be interpreted via the mechanism of unselective binding.

31. By moving first to the specifier of the lower CP, we can however reduce to two the number of bounding nodes crossed during the derivation of the complex NP case in (44b), providing a possible explanation of why the violation in this case seems less severe than the violation in extraction from a relative clause.

32. Reinhart (1981) was the first to propose that the generation of *wh*-island violations derives from the possibility of moving multiple *wh*-elements to the front of a single clause rather than from a parameterization in the locality conditions on movement, as suggested by Rizzi (1982, chap. 2). It is interesting to note that in the context of the TAG-based derivational architecture we are exploring, this is the only analytical possibility.

33. Two notes are in order here.

First, for this implication to go through, the multiple fronting must involve movement of all *wh*-phrases to a position within the C domain. This excludes languages like Polish and Serbo-Croatian, which, according to Rudin (1988), involve movement of one *wh*-element to the specifier of CP, the others adjoining to TP.

Second, note that the reasoning in this argument parallels the reasoning we applied in chapter 3 in discussing examples like (i).

(i) *There seems a man to be here.

There, we argued that the unavailability of TECs in English, as compared to Icelandic, leads to the observed contrast in acceptability. TECs can be thought of as a multiple specifier construction, like the multiple *wh*-questions under discussion.

34. The more general hypothesis that ill-formedness of some structure as an independent monoclausal sentence implies ill-formedness of an elementary tree is clearly too strong. In the derivation of (5), for example, we made crucial use of the elementary tree in (3), a structure violating the so-called Doubly Filled Comp Filter. Nonetheless, there seems to be something right about the implication in the multiple *wh*-movement case we are currently exploring. I leave for future work a characterization of those cases in which such implications are accurate, though the system of feature checking explored in chapter 4 and in section 5.3 will surely play a significant role.

35. Unless otherwise noted, Romanian examples in the remainder of this section are drawn from Comorovski 1996, 2–3, 164, and Bulgarian examples are drawn from Richards 1997, 42–43.

36. Some Bulgarian speakers do not exhibit the contrast in (60), finding both sentences unacceptable (Marina Todorova, personal communication). Such speakers do not display the same sharp contrast in acceptability on the monoclausal multiple *wh*-questions in (58): any difference between the two is pragmatic, with (58b) requiring that the object *wh*-phrase have a distinctive discourse status, perhaps that of topic. I leave open the analysis of the grammar of this class of speakers.

37. Richards (1997, 42) cites the following examples as exhibiting a pattern similar to the one seen in (62), with both orderings of *wh*-phrases possible.

(i) a. Koja  kniga$_i$ te   popita učitelja [kogo$_j$ ubedi     Ivan $t_j$ da publikuva $t_i$]?
       which book   you asked teacher who   convinced Ivan    to publish
       'Which book did the teacher ask you who Ivan convinced to publish (it)?'
    b. Kogo$_i$ te   popita učitelja [koja  kniga$_j$ ubedi     Ivan $t_i$ da publikuva $t_j$]?
       who    you asked teacher which book   convinced Ivan    to publish
       'Who did the teacher ask you which book Ivan convinced (them) to
       publish?'

Assuming that *kogo* 'who' and *koja kniga* 'which book' are generated in distinct elementary trees (but see note 22), these cases will have a somewhat different analysis from the one we provided for (62), resting perhaps on distinct layers of CP projection for the outer and inner *wh*-phrases.

38. Alternatively, the preposed PP might occupy the specifier of some other functional projection within a more elaborated CP, along lines suggested by Rizzi (1997).

39. Analogous examples in Romanian are well formed, with adjoining at C′ below both *wh*-phrases (Comorovski 1996, 2).

(i) a. Cine ce    crezi     că  a   văzut?
       who  what  think.2SG that has seen
       'Who do you think saw what?'
    b. Cine despre ce    crezi     că  mi-a        povestit?
       who  about  what  think.2SG that me.DAT-has told
       'Who do you think told me about what?'

40. Kroch's (1987) derivation of the impossibility of extraction from a complex NP assumed that complex NPs are adjoined in the same way as relative clauses. This was necessary given Kroch's conception of elementary trees, which, lacking a principle analogous to the CETM, could not rule out (71) as a possible elementary tree.

41. Recall that this Markovian/context-free condition on TAG derivations, which requires that "auxiliary trees be born" prior to the TAG derivation "and not made," played a significant role in chapter 3 in deriving the impossibility of superraising. See also the discussion in section 1.3.

42. Or equivalently, in the terms of the constraint that Merge be accompanied by the satisfaction of some selectional requirement, the C′ frontier nonterminal node neither is selected nor selects anything itself.

43. In contrast, the ill-formedness of (81b) might be tied to Subjacency, since movement will necessarily cross both DP and TP. As has often been noted, however, the degree of ungrammaticality in this case is more severe than in other cases of simple Subjacency violations, suggesting that some other condition is violated as well. Thus far, I have not provided an analysis for even well-formed cases of extraction from DP objects like the following:

(i) I wonder which book John wrote a review of?

I return to such cases, and the subject-object contrast, below. For the remainder of this section, I focus on sentential subjects.

44. Stepanov (2000) argues for the same distinction, but with different theoretical conclusions.

45. Kroch's formulation of the ECP is more complex. He provides a disjunctive formulation in which empty elements can satisfy either the ECP via antecedent government (i.e., binding within an elementary tree) or a form of head government. Since foot nodes lack an antecedent, it is head government that will always be relevant in such cases. This head government requirement, however, requires that the foot node's g-projection, in the sense of Kayne 1984, chap. 8, extend up to the root of the auxiliary tree. This proposal was made in a context without the CETM and $\theta$-Criterion as constraints on elementary trees. Once these are introduced, such complication is no longer necessary, as head government of a foot node is sufficient to ensure that its g-projection is the auxiliary tree's root.

46. Though the question is beyond the scope of this work, it would be interesting to consider what becomes of these correlations in the context of the theory of word order variation in Kayne 1994, where differing orders are derived from an underlying SVO structure via movement.

47. As already noted, the TAG-based analysis eschews the use of intermediate traces of *wh*-movement, the effects successive-cyclic movement being accomplished via Adjoining. In fact, this allows us to avoid the complexities that arise when such intermediate traces are required to satisfy the ECP (Lasnik and Saito 1992).

48. MC-TAG has also been exploited in analyses of extraposition (Kroch and Joshi 1987), West Germanic verb raising (Kroch and Santorini 1991), Japanese causative constructions (Heycock 1987), Romance clitic climbing (Bleam 2000), and verb movement (Frank 1992).

49. Other conceptions of MC-TAG, in which the different components of a tree set are not obliged to adjoin or substitute into the same elementary tree, are possible, and are demonstrably more powerful. Heycock (1987) and Bleam (2000) argue that one such extension is necessary to analyze, respectively, Japanese causatives and Romance clitic climbing; but see Kulick, Frank, and Vijay-Shanker 2000, Frank, Kulick, and Vijay-Shanker 2000, and Kulick 2000 for less powerful alternatives.

50. I assume that there are some cases of variable binding that are not established syntactically and hence are not subject to syntactic locality restrictions of any sort.

51. The use of such degenerate auxiliary trees raises the issue of the role of Greed in the context of MC-TAG derivations, as it is unclear what feature could be checked by the adjoining of such trees. One possibility is that the degenerate DP substitutes rather than adjoins into the specifier of CP. Since Greed does not constrain Substitution, no features would need to be checked. This alternative may also have interpretive advantages, as the *wh*-phrase would be substituted into a part of the tree set headed by the predicate that assigns it a θ-role. I leave the resolution of this issue for future work.

52. See Frank, Kulick, and Vijay-Shanker 2000 for further discussion and generalization of the use of c-command links.

53. This style of MC-TAG derivation offers no way to generate examples like the Bulgarian sentence in (i) (from Richards 1997, 25).

(i) ?Koj   senator$_j$ koja  kniga$_i$ $t_j$ otreče [mâlvata  če   iska    da zabrani $t_i$]?
    which senator  which book        denied  the rumor that wanted to ban
    'Which senator denied the rumor that he wanted to ban which book?'

Richards argues that such examples provide evidence for his Principle of Minimal Compliance, according to which movement to a certain position P may cross a strong island so long as another instance of movement to P satisfies locality principles. If such examples are indeed well formed, we will need to make use of a mechanism different from those we have considered here to establish such radically nonlocal *wh*-dependencies. One possibility is that the locality-violating *wh*-elements are base-generated in a matrix topic position and serve to bind a covert variable in the apparent base position. As we have seen, unselective binding of this sort, which I have taken to be implicated in English multiple *wh*-questions, does not obey island effects, as it is a semantically rather than syntactically established dependency. Further, if such topic *wh*-elements are incapable of checking the *wh*-features on the matrix C, this would explain why the possibility of such nonlocal dependencies relies on the presence of a movement-derived, and hence local, *wh*-dependency, as Richards notes.

(ii) *Koja kniga$_i$ otreče senatorât [mâlvata  če   iska    da zabrani $t_i$]?
     which book   denied the senator the rumor that wanted to ban
     'Which book did the senator deny the rumor that he wanted to ban?'

54. This derivation crucially depends on the possibility of attaching relative clauses to the outermost DP layer of the nominal extended projection, rather than properly within it at NP, as is usually assumed. If this is not permitted, the derivation is blocked by the restriction that both pieces of a multicomponent tree set must attach to a single, underived elementary tree. The structure in (94) cannot form an elementary tree, as it contains both nominal and verbal extended projections and hence violates the CETM.

55. Tree sets like the one in (93) may, however, be appropriate in the context of parasitic gap constructions, where the DP to which the degenerate auxiliary tree adjoins would need to head an independently established *wh*-dependency. Since both halves of the tree set must adjoin into the same underived auxiliary tree, this

implies a strict locality relation on the adjunct hosting the parasitic gap and the *wh*-operator that licenses it, as suggested in Aoun and Clark 1984 and Frank 1991 (cf. Chomsky 1986). This locality requirement appears to run into trouble with cases of the following sort, in which the parasitic-gap-containing adjunct is attached to a matrix clause, while the licensing gap is in the embedded clause.

(i) Which paper did Alice recommend that we reject *t* [without PRO first reading *e* herself]?

If the licensing dependency is generated in the embedded clause's elementary tree, as in the TAG analysis of "short" *wh*-movement assumed in this chapter, there will be no DP in the specifier of CP of the matrix clause's elementary tree to which the degenerate DP auxiliary tree could adjoin at the same time that the adverbial adjoins to the matrix clause. This suggests the perhaps surprising conclusion that cases like (i) must involve long movement; that is, they involve an MC-TAG derivation in which the *wh*-phrase is generated in the main clause and is "licensed" by the adjoining of a multicomponent tree set from the embedded clause as in the derivation of example (87). In fact, there is evidence from interpretive considerations of the sort discussed in section 5.7 suggesting that this is the correct analysis of such cases. I return to these in note 60.

56. Kroch (1989b) rules this tree out in terms of the ECP: the AdvP empty category is neither antecedent nor head governed within its elementary tree. Given the more articulated theory of elementary trees developed here, such reference to the ECP is no longer necessary. Note, though, that the current analysis does nothing to block long movement of subject DPs, something that is impossible in *wh*-island cases, though not in factives, which as nonbridge verbs will make use of the multicomponent analysis suggested here.

(i) a. *Who$_i$ did you ask whether $t_i$ had visited Louise?
    b. ?Who$_i$ did you doubt $t_i$ had visited Louise?

It is likely that the source of ill-formedness in (ia) is the same as that in comp-trace effects. Thus, whatever account is given of such effects in the elementary-tree-local context can be applied here as well as a condition on the distribution of pro. One potential wrinkle comes from French, which, as noted by Rouveret (1980), blocks extraction from subject position of complements to the factive class of nonbridge verbs.

(ii) *Qui$_i$ regrettes-tu qui $t_i$ t'ait    vu   à la  fête?
     who regret-you   that    you-has seen at the party
     'Who do you regret saw you at the party?'

Consideration of a broader range of data muddies the picture, however. In contrast to the impossibility of extraction in (ii), some nonbridge predicates such as *douter* 'doubt' permit subject extraction freely, while others like *sûr* 'sure' permit it only marginally (Kayne 1976, 294).

(iii) a. Qui$_i$ doutes-tu  qui $t_i$ soit parti?
       who doubt-you that   is   left
       'Who do you doubt left?'

     b. ?la  fille que je suis sûr  qui  arrivera    la  première
        the girl that I  am  sure that will arrive the first
        'the girl who I am sure will arrive first'

I have nothing to offer about why French nonbridge predicates do not behave as uniformly as their English counterparts, and I leave the resolution of this puzzle for future work.

57. Cinque attributes this example to M. A. Browning. Similar examples are discussed in Frampton 1990.

58. One potential difficulty for this analysis relates to the prohibition discussed in chapter 3 against raising out of clausal complements to nominals. Unless further restricted, the use of multicomponent tree sets will allow us to derive impossible cases like (i), by substituting a TP infinitival complement with pro subject and adjoining a DP degenerate auxiliary to the DP node in the specifier of DP position of the nominal elementary tree.

(i) *Leon's appearance to have left surprised me.

Such cases can easily be avoided, however, if we assume, following Cinque, that pro in these cases must be bound by an element in an Ā-position. This will have the effect of blocking the adjoining of the degenerate auxiliary to the DP node in the specifier of DP position.

59. Longobardi (1990), in contrast, assumes that the intermediate trace position is necessary if the AQ is to undergo scope reconstruction to the front of the lower clause, which he takes to be the source of the quantificational reading.

60. These interpretive distinctions also argue in favor of a long movement analysis of *wh*-movement in parasitic-gap-containing examples like (i) from note 55. Note first that in the absence of a parasitic gap, AQs may receive either quantificational or referential interpretations in such structures.

(i) How many papers did Alice recommend that we reject $t$ [without PRO first reading the journal's acceptance policy herself]?

When the parasitic gap is introduced, however, only the referential reading is possible, suggesting that long movement is at issue.

(ii) How many papers did Alice recommend that we reject $t$ [without PRO first reading $e$ herself]?

In the TAG context, this implies an MC-TAG derivation, in which the *wh*-DP is generated in the matrix clause. As discussed in note 55, this is necessary to satisfy the elementary tree locality requirement on the adjoining of the two parts of the multicomponent tree set that I am taking to be involved in the formation of parasitic dependencies. Note that if the adjunct is attached instead to the embedded clause, the ambiguity in AQ interpretation returns.

(iii) How many papers did Alice recommend that we reject $t$ [without PRO first reading $e$ ourselves]?

Since the adjunct clause will now be adjoined to the lower clause, we need no longer make use of an MC-TAG analysis for the *wh*-dependency, thereby licensing a quantificational interpretation.

Notes to Pages 231–241                                                    291

**Chapter 6**

1. To make this argument formally precise, Rambow must assume that the grammar is able to generate a wide class of unacceptable sentences. On the face of it, this appears parallel to arguments based on unacceptable center-embedded sentences for the proposition that generating the string set of English requires at least a context-free grammar. See Joshi, Becker, and Rambow 2000 for arguments against drawing this parallel, and hence for rejecting Rambow's conclusions about the power needed to generate instances of German scrambling.

2. It is worth noting that it is nonetheless possible to incorporate the idea of (elementary-tree-local) LF movement into the current context by complicating the TAG portion of the derivation along the lines suggested by Schabes and Shieber (1990). Specifically, suppose we take Spell-Out to be an operation that applies during the elementary tree derivation, to produce both a PF elementary structure and another phrase marker that could continue to be the target of Merge and Move. In this way, the elementary tree derivation would produce not a single phrase marker, but a pair of elementary structures, one corresponding to PF and one corresponding to LF. In Schabes and Shieber's synchronous TAG formalism, the basic objects are pairs of elementary trees, which are combined during the derivation in a pairwise fashion: the first element from a pair combines via Adjoining or Substitution with the first element of another pair, and similarly for the second elements of each pair. The result of such a derivation, then, is a pair of structures, whose derivations must have been carried out in parallel fashion. It is straightforward to see how such a system could be used to combine the PF-LF pairs derived from the elementary tree derivation. While it is intriguing to think about how the synchrony imposed on the LF and PF derivations might serve to further constrain well-formedness, I will put this possibility aside because of the complications it introduces into the TAG formalism.

3. Working from this idea, Candito and Kahane (1998) propose a very simple process for computing one aspect of interpretation from the TAG derivation, namely, that of recovering predicate argument relations. They suggest that a Substitution link in a derivation tree be interpreted as a predicate-argument dependency between the elementary tree that is the locus of substitution and the substituted elementary tree, respectively. They take Adjoining to trigger a similar interpretation, but with the dependency reversed, so that the adjoined element is the predicate and the locus of adjoining is the argument. As Candito and Kahane note, however, such a procedure runs into problems with the TAG derivation of examples like (ia) with derivation structure (ib).

(i) a. What do you think John was likely to buy?

  b.     what John to buy

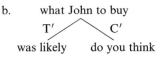

Following Candito and Kahane's proposal, we derive the incorrect interpretation according to which the *buy* predication is an argument of both *likely* and *think*.

One fundamental problem with this proposal is that it does not attend to the location in the elementary tree at which the structural combination takes place, something that is in any case necessary to assign correct θ-roles to the subject and object of a transitive verb. This means that our compositional semantics for derivation structures will need to allow ways of combining semantic objects that attend to their internal structure. I leave to the future the task of working out what such a system would look like.

4. See, for example, note 16 of chapter 3, which suggests treating certain cases of scope ambiguity in this way.

5. I leave open the question of how to resolve the conflict between the CETM and the proposal that the entire structure of an idiom lies within a single elementary tree.

6. Indeed, given the conception of elementary trees I have adopted here in which it is thematic rather than Case relations that are localized within an elementary tree, even apparently local anaphoric dependencies like reflexive and reciprocal binding cannot be resolved within an elementary tree. Both of the following examples involve a reflexive or reciprocal that is bound outside its (bracketed) elementary tree:

(i)  a.  Joe [seems to himself] to be the best candidate for the job.
     b.  Lucy expects [herself to win the election].

# References

Abeillé, Anne. 1988. Parsing French with Tree Adjoining Grammar: Some linguistic accounts. In *Proceedings of the 12th International Conference on Computational Linguistics*, 1–12. Budapest.

Abeillé, Anne. 1991. Une grammaire lexicalisée d'arbres adjoints pour le français. Ph.D. thesis, Université Paris 7.

Abeillé, Anne. 1993. *Les nouvelles syntaxes*. Paris: Armand Colin.

Abeillé, Anne, and Yves Schabes. 1989. Parsing idioms with a lexicalized tree adjoining grammar. In *Proceedings of the Fourth Conference of the European Chapter of the Association for Computational Linguistics*, 161–165. Manchester.

Abney, Steven. 1987. The English noun phrase in its sentential aspect. Ph.D. thesis, MIT.

Alexiadou, Artemis. 1999. Remarks on the syntax of process nominals: An ergative pattern in nominative-accusative languages. In Pius Tamanji, Masako Hirotani, and Nancy Hall, eds., *NELS 29*, 1–15. GLSA, University of Massachusetts, Amherst.

Anderson, Stephen. 1993. Wackernagel's revenge: Clitics, morphology, and the syntax of second position. *Language* 69, 68–98.

Andrews, Avery. 1990. The VP-complement analysis in modern Icelandic. In Joan Maling and Annie Zaenen, eds., *Modern Icelandic syntax*, 165–185. Syntax and Semantics 24. San Diego, Calif.: Academic Press.

Aoun, Joseph, and Robin Clark. 1984. On non-overt operators. Manuscript, University of Southern California and UCLA.

Aoun, Joseph, and Yen-hui Audrey Li. 1993. *Wh*-elements in situ: Syntax or LF? *Linguistic Inquiry* 24, 199–238.

Bach, Emmon. 1977. "The position of embedding transformations in a grammar" revisited. In Antonio Zampolli, ed., *Linguistic structures processing*, 31–51. Amsterdam: North Holland.

Badecker, William, and Robert Frank. 1999. Modeling sentence planning in Lexicalized Tree-Adjoining Grammar. Paper presented at the Speech Production Conference, University of Southern California.

Baker, C. L. 1970. Notes on the description of English questions: The role of an abstract question morpheme. *Foundations of Language* 6, 197–219.

Baker, Mark. 1988. *Incorporation: A theory of grammatical function changing.* Chicago: University of Chicago Press.

Baker, Mark, and Osamuyimen Thompson Stewart. 1997. Unaccusativity and the adjective-verb distinction: Edo evidence. In Kiyomi Kusumoto, ed., *NELS 27*, 33–47. GLSA, University of Massachusetts, Amherst.

Baltin, Mark. 1985. Review article: *The mental representation of grammatical relations. Language* 61, 863–880.

Baltin, Mark. 1986. Adverb preposing and extraction constraints. Manuscript, New York University.

Becker, Tilman, Owen Rambow, and Michael Niv. 1992. The derivational generative power of scrambling is beyond LCFRS. Technical report IRCS 92-38, Institute for Research in Cognitive Science, University of Pennsylvania.

Belletti, Adriana. 1988. The Case of unaccusatives. *Linguistic Inquiry* 19, 1–34.

Bennis, Hans. 1986. *Gaps and dummies.* Dordrecht: Foris.

Bernstein, Judy. 1991. DPs in French and Walloon: Evidence for parametric variation in nominal head movement. *Probus* 3, 101–126.

Bleam, Tonia. 2000. Clitic climbing and the power of Tree Adjoining Grammar. In Anne Abeillé and Owen Rambow, eds., *Tree adjoining grammars: Formalisms, linguistic analysis, and processing*, 193–220. Stanford, Calif.: CSLI.

Bobaljik, Jonathan David, and Dianne Jonas. 1996. Subject positions and the role of TP. *Linguistic Inquiry* 27, 195–236.

Bobaljik, Jonathan David, and Höskuldur Thráinsson. 1998. Two heads aren't always better than one. *Syntax* 1, 37–71.

Boeckx, Cedric. 1999. Raising in Romance. WWW document, available at http://addendum.mit.edu/chomskydisc/Boeckx2.html.

Bolinger, Dwight. 1978. Asking more than one thing at a time. In Henry Hiż, ed., *Questions*, 107–150. Dordrecht: Reidel.

Bošković, Željko. 1997. On certain violations of the Superiority Condition, AgrO, and economy of derivation. *Journal of Linguistics* 33, 227–254.

Bowers, John. 1993. The syntax of predication. *Linguistic Inquiry* 24, 591–656.

Bresnan, Joan. 1982a. Control and complementation. In Joan Bresnan, ed., *The mental representation of grammatical relations*, 282–390. Cambridge, Mass.: MIT Press.

Bresnan, Joan, ed. 1982b. *The mental representation of grammatical relations.* Cambridge, Mass.: MIT Press.

Bresnan, Joan. 1994. Locative inversion and the architecture of Universal Grammar. *Language* 70, 72–131.

Büring, Daniel, and Katharina Hartmann. 1994. The dark side of *wh*-movement. *Linguistische Berichte* 149, 56–74.

Burzio, Luigi. 1986. *Italian syntax*. Dordrecht: Reidel.

Burzio, Luigi. 1989. On the non-existence of disjoint reference principles. *Rivista di Grammatica Generativa* 14, 3–27.

Burzio, Luigi. 1991. The morphological basis of anaphora. *Journal of Linguistics* 27, 81–105.

Burzio, Luigi. 1992. On the morphology of reflexives and impersonals. In Christiane Laeufer and Terrell A. Morgan, eds., *Theoretical analyses in Romance linguistics*, 399–414. Amsterdam: John Benjamins.

Burzio, Luigi. 1994. Case uniformity. Manuscript, Johns Hopkins University.

Burzio, Luigi. 2000. Anatomy of a generalization. In Eric Reuland, ed., *Arguments and case: Explaining Burzio's generalization*, 195–240. Amsterdam: John Benjamins.

Candito, Marie-Hélène, and Sylvain Kahane. 1998. Can the TAG derivation tree represent a semantic graph? An answer in light of Meaning-Text Theory. In *Proceedings of the Fourth International Workshop on Tree Adjoining Grammars and Related Formalisms*, 25–28. Technical report IRCS 98-12, Institute for Research in Cognitive Science, University of Pennsylvania.

Cardinaletti, Anna, and Maria Teresa Guasti, eds. 1995. *Small clauses*. Syntax and Semantics 18. San Diego, Calif.: Academic Press.

Carlson, Greg. 1977. Reference to kinds in English. Ph.D. thesis, University of Massachusetts, Amherst.

Castillo, Juan Carlos, John Drury, and Kleanthes K. Grohmann. 1999. Merge over Move and the Extended Projection Principle. In Sachiko Aoshima, John Drury, and Tuomo Neuvonen, eds., *University of Maryland working papers in linguistics 8*, 66–103. Department of Linguistics, University of Maryland, College Park.

Castillo, Juan Carlos, and Juan Uriagereka. 2000. A note on successive cyclicity. In Cilene Rodrigues, Maximiliano Guimaraes, Luisa Meroni, and Itziar San Martin, eds., *University of Maryland working papers in linguistics 9*, 1–13. Department of Linguistics, University of Maryland, College Park.

Chomsky, Noam. 1955. *The logical structure of linguistic theory*. Distributed by Indiana University Linguistics Club. [Published in part 1975, New York: Plenum.]

Chomsky, Noam. 1956. Three models for the description of language. *IRE Transactions on Information Theory* 2, 113–124.

Chomsky, Noam. 1957. *Syntactic structures*. The Hague: Mouton.

Chomsky, Noam. 1964. *Current issues in linguistic theory*. The Hague: Mouton.

Chomsky, Noam. 1965. *Aspects of the theory of syntax*. Cambridge, Mass.: MIT Press.

Chomsky, Noam. 1970. Remarks on nominalization. In Roderick A. Jacobs and Peter S. Rosenbaum, eds., *Readings in English transformational grammar*, 184–221. Waltham, Mass.: Ginn.

Chomsky, Noam. 1973. Conditions on transformations. In Stephen Anderson and Paul Kiparsky, eds., *A festschrift for Morris Halle*, 232–286. New York: Holt, Rinehart and Winston.

Chomsky, Noam. 1977. On *wh*-movement. In Peter Culicover, Thomas Wasow, and Adrian Akmajian, eds., *Formal syntax*, 71–132. New York: Academic Press.

Chomsky, Noam. 1981. *Lectures on government and binding*. Dordrecht: Foris.

Chomsky, Noam. 1982. Some concepts and consequences of the theory of government and binding. Cambridge, Mass.: MIT Press.

Chomsky, Noam. 1986. *Barriers*. Cambridge, Mass.: MIT Press.

Chomsky, Noam. 1991. Some notes on economy of representation and derivation. In Robert Freidin, ed., *Principles and parameters in comparative grammar*, 417–454. Cambridge, Mass.: MIT Press.

Chomsky, Noam. 1993. A minimalist program for linguistic theory. In Kenneth Hale and Samuel Jay Keyser, eds., *The view from Building 20*, 1–52. Cambridge, Mass.: MIT Press.

Chomsky, Noam. 1995. Categories and transformations. In *The Minimalist Program*, 219–394. Cambridge, Mass.: MIT Press.

Chomsky, Noam. 2000. Minimalist inquiries: The framework. In Roger Martin, David Michaels, and Juan Uriagereka, eds., *Step by step: Essays on minimalist syntax in honor of Howard Lasnik*, 89–155. Cambridge, Mass.: MIT Press.

Chomsky, Noam. 2001. Derivation by phase. In Michael Kenstowicz, ed., *Ken Hale: A life in language*, 1–52. Cambridge, Mass.: MIT Press.

Chomsky, Noam, and Howard Lasnik. 1993. The theory of principles and parameters. In Joachim Jacobs, Arnim von Stechow, Wolfgang Sternefeld, and Theo Vennemann, eds., *Syntax: An international handbook of contemporary research*, 506–569. Berlin: Walter de Gruyter.

Chung, Sandra, and James McCloskey. 1987. Government, barriers, and small clauses in modern Irish. *Linguistic Inquiry* 18, 173–237.

Cinque, Guglielmo. 1978. Towards a unified treatment of island constraints. In Wolfgang U. Dressler and Wolfgang Meid, eds., *Proceedings of the Twelfth International Congress of Linguists*, 344–348. Innsbrucker Beiträge zur Sprachwissenschaft.

Cinque, Guglielmo. 1982. On the theory of relative clauses and markedness. *The Linguistic Review* 1, 274–294.

Cinque, Guglielmo. 1990. *Types of Ā-dependencies*. Cambridge, Mass.: MIT Press.

Cinque, Guglielmo. 1994. On the evidence for partial N-movement in the Romance DP. In Guglielmo Cinque, Jan Koster, Jean-Yves Pollock, Luigi Rizzi, and Raffaella Zanuttini, eds., *Paths towards Universal Grammar: Studies in honor of Richard S. Kayne*, 85–110. Washington, D.C.: Georgetown University Press.

Cinque, Guglielmo. 1999. *Adverbs and functional heads: A cross-linguistic perspective*. New York: Oxford University Press.

Cole, Peter, and Gabriella Hermon. 1998. The typology of *wh*-movement: *Wh*-questions in Malay. *Syntax* 1, 221–258.

Collins, Chris. 1997. *Local economy*. Cambridge, Mass.: MIT Press.

Comorovski, Ileana. 1986. Multiple *wh*-movement in Romanian. *Linguistic Inquiry* 17, 171–177.

Comorovski, Ileana. 1996. *Interrogative phrases and the syntax-semantics interface*. Dordrecht: Kluwer.

Cooper, Robin. 1983. *Quantification and syntactic theory*. Dordrecht: Reidel.

Couquaux, Daniel. 1982. French predication and linguistic theory. In Robert May and Jan Koster, eds., *Levels of syntactic representation*, 33–64. Dordrecht: Foris.

Culy, Christopher. 1985. The complexity of the vocabulary of Bambara. *Linguistics and Philosophy* 8, 345–351.

Dikken, Marcel den. 1993. Predicate inversion and minimality. Manuscript, Free University Amsterdam.

Emonds, Joseph. 1978. The verbal complex V'-V in French. *Linguistic Inquiry* 9, 151–175.

Erteschik-Shir, Nomi. 1973. On the nature of island constraints. Ph.D. thesis, MIT.

Fanselow, Gisbert. 1997. Minimal links. Paper presented at the Workshop on the Minimal Link Condition, University of Potsdam.

Feng, Shengli. 1995. Prosodic structure and prosodically constrained syntax in Chinese. Ph.D. thesis, University of Pennsylvania.

Feng, Shengli. 1996. Prosodically constrained syntactic changes in early archaic Chinese. *Journal of East Asian Linguistics* 5, 323–371.

Feng, Shengli. 2000. Prosodically constrained bare-verb in Ba constructions. Manuscript, University of Kansas.

Ferreira, Fernanda. 2000. Syntax in language production: An approach using tree-adjoining grammars. In Linda Wheeldon, ed., *Aspects of language production*, 291–330. Philadelphia: Psychology Press.

Fillmore, Charles. 1963. The position of embedding transformations in a grammar. *Word* 19, 208–231.

Fillmore, Charles. 1968. The case for case. In Emmon Bach and Robert T. Harms, eds., *Universals in linguistic theory*, 1–88. New York: Holt, Rinehart and Winston.

Fox, Danny. 1999. Reconstruction, binding theory, and the interpretation of chains. *Linguistic Inquiry* 30, 157–196.

Frampton, John. 1990. Parasitic gaps and the theory of *wh*-chains. *Linguistic Inquiry* 21, 49–77.

Frank, Robert. 1991. Parasitic gaps and locality conditions. In Lise M. Dobrin, Lynn Nichols, and Rosa M. Rodriguez, eds., *CLS 27*, 167–181. Chicago Linguistic Society, University of Chicago.

Frank, Robert. 1992. Syntactic locality and Tree Adjoining Grammar: Grammatical, acquisition, and processing perspectives. Ph.D. thesis, University of Pennsylvania.

Frank, Robert. 1998. Structural complexity and the time course of grammatical development. *Cognition* 66, 249–301.

Frank, Robert. 2000. From regular to context-free to mildly context-sensitive tree rewriting systems: The path of child language acquisition. In Anne Abeillé and Owen Rambow, eds., *Tree adjoining grammars: Formalisms, linguistic analysis, and processing*, 101–120. Stanford, Calif.: CSLI.

Frank, Robert, and William Badecker. 2001. Modeling incremental syntactic encoding with Tree-Adjoining Grammar (iTAG): How grammar constrains production and how production constrains grammar. Paper presented at the 14th Annual CUNY Conference on Human Sentence Processing, University of Pennsylvania.

Frank, Robert, and Anthony Kroch. 1994. Nominal structures and structural recursion. *Computational Intelligence* 10, 453–470.

Frank, Robert, and Anthony Kroch. 1995. Generalized transformations and the theory of grammar. *Studia Linguistica* 49, 103–151.

Frank, Robert, Seth Kulick, and K. Vijay-Shanker. 2000. Monotonic c-command: A new perspective on Tree Adjoining Grammar. *Grammars* 3, 151–173.

Frank, Robert, and K. Vijay-Shanker. 2001. Primitive c-command. *Syntax* 4, 164–204.

Freidin, Robert. 1986. Fundamental issues in the theory of binding. In Barbara Lust, ed., *Studies in the acquisition of anaphora*, vol. 1, 151–188. Dordrecht: Reidel.

Freidin, Robert, and Rex A. Sprouse. 1991. Lexical Case phenomena. In Robert Freidin, ed., *Principles and parameters in comparative grammar*, 392–416. Cambridge, Mass.: MIT Press.

Fukui, Naoki, and Margaret Speas. 1986. Specifiers and projection. In Naoki Fukui, Tova R. Rapoport, and Elizabeth Sagey, eds., *Papers in theoretical linguistics*, 128–172. MIT Working Papers in Linguistics 8. MITWPL, MIT.

Gazdar, Gerald, Ewan Klein, Geoffrey K. Pullum, and Ivan Sag. 1985. *Generalized Phrase Structure Grammar*. Cambridge, Mass.: Harvard University Press.

George, Leland M., and Jaklin Kornfilt. 1981. Finiteness and boundedness in Turkish. In Frank Heny, ed., *Binding and filtering*, 105–127. Cambridge, Mass.: MIT Press.

Grewendorf, Günther. 2001. Multiple *wh*-fronting. *Linguistic Inquiry* 32, 87–122.

Grimshaw, Jane. 1990. *Argument structure*. Cambridge, Mass.: MIT Press.

Grimshaw, Jane. 1991. Extended projection. Manuscript, Brandeis University.

Grimshaw, Jane. 1997. Projection, heads, and optimality. *Linguistic Inquiry* 28, 373–422.

Grimshaw, Jane, and Ralf-Armin Mester. 1985. Complex verb formation in Eskimo. *Natural Language and Linguistic Theory* 3, 1–19.

Groat, Erich, and John O'Neil. 1996. Spell-Out at the LF interface. In Werner Abraham, Samuel David Epstein, Höskuldur Thráinsson, and C. Jan-Wouter Zwart, eds., *Minimal ideas*, 113–139. Amsterdam: John Benjamins.

Grosu, Alexander, and Julia Horvath. 1984. The GB Theory and raising in Rumanian. *Linguistic Inquiry* 15, 348–353.

Haegeman, Liliane. 1992. *Generative syntax: Theory and description. A case study from West Flemish.* Cambridge: Cambridge University Press.

Haider, Hubert. 1983. *Deutsche Syntax, generativ.* Tübingen: Narr.

Haider, Hubert. 2000. Towards a superior account of superiority. In Uli Lutz, Gereon Müller, and Arnim von Stechow, eds., *Wh-scope marking*, 231–248. Amsterdam: John Benjamins.

Hale, Kenneth, and Samuel Jay Keyser. 1993. On argument structure and the lexical expression of syntactic relations. In Kenneth Hale and Samuel Jay Keyser, eds., *The view from Building 20*, 53–109. Cambridge, Mass.: MIT Press.

Harley, Heidi, and Seth Kulick. 1998. TAG and raising in VSO languages. In *Proceedings of the Fourth International Workshop on Tree Adjoining Grammars and Related Frameworks (TAG+4)*, 62–65. Technical report IRCS 98-12, Institute for Research in Cognitive Science, University of Pennsylvania.

Harris, Zelig. 1957. Co-occurrence and transformation in linguistic structure. *Language* 33, 283–340.

Heck, Fabian, and Gereon Müller. 2000. Successive cyclicity, long-distance superiority, and local optimization. In Roger Billery and Brook Danielle Lillehaugen, eds., *Proceedings of the Nineteenth West Coast Conference on Formal Linguistics*, 218–231. Stanford, Calif.: CSLI.

Hegarty, Michael. 1992. Adjunct extraction and chain configurations. Ph.D. thesis, MIT.

Hegarty, Michael. 1993a. Deriving clausal structure in Tree Adjoining Grammar. Manuscript, University of Pennsylvania.

Hegarty, Michael. 1993b. *Wh* fronting and the composition of phrase structure in Tree Adjoining Grammar. Manuscript, University of Pennsylvania.

Henry, Alison. 1995. *Belfast English and Standard English.* New York: Oxford University Press.

Heycock, Caroline. 1987. The structure of the Japanese causative. Technical report MS-CIS-87-55, Department of Computer and Information Sciences, University of Pennsylvania.

Heycock, Caroline. 1991. Layers of predication: The non-lexical syntax of clauses. Ph.D. thesis, University of Pennsylvania. [Published 1994, New York: Garland.]

Heycock, Caroline. 1995. The internal structure of small clauses: New evidence from inversion. In Jill N. Beckman, ed., *NELS 25*, 223–238. GLSA, University of Massachusetts, Amherst.

Higginbotham, James. 1985. On semantics. *Linguistic Inquiry* 16, 547–594.

Higgins, Francis Roger. 1973. The pseudo-cleft construction in English. Ph.D. thesis, MIT. [Published 1979, New York: Garland.]

Holmberg, Anders, and Christer Platzack. 1995. *The role of inflection in Scandinavian syntax*. New York: Oxford University Press.

Hornstein, Norbert. 1999. Movement and control. *Linguistic Inquiry* 30, 69–96.

Huang, C.-T. James. 1982. Logical relations in Chinese and the theory of grammar. Ph.D. thesis, MIT.

Iatridou, Sabine. 1993. On nominative Case assignment and a few related things. In Colin Phillips, ed., *Papers on Case and agreement II*, 175–196. MIT Working Papers in Linguistics 19. MITWPL, MIT.

Jacobson, Pauline. 1990. Raising as function composition. *Linguistics and Philosophy* 13, 423–475.

Jaeggli, Osvaldo. 1980. Remarks on *to*-contraction. *Linguistic Inquiry* 11, 239–247.

Jaeggli, Osvaldo. 1982. *Topics in Romance syntax*. Dordrecht: Foris.

Jonas, Dianne. 1992. Checking theory and nominative Case in Icelandic. In Susumu Kuno and Höskuldur Thráinsson, eds., *Harvard working papers in linguistics 1*, 175–195. Department of Linguistics, Harvard University.

Jonas, Dianne. 1996. Clause structure, expletives and verb movement. In Werner Abraham, Samuel David Epstein, Höskuldur Thráinsson, and C. Jan-Wouter Zwart, eds., *Minimal ideas*, 167–188. Amsterdam: John Benjamins.

Joshi, Aravind K. 1985. How much context-sensitivity is required to provide reasonable structural descriptions: Tree adjoining grammars. In David Dowty, Lauri Karttunen, and Arnold Zwicky, eds., *Natural language parsing: Psychological, computational, and theoretical perspectives*, 206–250. Cambridge: Cambridge University Press.

Joshi, Aravind K. 1989. A possible mathematical specification of *degree-0* or *degree-0 plus a little* learnability. *Behavioral and Brain Sciences* 12, 345–347.

Joshi, Aravind K. 1990. Processing crossed and nested dependencies: An automaton perspective on the psycholinguistic results. *Language and Cognitive Processes* 5, 1–27.

Joshi, Aravind K., Tilman Becker, and Owen Rambow. 2000. Complexity of scrambling: A new twist on the competence-performance distinction. In Anne Abeillé and Owen Rambow, eds., *Tree adjoining grammars: Formalisms, linguistic analysis, and processing*, 167–181. Stanford, Calif.: CSLI.

Joshi, Aravind K., and Seth Kulick. 1997. Partial proof trees as building blocks for a categorial grammar. *Linguistics and Philosophy* 20, 637–667.

Joshi, Aravind K., Leon Levy, and Masako Takahashi. 1975. Tree adjunct grammars. *Journal of the Computer and System Sciences* 10, 136–163.

Kallmeyer, Laura, and Aravind K. Joshi. 1999. Factoring predicate argument and scope semantics: Underspecified semantics with LTAG. In Paul Dekker, ed.,

*Proceedings of the 12th Amsterdam Colloquium*, 169–174. Amsterdam: Institute for Logic, Language and Computation.

Kallmeyer, Laura, and Aravind K. Joshi. To appear. Factoring predicate argument and scope semantics: Underspecified semantics with LTAG. *Language and Computation*.

Kasper, Robert, Bernd Kiefer, Klaus Netter, and K. Vijay-Shanker. 1995. Compilation of HPSG to TAG. In *Proceedings of the 33rd Annual Meeting of the Association for Computational Linguistics*, 92–99. Cambridge, Mass.

Kayne, Richard. 1976. French relative 'que'. In Marta Luján and Fritz G. Hensey, eds., *Current studies in Romance linguistics*, 255–299. Washington, D.C.: Georgetown University Press.

Kayne, Richard. 1984. *Connectedness and binary branching*. Dordrecht: Foris.

Kayne, Richard. 1994. *The antisymmetry of syntax*. Cambridge, Mass.: MIT Press.

Kayne, Richard. 1998. Overt versus covert movement. *Syntax* 1, 128–191.

Kayne, Richard, and Jean-Yves Pollock. 1978. Stylistic inversion, successive cyclicity, and Move NP in French. *Linguistic Inquiry* 9, 595–621.

Kim, Albert E., B. Srinivas, and John C. Trueswell. To appear. The convergence of lexicalist perspectives in psycholinguistics and computational linguistics. In Suzanne Stevenson and Paola Merlo, eds., *Sentence processing and the lexicon: Formal, computational, and experimental perspectives*. Amsterdam: John Benjamins.

Koopman, Hilda, and Dominique Sportiche. 1991. The position of subjects. *Lingua* 85, 139–160.

Koster, Jan. 1978. Why subject sentences don't exist. In Samuel Jay Keyser, ed., *Recent transformational studies in European languages*, 53–64. Cambridge, Mass.: MIT Press.

Kroch, Anthony. 1987. Unbounded dependencies and subjacency in a tree adjoining grammar. In Alexis Manaster-Ramer, ed., *The mathematics of language*, 143–172. Amsterdam: John Benjamins.

Kroch, Anthony. 1989a. Amount quantification, referentiality, and long *wh*-movement. Manuscript, University of Pennsylvania.

Kroch, Anthony. 1989b. Asymmetries in long distance extraction in a tree adjoining grammar. In Mark Baltin and Anthony Kroch, eds., *Alternative conceptions of phrase structure*, 66–98. Chicago: University of Chicago Press.

Kroch, Anthony, and Aravind K. Joshi. 1985. The linguistic relevance of Tree Adjoining Grammar. Technical report MS-CS-85-16, Department of Computer and Information Sciences, University of Pennsylvania.

Kroch, Anthony, and Aravind K. Joshi. 1987. Analyzing extraposition in a tree adjoining grammar. In Geoffrey Huck and Almerindo Ojeda, eds., *Discontinuous constituents*, 107–149. Syntax and Semantics 20. Orlando, Fla.: Academic Press.

Kroch, Anthony, and Beatrice Santorini. 1991. The derived constituent structure of the West Germanic verb raising construction. In Robert Freidin, ed., *Principles and parameters in comparative grammar*, 269–338. Cambridge, Mass.: MIT Press.

Kroch, Anthony, Beatrice Santorini, and Caroline Heycock. 1988. Bare infinitives and external arguments. In James Blevins and Juli Carter, eds., *Proceedings of NELS 18*, vol. 1, 271–285. GLSA, University of Massachusetts, Amherst.

Kulick, Seth. 1998. Constrained non-locality in syntax: Long-distance dependencies in Tree Adjoining Grammar. Thesis proposal, University of Pennsylvania.

Kulick, Seth. 1999. Long transformations in TAG and HPSG. In Geert-Jan M. Kruijff and Richard T. Oehrle, eds., *Proceedings of Formal Grammar 1999*, 61–72. Utrecht.

Kulick, Seth. 2000. Constraining non-local dependencies in Tree Adjoining Grammar: Computational and linguistic perspectives. Ph.D. thesis, University of Pennsylvania.

Kulick, Seth, Robert Frank, and K. Vijay-Shanker. 2000. Defective complements in Tree Adjoining Grammar. In Alexander Williams and Elsi Kaiser, eds., *Penn working papers in linguistics 6(3)*, 35–73. Department of Linguistics, University of Pennsylvania.

Kuroda, S.-Y. 1988. Whether we agree or not: A comparative syntax of English and Japanese. *Lingvisticae Investigationes* 12, 1–47.

Laka, Itziar. 1990. Negation in syntax: On the nature of functional categories and projections. Ph.D. thesis, MIT.

Larson, Richard. 1988. On the double object construction. *Linguistic Inquiry* 19, 335–391.

Lasnik, Howard. 1995. Case and expletives revisited: On Greed and other human failings. *Linguistic Inquiry* 26, 615–635.

Lasnik, Howard. 1999. On a scope reconstruction paradox. WWW document, available at http://addendum.mit.edu/celebration/lasnik.html.

Lasnik, Howard, and Mamoru Saito. 1991. On the subject of infinitives. In Lise M. Dobrin, Lynn Nichols, and Rosa M. Rodriguez, eds., *CLS 27*, 324–343. Chicago Linguistic Society, University of Chicago.

Lasnik, Howard, and Mamoru Saito. 1992. *Move α*. Cambridge, Mass.: MIT Press.

Lebeaux, David. 1988. Language acquisition and the form of the grammar. Ph.D. thesis, University of Massachusetts, Amherst.

Legate, Julie Anne. 1998. Verb phrase types and the notion of a phase. Manuscript, MIT.

Lema, José, and Maria-Luisa Rivero. 1990. Long head movement: ECP vs. HMC. In Juli Carter, Rose-Marie Déchaine, Bill Philip, and Tim Sherer, eds., *Proceedings of NELS 20*, 333–347. GLSA, University of Massachusetts, Amherst.

Lightfoot, David. 1991. *How to set parameters: Arguments from language change.* Cambridge, Mass.: MIT Press.

Longobardi, Giuseppe. 1990. Extraction from NP and the proper notion of head government. In Alessandra Giorgi and Giuseppe Longobardi, eds., *The syntax of noun phrases*, 57–112. Cambridge: Cambridge University Press.

Longobardi, Giuseppe. 1994. Reference and proper names: A theory of N-movement in syntax and Logical Form. *Linguistic Inquiry* 25, 609–665.

Maling, Joan. 1990. Inversion in embedded clauses in modern Icelandic. In Joan Maling and Annie Zaenen, eds., *Modern Icelandic syntax*, 71–91. Syntax and Semantics 24. San Diego, Calif.: Academic Press.

Maling, Joan, and Rex A. Sprouse. 1995. Structural Case, specifier-head relations, and the Case of predicate NPs. In Hubert Haider, Susan Olsen, and Sten Vikner, eds., *Studies in comparative Germanic syntax*, 167–185. Dordrecht: Kluwer.

Marantz, Alec. 1984. *On the nature of grammatical relations.* Cambridge, Mass.: MIT Press.

May, Robert. 1985. *Logical Form.* Cambridge, Mass.: MIT Press.

McCawley, James. 1968. Concerning the base component of a transformational grammar. *Foundations of Language* 4, 243–269.

McCawley, James. 1970. English as a VSO language. *Language* 46, 286–299.

McCloskey, James. 1979. *Transformational syntax and model theoretic semantics.* Dordrecht: Reidel.

McCloskey, James. 1991. *There*, *it*, and agreement. *Linguistic Inquiry* 22, 563–567.

McCloskey, James. 2000. Quantifier float and *wh*-movement in an Irish English. *Linguistic Inquiry* 31, 57–84.

McDaniel, Dana. 1989. Partial and multiple *wh*-movement. *Natural Language and Linguistic Theory* 7, 565–604.

McGinnis, Martha. 1998. Locality and inert case. In Pius Tamanji and Kiyomi Kusumoto, eds., *NELS 28*, vol. 1, 267–281. GLSA, University of Massachusetts, Amherst.

Melvold, Judith. 1986. Factivity and definiteness. Manuscript, MIT.

Michaelis, Jens, and Marcus Kracht. 1997. Semilinearity as a syntactic invariant. In Christian Retoré, ed., *Logical aspects of computational linguistics*, 329–345. New York: Springer-Verlag.

Miller, George, and Noam Chomsky. 1963. Finitary models of language users. In R. Duncan Luce, Robert R. Bush, and Eugene Galanter, eds., *Handbook of mathematical psychology, volume 2*, 419–491. New York: Wiley.

Miller, Philip. 1991. Scandinavian extraction phenomena revisited: Weak and strong generative capacity. *Linguistics and Philosophy* 14, 101–113.

Moro, Andrea. 1988. Per una teoria unificata delle frase copulari. *Rivista di Grammatica Generativa* 13, 81–110.

Moro, Andrea. 1990. The raising of predicates: Copula, expletives and existence. Manuscript, Università di Venezia and MIT.

Moro, Andrea. 1997. *The raising of predicates: Predicative noun phrases and the theory of clause structure*. Cambridge: Cambridge University Press.

Motapanyane, Virginia. 1994. An A-position for Romanian subjects. *Linguistic Inquiry* 25, 729–734.

Munro, Pamela, and Lynn Gordon. 1982. Syntactic relations in western Muskogean: A typological perspective. *Language* 58, 81–115.

Muysken, Pieter. 1982. Parametrizing the notion "head." *Journal of Linguistic Research* 2, 57–75.

Napoli, Donna Jo. 1993. *Syntax: Theory and problems*. New York: Oxford University Press.

Nissenbaum, Jon. 1998. Movement and derived predicates: Evidence from parasitic gaps. In Uli Sauerland and Orin Percus, eds., *The interpretive tract*, 247–295. MIT Working Papers in Linguistics 25. MITWPL, MIT.

Ouhalla, Jamal. 1991. *Functional categories and parametric variation*. London: Routledge.

Perlmutter, David M., ed. 1983. *Studies in Relational Grammar 1*. Chicago: University of Chicago Press.

Pesetsky, David. 1987. *Wh*-in-situ: Movement and unselective binding. In Eric Reuland and Alice ter Meulen, eds., *The representation of (in)definiteness*, 98–129. Cambridge, Mass.: MIT Press.

Pollard, Carl, and Ivan Sag. 1987. *Information-based syntax and semantics*. Vol. 1: *Fundamentals*. Stanford, Calif.: CSLI.

Pollard, Carl, and Ivan Sag. 1994. *Head-Driven Phrase Structure Grammar*. Stanford, Calif.: CSLI.

Pollock, Jean-Yves. 1989. Verb movement, Universal Grammar, and the structure of IP. *Linguistic Inquiry* 20, 365–424.

Postal, Paul M. 1974. *On raising*. Cambridge, Mass.: MIT Press.

Postal, Paul M., and Geoffrey K. Pullum. 1978. Traces and the description of English complementizer contraction. *Linguistic Inquiry* 9, 1–29.

Progovac, Ljiljana. 1988. *A binding approach to polarity sensitivity*. Ph.D. thesis, University of Southern California.

Pullum, Geoffrey K. 1985. On two recent attempts to show that English is not a CFL. *Computational Linguistics* 10, 182–186.

Quicoli, A. Carlos. 1996. Inflection and parametric variation: Portuguese vs. Spanish. In Robert Freidin, ed., *Current issues in comparative grammar*, 46–80. Dordrecht: Kluwer.

Radzinski, Daniel. 1991. Chinese number-names, tree-adjoining languages, and mild context-sensitivity. *Computational Linguistics* 17, 277–299.

Rambow, Owen. 1992. A linguistic and computational analysis of the third construction. In *Proceedings of the 30th Annual Meeting of the Association for Computational Linguistics*, 297–299. Newark, Del.

Rambow, Owen. 1993. Mobile heads and strict lexicalization. Master's thesis, University of Pennsylvania.

Rambow, Owen. 1994. Formal and computational aspects of natural language syntax. Ph.D. thesis, University of Pennsylvania.

Rambow, Owen, and Aravind K. Joshi. 1994. A processing model for free word order languages. In Charles Clifton, Jr., Lyn Frazier, and Keith Rayner, eds., *Perspectives on sentence processing*, 267–301. Hillsdale, N.J.: Lawrence Erlbaum.

Rambow, Owen, and Beatrice Santorini. 1995. Incremental phrase structure generation and a universal theory of V2. In Jill N. Beckman, ed., *NELS 25*, 373–387. GLSA, University of Massachusetts, Amherst.

Rambow, Owen, K. Vijay-Shanker, and David Weir. 2001. D-tree substitution grammars. *Computational Linguistics* 27, 87–122.

Rapoport, Tova. 1987. Copular, nominal, and small clauses: A study of Israeli Hebrew. Ph.D. thesis, MIT.

Raposo, Eduardo. 1987. Case theory and Infl-to-Comp: The inflected infinitive in European Portuguese. *Linguistic Inquiry* 18, 85–109.

Raposo, Eduardo. 1989. Prepositional infinitival constructions in European Portuguese. In Osvaldo Jaeggli and Kenneth J. Safir, eds., *The null subject parameter*, 277–305. Dordrecht: Kluwer.

Reinhart, Tanya. 1981. A second COMP position. In Adriana Belletti, Luciana Brandi, and Luigi Rizzi, eds., *Theory of markedness in generative grammar: Proceedings of the 1979 GLOW Conference*, 517–551. Scuole Normale Superiore, Pisa.

Reinhart, Tanya. 1986. Center and periphery in the grammar of anaphora. In Barbara Lust, ed., *Studies in the acquisition of anaphora*, vol. 1, 123–150. Dordrecht: Reidel.

Reinhart, Tanya. 1994. WH-in-situ in the framework of the Minimalist Program. Technical report OTS-WP-TL-94-003. OTS, Universiteit Utrecht.

Reinhart, Tanya. 1995. Interface strategies. Technical report OTS-WP-TL-95-002, OTS, Universiteit Utrecht.

Reis, Marga, and Inger Rosengren. 1992. What do WH-imperatives tell us about WH-movement? *Natural Language and Linguistic Theory* 10, 79–118.

Richards, Norvin. 1997. What moves where when in which language. Ph.D. thesis, MIT.

Riemsdijk, Henk van. 1996. The extension of projections. Manuscript, Tilburg University.

Ritter, Elizabeth. 1991. Two functional categories in noun phrases: Evidence from modern Hebrew. In Susan Rothstein, ed., *Perspectives on phrase structure:*

*Heads and licensing*, 37–62. Syntax and Semantics 25. San Diego, Calif.: Academic Press.

Rivero, María-Luisa. 1991. Long head movement and negation: Serbo-Croatian vs. Slovak vs. Czech. *The Linguistic Review* 8, 319–351.

Rivero, María-Luisa. 1993. Finiteness and second position in long head movement languages: Breton and Slavic. Manuscript, University of Ottawa.

Rizzi, Luigi. 1981. Nominative marking in Italian infinitives and the Nominative Island Constraint. In Frank Heny, ed., *Binding and filtering*, 129–157. Cambridge, Mass.: MIT Press.

Rizzi, Luigi. 1982. *Issues in Italian syntax*. Dordrecht: Foris.

Rizzi, Luigi. 1990. *Relativized Minimality*. Cambridge, Mass.: MIT Press.

Rizzi, Luigi. 1996. Residual verb second and the WH Criterion. In Adriana Belletti and Luigi Rizzi, eds., *Parameters and functional heads*, 63–90. New York: Oxford University Press.

Rizzi, Luigi. 1997. The fine structure of the left periphery. In Liliane Haegeman, ed., *Elements of grammar*, 281–337. Dordrecht: Kluwer.

Roberts, Ian. 1994. Two types of head movment in Romance. In David Lightfoot and Norbert Hornstein, eds., *Verb movement*, 207–242. Cambridge: Cambridge University Press.

Rögnvaldsson, Eiríkur, and Höskuldur Thráinsson. 1990. On Icelandic word order once more. In Joan Maling and Annie Zaenen, eds., *Modern Icelandic syntax*, 3–40. Syntax and Semantics 24. San Diego, Calif.: Academic Press.

Rosen, Sarah. 1989. Two types of noun incorporation: A lexical analysis. *Language* 65, 294–317.

Rosenbaum, Peter. 1967. *The grammar of English predicate complement constructions*. Cambridge, Mass.: MIT Press.

Ross, John Robert. 1967. Constraints on variables in syntax. Ph.D. thesis, MIT. [Published 1986 as *Infinite syntax*. Norwood, N.J.: Ablex.]

Rouveret, Alain. 1980. Sur la notion de proposition finie, gouvernement, et inversion. *Langages* 60, 75–107.

Rudin, Catherine. 1988. On multiple questions and multiple *wh*-fronting. *Natural Language and Linguistic Theory* 6, 445–501.

Ruwet, Nicolas. 1982. Les phrases copulatives en français. In *Grammaire des insultes et autres études*, 207–238. Paris: Seuil.

Sadock, Jerrold M. 1991. *Autolexical syntax: A theory of parallel grammatical representations*. Chicago: University of Chicago Press.

Schabes, Yves, and Stuart Shieber. 1990. Synchronous tree adjoining grammars. In *Proceedings of the 13th International Conference on Computational Linguistics*, vol. 3, 1–6. Helsinki.

Schabes, Yves, and Stuart Shieber. 1994. An alternative conception of tree adjoining derivation. *Computational Linguistics* 20, 91–124.

Schütze, Carson T. 1997. INFL in child and adult language: Agreement, Case, and licensing. Ph.D. thesis, MIT.

Sells, Peter. 1991. Raising from nominal complements in Japanese. Paper presented at the 65th Annual Meeting of the Linguistic Society of America, Chicago.

Shieber, Stuart. 1985. Evidence against the context-freeness of natural language. *Linguistics and Philosophy* 8, 333–343.

Shieber, Stuart. 1986. *An introduction to unification-based approaches to grammar.* Stanford, Calif.: CSLI.

Shima, Etsuro. 1999. Two types of *wh*-features. *Lingua* 107, 189–206.

Sigurðsson, Halldór Ármann. 1989. Verbal syntax and Case in Icelandic. Ph.D. thesis, University of Lund.

Sigurðsson, Halldór Ármann. 1991. Icelandic Case-marked PRO and the licensing of lexical arguments. *Natural Language and Linguistic Theory* 9, 327–363.

Sigurðsson, Halldór Ármann. 1992. The case of quirky subjects. *Working Papers in Scandinavian Syntax* 49, 1–26.

Sigurðsson, Halldór Ármann. 1996. Icelandic finite verb agreement. *Working Papers in Scandinavian Syntax* 57, 1–46.

Sportiche, Dominique. 1996. Clitic constructions. In Johan Rooryck and Laurie Zaring, eds., *Phrase structure and the lexicon*, 213–276. Dordrecht: Kluwer.

Steedman, Mark. 1987. Combinatory grammars and parasitic gaps. *Natural Language and Linguistic Theory* 5, 403–439.

Steedman, Mark. 1996. *Surface structure and interpretation.* Cambridge, Mass.: MIT Press.

Stepanov, Arthur. 2000. Extractability, CED and word order. Paper presented at the 24th Penn Linguistic Colloquium, University of Pennsylvania.

Stowell, Tim. 1978. What was there before there was there. In Donca Farkas, Wesley M. Jacobsen, and Karol W. Todrys, eds., *Papers from the Thirteenth Regional Meeting, Chicago Linguistic Society*, 458–471. Chicago Linguistic Society, University of Chicago.

Stowell, Tim. 1981. *Origins of phrase structure.* Ph.D. thesis, MIT.

Stowell, Tim. 1989. Subjects, specifiers and X-bar theory. In Mark Baltin and Anthony Kroch, eds., *Alternative conceptions of phrase structure*, 232–262. Chicago: University of Chicago Press.

Takahashi, Daiko. 1994. *Minimality of movement.* Ph.D. thesis, University of Connecticut, Storrs.

Tanaka, Hidekazu. 1999. Raised objects and superiority. *Linguistic Inquiry* 30, 317–325.

Taraldsen, Knut Tarald. 1995. On agreement and nominative objects in Icelandic. In Hubert Haider, Susan Olsen, and Sten Vikner, eds., *Studies in comparative Germanic syntax*, 307–327. Dordrecht: Kluwer.

Thráinsson, Höskuldur. 1979. On complementation in Icelandic. Ph.D. thesis, Harvard University. [Published 1979, New York: Garland.]

Thráinsson, Höskuldur. 1985. V1, V2, V3 in Icelandic. In Hubert Haider and Martin Prinzhorn, eds., *Verb-second phenomena in Germanic languages*, 169–194. Dordrecht: Foris.

Torrego, Esther. 1983. More effects of successive-cyclic movement. *Linguistic Inquiry* 14, 561–565.

Torrego, Esther. 1984. On inversion in Spanish and some of its effects. *Linguistic Inquiry* 15, 103–130.

Travis, Lisa deMena. 1984. Parameters and the effects of word order variation. Ph.D. thesis, MIT.

Trithart, Mary Lee. 1977. Relational Grammar and Chichewa subjectivization rules. Distributed by Indiana University Linguistics Club.

Ura, Hiroyuki. 1996. Multiple feature-checking: A theory of grammatical function splitting. Ph.D. thesis, MIT.

Uriagereka, Juan. 1999. Multiple Spell-Out. In Samuel David Epstein and Norbert Hornstein, eds., *Working minimalism*, 217–250. Cambridge, Mass.: MIT Press.

Vijay-Shanker, K. 1987. A study of tree adjoining grammars. Ph.D. thesis, University of Pennsylvania.

Vijay-Shanker, K., and Aravind K. Joshi. 1985. Some computational properties of Tree Adjoining Grammar. In *Proceedings of the 23rd Annual Meeting of the Association for Computational Linguistics*, 82–93. Chicago.

Vijay-Shanker, K., and Aravind K. Joshi. 1988. Feature structure based tree adjoining grammars. In *Proceedings of the 12th International Conference on Computational Linguistics*, 714–719. Budapest.

Vikner, Sten. 1995. *Verb movement and expletive subjects in the Germanic languages*. New York: Oxford University Press.

Watanabe, Akira. 1992. *Wh*-in-situ, Subjacency, and chain formation. MIT Occasional Papers in Linguistics 2, MITWPL, MIT.

Weir, David. 1988. Characterizing mildly context-sensitive grammar formalisms. Ph.D. thesis, University of Pennsylvania.

Wilder, Chris, and Hans-Martin Gärtner. 1997. Introduction. In Chris Wilder, Hans-Martin Gärtner, and Manfred Bierwisch, eds., *The role of economy principles in linguistic theory*, 1–35. Berlin: Akademie Verlag.

Williams, Edwin. 1982. The NP cycle. *Linguistic Inquiry* 13, 277–295.

Williams, Edwin. 1983. Against small clauses. *Linguistic Inquiry* 14, 287–308.

Williams, Edwin. 1994. *Thematic structure in syntax*. Cambridge, Mass.: MIT Press.

XTAG Research Group. 1992. A lexicalized tree adjoining grammar for English. Technical report IRCS 98-18, Institute for Research in Cognitive Science, University of Pennsylvania.

Zanuttini, Raffaella. 1997. *Negation and clausal structure: A comparative study of Romance languages*. New York: Oxford University Press.

# Index

A-movement. *See* Movement, A-movement
A-positions, 156. *See also* Movement, A-movement
A′-movement. *See* Movement, A′-movement
Abeillé, A., 22–23, 41, 60–62, 241, 249n24
Abney, S., 39, 94, 248n15, 251n6
Acc-*ing* gerunds. *See* Gerunds
Adjoining, 16, 21–23, 27–28, 42, 53–54, 78, 91, 246n5, 249n24, 250n29, 254n21, 255nn21,1,3, 256n5, 261nn24–25, 264n32, 270n23, 273n36, 277n57, 291n3
    versus adjunction, 21
    in C- versus T-domain, 180
    and c-command, 251n5
    and clausal complements, 60
    constraints on, 34 (*see also* Features, top- versus bottom-, unification of; greed, and adjoining)
    and dislocation of *wh*-elements, 176
    as dominance/c-command preserving expansion of tree- structure, 248n17
    and the Extension Condition, 257n12 (*see also* Extension Condition)
    and feature identification, 162
    and Greed/derivational economy, 31, 158–160, 168, 170–171, 186, 191, 194–195, 227, 277n56, 279n5 (*see also* Greed)
    and homogeneous dependencies, 177
    interactions with local dependencies, 234
    and locality, 80 (*see also* Elementary trees; Locality)
    and long-movement from NPs, 227, 230 (*see also* Islands)
    and MC-TAG, 221 (*see also* MC-TAG)
    and Merge/Move, 23 (*see also* Merge; Move)
    and modification, 19 (*see also* Modification)
    versus movement, 111, 175
    and the projection principle, 64
    and raising, 70, 73, 83, 110, 112, 258n14 (*see also* Raising)
    and recursive structures, 77
    requirements of, 100
    schematic example of, 19
    and small clause structures, 107 (*see also* Small clauses)
    versus Substitution, 18, 59
    and successive-cyclic movement, 80, 177, 278n62, 287n47 (*see also* Cyclicity; Movement)
    and superraising, 75 (*see also* Raising; Superraising)
    and theta-roles, 65 (*see also* Theta- criterion; Theta- roles)
    and top versus bottom features, 163–164, 167 (*see also* Features)
    and unbounded dependencies, 199
    as universal, 22
    and verb raising/adverb placement, 40
Adjunct Condition, 175. *See also* Islands
Adjunct islands. *See* Islands
Adjunction, 10–11, 63–64
    versus adjoining, 20
    Chomsky-adjunction, 20
    as subcase of Merge, 11
    and theta-identification, 63
Agree, 159. *See also* Agreement; Features; Phi-features
Agreement, 8, 11, 48, 142, 144–145, 151, 252n9, 253nn14–15, 272nn34,36, 277n57
    between dative subjects and T, 140–141
    default, 142–143, 149, 272n35
    across distinct elementary trees, 145, 152
    and ECM accusative, 145
    and expletives, 153
    and extended projections, 48–49
    gender and number agreement on determiners, 49

**Current Studies in Linguistics**
Samuel Jay Keyser, general editor